Mighty Winds ... Mighty Champions

The official history of The Royal Liverpool Golf Club

Joe Pinnington

Photography by Guy Woodland

Published by Guy Woodland in collaboration with *Cities500*

Mighty Winds ... Mighty Champions
The official history of The Royal Liverpool Golf Club

Joe Pinnington
Photography by Guy Woodland

ISBN 1-905547-02-1
EAN 978-1-905547-02-9

Publisher: Guy Woodland
Editor: Alastair Machray

Research: Alastair Machray, Roger Greenway, Mark Brocklehurst, Tom Behan, Bob Chadwick, Barry Shortall, Ian Brown, Chris Moore
Design: Tynwald Design www.tynwalddesign.co.uk
Proof reading: Judy Tasker
Additional photography: Paul McMullin, Studio H
Archive photographs: Ian Boumphrey, The Royal Liverpool Golf Club
Printed and bound: Bookprint SL, Barcelona, Spain

First published in June 2006 by Guy Woodland

4 Warren Park, 85 Grove Road, Wirral CH45 3HG, UK
Tel: + 44 (0) 151 639 0960
e.mail: info@cities500.com www.guywoodland.co.uk

The Club Gold Medal

April Stern, *2006 Captain The Royal Liverpool Ladies Golf Club*

Andrew Cross, *2006 Captain The Royal Liverpool Golf Club*

Subscribers

A
Sandy Adelman
Craig Ammerman
B
John A Bambery
Chris Banwell
Michael & Annabel Barton
David Beazley
John Beharrell
Dr Blyth T Bell
Hans Bergdahl
DA Berstock
Patrick Bingham
Steve Binns, MBE
Keith Blackman
Campbell Boal
Nicholas Botting
Michael Brabner
Austin M Brown
C
Heather Caley
Peter Canevali
Bob Chadwick
Mark R Clelland
Michael WA Coffey
Newcombe Cole III
Andrew Collinge
Tony Colvin
Liam Connolly
Frank Cougan
Peter E Crabtree
John Crawshaw
John Creagh
Andy Cross
D
The Lord Daresbury
Dr Simon Delaney
Tom A Dickinson
Keith V Dodman
David W Dorman
Valentine P Duggins
Sean Duncan
E
Jo Earlam
Nick Earlam
Gordon M Edwards
Nicholas H Ellis
Dick Estey
Andy Evans
F
William JD Farmer
Matthew Fletcher
Duncan Frazer
Thomas Frick
G
Philip Gawith
Antonio Gonzalez Lobon
HRJ Grant
Jeremy Greenfield
John Greenhalgh
David Greensmith
Roger K Greenway
Paul Griffies
Michael Groves
H
John W Hall
Stephen Roy Hankinson
Andrew Harvey
Peter Heath
John Heggarty
James M Hennessy
Michael S Hennessy
Sir David Henshaw
Dr Donald Holmes
John T Holt
Charles AC Hurst
J
Sands Johnson
Alastair J Johnston
K
Michael Kane
Barry Kay
Jon W Kilgore
John Koontz
L
Nicholas Leefe
David Low
Jeremy NS Lowe
M
Rob McBurney
Malcolm & Diddle McCallister
Edward McGonagle
Alastair Machray
William Marle
Graeme Marrs
Gerry Maxwell
Nikhil Mehta
Robin Meyer
John Crow Miller
Peter W Mills QC
John Milton
Clive A Mitchell
CT Moore, CBE
Andrew Moreton
John F Moreton
Hugh Morland
Nicholas FM Moss
Jeremy Mounsey
Paul Muddyman
N
Michael Neary
Paul Nichols
John Norbury
David Norman
Douglas Norval
Nigel Notley
O
Kieran O'Brian
Tony Ogden
Lennart Olsson
Rickard Ovin
Barry Owen
Robert TH Owen
P
MJ Paddon
Win Padgett
Michael J Pearson
Nick Peel
Tony Petersson
Alexandra Pinnington
Joe Pinnington
Kim Pinnington
GSF Piper
Tim Piper
Sir David Plastow
Karen Porter
Derek Pott
Angus Prain
Corinne Pringle
R
Cameron Jay Rains
Martha P Reddington
Peter Renison
Lee Richardson
Roger T Robinson
Pieter Roef
The Royal Liverpool Village Play
S
John Seal
Eddy Shah
Arnold Slater
Douglas Stark
Philip Stern
Geoffrey Joseph Stockwell
Anthony Stoker
T
Philip A Truett
John & Liz Turner
Jonathan R Turner
Timothy J Turner
V
David Vaughan
Gary Vaulks
Peter F Veitch
W
Nicholas Wainwright
Liam Walker
Cieran Walsh
Roger Warbrick
Mark Wehring
Mike Welch
Tim White
Mrs Malcolm Williams
NC Williams
Peter Wilson
David KC Wright
Walter S Wright
Peter Wynn Jones
Y
Tim Yeo
HRH The Duke of York
Bill Young
Z
Gordon Ziegler Jnr

Partners

We gratefully acknowledge the following companies, without whose support this project would not have been possible:

Andrew Collinge

Boodles

Brabners Chaffe Street

Coulter Hurst & Co.

DLA Piper Rudnick Gray Cary

Finch

Fujifilm Colourants Limited

Hobs Reprographic PLC

House of Hilbre

Mason Owen

The Owen Ellis Partnership

Plexus Cotton

Rensburg Sheppards

The Royal Liverpool Golf Club

Tilney Investment Management

Wirral Metropolitan Borough Council

Acknowledgements

At this place of Mighty Winds and Mighty Champions it is essential not to be blown off course. So let me begin by explaining the background and thanking some important people.

The council of The Royal Liverpool Golf Club asked me if I would write the history of the Club back in October 2003. Nicko Williams, the Chairman, being of a persuasive nature, thought it was a cracking idea. It was also a mighty task. I gathered seven enthusiastic fellow members to help with the research. I must particularly thank Roger Greenway who contributed the chapter 1900-1913, Barry Shortall chapter 1914-1939 and Bob Chadwick 1967-1987. There were valuable contributions from Mark Brocklehurst, Tom Behan and Ian Brown, backed up by the Secretary, Chris Moore.

Our publisher, Guy Woodland, has taken the marvellous new photographs that appear throughout the book. I would also like to thank Ian Boumphrey, who publishes *Yesterday's Wirral,* for providing such useful information – and all his old pictures.

Also Jay Rains, a member of Hoylake and a former Chairman of the United States Golf Association's Museum Committee, for his research and his contribution to Chapter 14, 'A View From America', which is just tremendous.

My particular thanks must go to Alastair Machray. His professional input has been a major contribution during the production of the book. His research and ideas for the content and his thoughts and support in all matters have been invaluable.

Then there's Guy Farrar, who wrote the only serious previous history of the Club. His work, published in 1933, provided information, but, more importantly perhaps, inspiration.

Let me praise too, two bookends of the golfing establishment. *The Times* golf correspondents, Bernard Darwin and John Hopkins. Today's man Hopkins provided the foreword to this book, while Darwin, *non pareil* in his appreciation of links golf, provided the title *'Mighty Winds … Mighty Champions'*.

Finally, and most crucially, let me thank Harold Hilton, and Johnny Ball and the thousands of golfers good and bad who have followed in their footsteps over what Darwin called "this dear, flat, historic expanse of Hoylake".

Joe Pinnington

Joe Pinnington, June 2006

PLAYERS' ENTRANCE
PROFESSIONAL & STARTER
Royal Liverpool Ladies Golf Club

Contents

Opposite: The ivy strewn clubhouse in high summer

Right: His Royal Highness The Duke of York

Overleaf: 10th hole

BUCKINGHAM PALACE

Hoylake commands a particular place in my golfing life. It was over the famous links of Royal Liverpool that I played my first full public game of golf whilst serving in the Royal Navy as Flight Commander on *HMS Campbeltown*. We were made most welcome under a standing arrangement by the Club for naval golfers visiting Liverpool.

Since that happy introduction to this historic Club, I have returned to play there on many occasions and I am now very proud to be its Patron.

I was pleased to inaugurate my annual Duke of York's Young Championship at Hoylake in 2001 with the willing co-operation of the Members. The event takes place after all the other junior tournaments have taken place across Europe in October. I played in a pre-tournament game with the author of this book, Joe Pinnington, when on the first hole we were hit by an almighty hailstorm. Putting through lying hailstones we continued to play with towels over our heads to protect our ears. I am pleased to say that we continued our game throughout the storm!

Hoylake holds many happy memories not only for me but also for many people over the years and I am delighted that its history is being re-written. This is the first update since 1932 and it is entirely appropriate that this book should be published the year The Open Championship returns to Hoylake after an absence of 39 years.

I know that this splendid publication will help fellow golfers understand the very special place that The Royal Liverpool Golf Club holds in golfing history.

Andrew

tribute

My fondness for Hoylake

by John Hopkins, Golf Correspondent, The Times

"It is a great honour for me, a stranger, to be asked to write some words of introduction to a book about Hoylake. As far as an alien can be a patriot, I am a Hoylake patriot; I love every cop of it and every breeze that blows across it, and I know no sensation more akin to home-coming than that of reaching Hoylake on a spring evening just in time to dash out on the links with a club or two before the darkness falls."

These are not my words but those of Bernard Darwin, a predecessor of mine as the golf correspondent of *The Times*. He wrote them, and many others, in the opening paragraph of his foreword for the first history of Royal Liverpool, one published in 1933. I have a copy beside me as I write. It is green, frayed and with a half-broken spine; just like a very old friend really.

Darwin's words seem to me to express my own feelings as well as if I had written them myself. I have a special fondness for Hoylake. I have been to the course no more than 20 times and played it only half as many, yet I have found myself forming an attachment to it that was as great as if I had been born overlooking it and had played it regularly since.

I cannot explain this affection, other than to say the Club has insinuated itself into my heart. Down the years I have found myself thinking of it when I least expected to. For example, I was reading a newspaper at Christmas time and in an article that had nothing to do with golf I came across a reference to Aunt Agatha, one of the larger-than-life characters created by PG Wodehouse, a hero of mine. "Aunt Agatha," Wodehouse wrote "had a voice of one who calls the cattle home across the sands of the Dee."

Hoylake is one of the aristocracy of golf clubs, and one of the most noble of those. Its full measure was first brought home to me at the Amateur Championship in 2000. The day after the final I flew to the US Open at Pebble Beach and as I settled back in my seat on the aeroplane I thought what a shame it was that, while Hoylake had hosted the first-ever international golf match between England and Scotland in 1902, the first match between Great Britain and Ireland and the USA (the forerunner of the Walker Cup) in 1921, and the first English Amateur Championship – as well as holding 10 Open Championships and generally doing more than its share of the initiating and staging of golf events – it had not held an Open since 1967. How disappointing it was that such a wonderful course, clearly in tip-top condition, was not scheduled to host The Open in the foreseeable future.

I wrote as much in both *The Times* and *Golf International*. I said I believed that the game's revered championships should be held on the game's best courses. I felt this way not just because that was how things were years ago, but because those courses provided vivid examinations for the modern players as well as offering a link with the past that should not be cut lightly, if at all. When a course as historically distinguished and good as Hoylake effectively disappears from public view it seems a shame, to say the least. A national treasure is less than half a treasure if it is not fully appreciated. "We are custodians of one of the great golf courses in the world. We have an obligation to share it," Harry McCaw – a past Captain of the Royal & Ancient Golf Club of St Andrews – said of his club, Royal County Down. The words could just as well have applied to Hoylake.

Happily, moves were afoot then to get Royal Liverpool back on to the rota of courses on which The Open could be staged, though I did not know it.

Far-sighted club members had struck up a relationship with far-sighted officials at the R & A and there had been much work going on behind the scenes involving a golf course architect, course changes, the local council, representatives of the railway network, the police and, of course, officials from Royal Liverpool itself. The result was that on 12 February 2001 it was announced that The Open, which had last been held at Hoylake when Roberto de Vicenzo won in 1967, would return to Hoylake. When it would return was not revealed. No matter. The intent to return was the main thing. And anyway, it did not take long for the due date to become clear, too.

In December 2002 came the further announcement. The 2006 Open would be staged at Hoylake. "Royal Liverpool is a club with a long and distinguished history and we are delighted that we are now able to bring The Open back to this wonderful course ..." Peter Dawson, now the Chief Executive but then the Secretary of the R & A, said: "Many people have contributed to the agreements that underpin today's announcement and it is right that Royal Liverpool, which is justly regarded as one of Britain's outstanding links, will again be put to the test by the world's top golfers." Dawson made this announcement personally to the 100 or so members gathered in the clubhouse, who were as pleased at the news as they were at the realisation that 2006 would be the 50th anniversary of Peter Thomson's hat trick of Open victories.

Preceding page: John Hopkins

Opposite: A chip onto the 6th green

All in all, a circle had been squared and everyone had reason to feel pleased with themselves. One of the most historic of all golf clubs, where John Ball Jnr and Harold Hilton were members and where Bobby Jones, the amateur, had won in 1930, his imperishable year, was back among the aristocracy of the competitive game. How fitting!

These words were begun in an hotel in San Diego, California, just about as far from Hoylake as it is possible to go. As I wrote them, in February 2005, I wondered what Darwin would make of all that was going on at Royal Liverpool at the moment as preparations for the 2006 Open moved on apace? What would he think of the changes to the course brought about by the R & A? What would he say about the caravanserai that will descend on Hoylake for the first Open here for 39 years? Indeed, what would he make of the fact that this foreword was being written on a laptop computer, the size of a briefcase, that shortly would be plugged in to a mobile telephone little bigger than a pack of cigarettes, after which a number would be dialled, a few buttons pressed and in little more time than it took Darwin to take a couple of practice swings, the words would have travelled from California to Wirral?

I have one other reason for holding Hoylake as high in my esteem as I do. I call it the Turner connection. Other clubs have their credentials; some strong, some overwhelming. None, so far as I know, can count among their admirers one of the best painters produced by this country, namely JMW Turner.

Turner was born in 1775 "... in London to working-class parents" goes the introduction accorded to him at the Turner, Whistler, Monet exhibition held at the Tate Britain gallery in London between February and May 2005. "During a career of over 50 years he produced an enormous range of landscapes in oils, watercolours and prints, collecting material through travels in Britain and Europe, especially Italy. Although his achievement was recognised

Opposite: A view from the 11th green across the broad reaches of the River Dee, during an evocative sunset over the Welsh hills by the art establishment, he was not admitted to its highest honours. His greatest champion was the critic, John Ruskin. Turner died at the age of 75. The work he bequeathed to the British nation had a profound influence on later painters, including Whistler and Monet."

What has Turner to do with Royal Liverpool? The answer is this: I think Turner acquired his remarkable ability to paint so vividly by spending time on the Wirral peninsula or across in north Wales and seeing the flaming sunsets that are so dramatic in this part of the world. Turner was able to keep the colours in his mind's eye until he came to use these images in his paintings. Think of 'Sun Setting Over a Lake' which he painted between 1840 and 1845, for example. Think of 'The Scarlet Sunset: a Town on a River', painted a few years earlier. Look at the colours in his painting entitled 'Venice: Looking Across the Lagoon at Sunset' and marvel at the colour in 'The Burning of the Houses of Lords and Commons'.

The critic Sam Smiles talks of Turner's ability to produce "sumptuous colour". "The notion of a Turner sky, usually applied to spectacular sunsets, is widely understood, linking the artist with effects of weather which he alone is deemed to have noticed and celebrated in his art," Smiles wrote. I have evidence to support my claim that Turner visited this part

A liverbird stands sentinel – the traditional mascot of the city of Liverpool. This one was originally on the grandstand of the old racecourse; it was donated by the Beazley family in 1938

of Merseyside. In a guide to the Wirral peninsula, a local author writes: "Local tradition has it that the immortal Turner came here to paint them [his sunsets]." I was told this on one of my first visits and I used it in one of my articles in *The Times*. A reader from the Wirral wrote to me and asked for the evidence to support my claim. "I found this comment fascinating and contacted the Tate gallery in London for clarification of your comments re Turner," he wrote. "However, they assured me that Turner never travelled to Merseyside and could find no trace of any sketches or paintings." I replied that I had not said he had done any sketches or paintings of this part of England, but that he had visited it on his travels and been inspired by what he saw. Turner was a considerable traveller.

Smiles tells us that he visited Bath and Malmesbury in the summer of 1791, Wales in 1792, the Midlands in 1794, south Wales and the Isle of Wight in 1795, the north of England in 1797 and Wales, again, in 1798 and 1799. Am I wrong to believe that on these travels, or at some other time, Turner was on the Wirral peninsula as dusk approached and was able to see the sun setting over Stanley Road with Hilbre island in the foreground and the Welsh hills and Snowdonia in the background? That is an image I carry in my mind's eye and until someone can prove to me that Turner never went near this end of the Wirral peninsula that is what I shall continue to believe.

"Hoylake golf is never, or so it seems to me, slack or casual; it is the golf of men rigorously brought up, who will always do their best and die if need be in the last of their own sacred ditches. This is a spirit which is often lacking in those trained in softer, less exacting surroundings, and it fills the visitor with admiration and a little awe. To play on such a course must make a man humble so that he wants to learn, and proud so that he determines to be worthy of his school. What better blend of qualities could a golfer desire? What better place is there to install them than this dear, flat, historic expanse of Hoylake, blown by mighty winds, breeder of mighty champions?"

Those were the words with which Darwin ended his foreword in 1933.

What a noble course it is! How stern a test of skill and strength! It may not at first sight be a beautiful one to the stranger who looks out with disappointed eyes on that expanse only broken here and there by its characteristic cops. To those who know it, it has a beauty of its own and let that suffice.

John Hopkins

John Hopkins, May 2006

Chapter One

Introduction

1st hole

It is an enormous privilege for me to captain The Royal Liverpool Golf Club in 2006, especially with the return of The Open after such a lengthy absence and, of course, with the publication of this wonderful book that provides an insightful and fascinating history of the Club.

The duties of the Captain are to be the Club's ambassador and figure head, representing it both at home and abroad; a responsibility I am looking forward to undertaking. I believe passionately that Hoylake has a unique place in the history of golf and it is truly one of the cradles of the game.

I've played golf since I was 13 and been a member of Hoylake since 1975. At one point for two years I was chairman of the committee in charge of competitions, which was again a terrific honour. I am extremely lucky to be a part of a marvellous team, which has worked tirelessly to improve the course and the clubhouse. They have been committed to attracting back The Open, which is another historic milestone in the Club's long history.

We are all delighted that the *Mighty Winds … Mighty Champions* book has come at a timely and appropriate moment to celebrate the distinguished traditions of this great club, which has had such an influence on the game at all levels. I know it has been a 'labour of love' for all those who have made valuable contributions.

Andy Cross

Andrew Cross, 2006 Captain, The Royal Liverpool Golf Club

Chapter Two

The First Professional Golf Tournament in England

On the 24th of April 1872 the first professional tournament of any importance took place outside Scotland – at Hoylake.

The members of The Royal Liverpool Golf Club had subscribed the sum of £103 and 15 shillings (£103.75). This was a great deal of money and a generous effort from the members of the newly-founded golf club. Was it a generous act or an indication of the determination to spread the word of golf throughout England to claim the high ground?

The leading members of the Club were certainly a dynamic bunch. They had already created many new competitions with splendid medals and trophies provided for the winners, which can be seen today in the Club's display cabinets. These were driven men who not only discussed but actually acted; they were men who did things, they were doers.

The Open Championship in 1872 carried a first prize of £8. The event at Hoylake would be worth £15 to the winner, with a silver medal and expenses for all competitors.

Sixteen professionals competed, having travelled from Scotland, Blackheath and Westward Ho! in Devon – a considerable distance and the only means of transport by rail. They played two rounds of 18 holes.

What is even more memorable about this first professional tournament was its winner, Young Tom Morris, the first really great golfer. He was a man ahead of his time and a man who would surely grace the pantheon of the finest golfers who have ever lived.

He had won three Open Championships on the run (1868-70) and so kept the champion's belt (now on show in the clubhouse of The Royal & Ancient Golf Club of St Andrews). In 1871 there was no tournament as Young Tom, having won three times, now owned the belt. However, it recommenced in 1872 with a new Championship Cup. Some things didn't change. Young Tom was the winner once again.

Preceding page: Golfers set to on the practice ground prior to the Easter Foursomes, 2005

Result of the First Professional Tournament:

Young Tom Morris	85...82...	=	167 (£15)
Davie Strath	82...86...	=	168 (£10)
Bob Andrews	85...86...	=	171 (£8)
John Allan	86...86...	=	172 (£7)
Jimmy Anderson	88...84...	=	172 (£6 shared)
Tom Dunn	86...88...	=	174 (£5)
*Old Tom Morris	92...84...	=	176
*David Park	92...84...	=	176

**For reasons unknown they played off. Park won and received £4.*

They won a total of £62.00 in prize money; the remainder was distributed in "expenses". Probably the first time this had ever happened and recognition that the members of this newly found golf club appreciated skill of the highest order.

There was no play-off between John Allan and Jimmy Anderson. It is likely they were happy to split the proceeds. Old Tom, though, probably had an eye to his bank balance and was in no mood for charity. The ploy, though, obviously backfired, as he lost.

It was a high-class field with four Open champions in the top eight and Young Tom winning twice as much money as he collected for winning The Open at Prestwick that same year. Even then, I am sure there were cries of professional sportsmen being overpaid, and I am sure there always will be. Surely, though, one cannot blame professional sportsmen for accepting an offer by those running the game?

The significance of that tournament has never been properly appreciated at Hoylake or in the world of golf. Perhaps it was the reluctance of the "powers that be" to accept that professional golfers were indeed a mighty skilled breed of men and not just artisans working at a game to make money.

It was to be a long time before the professional was socially accepted in the British Isles, in fact probably another 100 years. To the modern golfer this must seem absurd and I have little time for those who yearn for the bad old days of gentlemen and players.

Hoylake is honoured to have played a major part in the evolution of the professional game.

An interested figure at that event would have been the 11-year-old John Ball Tertius. His father, having taken up the game at the Club's formation had reduced his own

handicap from 36 to scratch in 12 months. John's father was not the most graceful of players, but he was effective. But what young Johnny saw was the likes of Young Tom and his fellow professionals and it must have made an indelible impression on him – all young players of any sport are great mimickers of their heroes. As young Johnny never really received any lessons of note, watching these early geniuses had an overwhelming influence.

While the event had huge appeal for this embryonic genius, it did not appeal to everyone. In certain parts of Scotland these new English golfers were considered far too big for their boots: Sassenach upstarts.

But the game that Scotland had invented and nourished required a fresh start and it was taking place on a once-primitive rabbit warren at The Royal Liverpool Golf Club, Hoylake. This was the beginning of the popularisation of the game in England and throughout the world. Liverpool, the trading centre of the world, spread the game to America and the old colonies.

With greater leisure time, the affluent Victorians took to the game and by the end of the century hundreds of new clubs were formed in England, Wales and Ireland, many of them inspired and driven by golfing missionaries from Hoylake.

It is appropriate that we can now put the record straight and celebrate our role in the genesis and development of professional golf.

I trust the Professional Golfers' Association accepts this late recognition and I am delighted to confirm that the honours board in the Club has been corrected, with Young Tom Morris's name inscribed. We look forward to similar golfers of distinction having their names added to this roll of honour in years to come.

The first professional tournament established Hoylake as a golf club with influence. That it should have taken place just three years into the Club's existence is a

1874

There have been many theories on the death of Young Tom Morris but let me quote from a newly found extract of the Revd Doctor AKH Boyd in 'Twenty-five Years at St Andrews'. Boyd was the minister of the parish church of St Andrews and his diaries often gave an eyewitness account of the golfing community.

"There was a pathetic event here at the beginning of September. The grand Old Tom Morris and his son Tom went together to North Berwick to play a great match on the links there. Tommy left his wife perfectly well. But on Saturday afternoon that fine young girl (she was no more) had her first child and at once ran down and died. A telegram was sent to Old Tom who told his son that they must leave at once. A fine yacht was put at their disposal and they were taken across the Firth of Forth. Tom did not tell his son that all was over till they were walking up from the harbour.

"I was in the house when they arrived. What can one say in such an hour? I never forget the young man's stony looks, and how, all of a sudden, he started up and cried "It's not true!" I have seen many sorrowful things, but not many like that Saturday night.

"Poor Tommy's heart was broken. On the morning of Christmas Day they found him dead in bed. So Tommy and his young wife were not long divided."

Preceding page: The 9th green

remarkable feature of a remarkable story: on the night of 15 May 1869 there was the most marvellous aurora over Hoylake and the surrounding areas, splendidly fitting as on that afternoon the Liverpool Golf Club was formed at the village's Royal Hotel.

The celestial display was a fine portent to the establishing of the second oldest golf course in England (Westward Ho!, that fine links in north Devon, being five years older). But this club at Hoylake was to have a significant role in world golf.

To the old colonies and the very old colonies of the United States of America, the connections between Liverpool and her trading outposts were inseparable. In America, for instance, we discover that even the legendary Charles Blair Macdonald, founder of the US Amateur, was a member of RLGC for 30 years.

Long before the founding of golf, Hoylake was a place of significance as a number of events took place that had an influence on world history.

In the late ninth century, the area was inhabited by Viking raiders. A number of the local towns confirm this with the suffix of 'by', the Norse name for a village. For instance, West Kirby, Greasby, Pensby, Irby, and others. Also the town called Thurstaston – meaning Thor's Stone – is a five-minute drive from Hoylake. Thor was the Norse god of sun and thunder. I do not believe the Vikings stayed too long, they were not that sort of people, but the hills close to the sea side of the course remind me of the ancient Viking graves one observes on visits to Sweden. From the 12th green at Hoylake one can see the Great Orme at Llandudno. Orme was an old Viking warrior.

During the reign of Charles II, in 1662, William Penn and his Quaker companions sailed for the Americas from the port of Hoylake. This was after the river Dee had silted up, so closing the port of Chester, and before Liverpool developed into the mighty trading port of the 18th and 19th centuries. Penn went on to found Pennsylvania and will be remembered as a key architect of the American way of life.

Thirty years on, in 1690, the sea lake was still deep enough for William of Orange to shelter about 100 boats off the coast. He gathered his 10,000 troops along the seaboard and then set sail for Ireland to fight the forces of James II at the Battle of the Boyne. The troops billeted on the land adjacent to the port and their crude accommodation was none other than the links that we play upon to this day.

By coincidence, at the same time in Scotland James II, the reigning monarch, was playing golf on the Leith links when he was approached and informed of the Irish Rebellion that was to have such a huge effect on Britain and Ireland for the next three centuries. One of the saddest results was that neither Dutch William nor any of the "wee, wee German Lairdies" had any interest in the game of golf and the development of the game in England was put back nearly 200 years.

James II was a keen golfer and before his enthronement, as Duke of York, he played many times on the Leith links whilst living in Edinburgh as commissioner for the king to the Scottish Parliament.

The Duke was challenged by two English noblemen to a game on the Leith links. The Duke could select any Scottish partner, but rather than choosing one of the courtiers or socialites he researched diligently to find the top local player and was informed that John Patersone was the finest golfer around. Patersone, a humble shoemaker, was duly enlisted to the astonishment of the ruling classes. It is quite apparent that the Duke was no fool and the golfing presence of the shoemaker was a deciding factor in the result. The Duke and the shoemaker won comfortably and the Duke gave John Patersone an equal share of the proceeds from the considerable wager.

Overjoyed with the money, he built a house at Number 100 Canongate, Edinburgh. On the wall the Duke had an escutcheon erected, bearing the arms of the Patersone family, with a crest in the form of a Dexter's hand holding a golf club. On it was written his name, with the motto "Far and Sure". The derivation of this motto was that if you bought your boots from John Patersone you would be able to walk "far and sure". This is, in fact, the motto of many golf clubs, including The Royal Liverpool.

I paid a visit to Canongate a few years back and found that the house had been razed to the ground but at the back, in the courtyard, is a stone with a Latin inscription that bears the above account. Further wording was "I hate no person" which is an anagram for John Patersone, with the J used as an I.

There are many golfing historians who think of the Duke and the shoemaker's triumph as the first international golf match.

Locating the precise origins of the game of golf is difficult. Etymologically, the origins of golf in those far-off

Above: Young Tom Morris, winner of the first professional golf tournament in 1872

Top: 1897 Open, Charles Hutchings drives

Below: 1897 Open, crowds gather for the presentation

Scotia days are not chronicled. In those days, the only events that were chronicled were those involving the reigning monarch and this depended on the ability of that king, very often a nonentity whose only instincts were for self-preservation.

Of one fact we are certain: the game of golf most certainly started in Scotland. There have been many variations of the game:

The Belgians had Chole and Crosse, which involved hitting a wooden ball with a stick. The French had Jeu de Mail, which was similar but a leather ball was used, stuffed with moss or hay.

The English played a game called Cambuta in the mid-14th century. A ball stuffed with feathers was propelled with a crooked stick. There is a stained glass window in Gloucester cathedral which features a man swinging a weapon. It is called 'the golfer' but in all probability it is a Cambuta player.

The Netherlands had Kolven, but that was usually played on ice.

Many other countries, particularly those from a totalitarian regime, have claimed the game of golf, including the old Soviet Union, China and even Morocco.

Surely, though, it could only be the Scots who could have invented such precise persecution with that faint glimmer of fun, hint of intrigue and, if all goes well, mild satisfaction? Surely it could only be the Scottish nation who could ever have had the imagination to inflict such misery on mankind when intending pleasure? We thank them for their contribution but wonder if it was a cunning, conspiratorial way of reducing even the most easy-going sportsman to a state of apoplectic gloom?

Not that the Scots have the monopoly on misery. Far from it. But there is little doubt that Scotland is the home of the game; golf was first played there and so ends the discussion.

Back at Hoylake and a further 100 years on, Sir John Stanley built the Royal Hotel on Stanley Road (the hotel's boundaries ran parallel to the current 17th green and 18th tee). It was 1792, and Sir John's intention was to capitalise upon the new fad of bathing in the sea. Hoylake was ideal, as the beach was long and shallow. Bathing meant paddling, with the odd splash thrown in. No strenuous butterfly or crawl.

The affluent classes homed in on Hoylake because at that time there was a conflict with the French and it was thought advisable not to holiday on the south coast in case there was some form of attack.

There were many accounts of the hotel and surrounding areas, notably recorded by Anna Seward, known as *'The Swan of Litchfield'*. She was regarded as a 'minor poetess' and wrote in a letter dated 5 September 1794: "The [hotel's] apartments are handsome and commodious, and the accommodation wonderfully comfortable for a situation without either town, or village, in its neighbourhood.

"The fine downs on which the edifice stands are level and extensive, affording the best walking imaginable. A light sandy soil leaves them [feet] almost instantly dry even after heavy rain. They extend to the cliffs all round the house, whose front side looks at the main ocean. Beyond the sand island it is open, and to the eye unbounded. On the left it flows

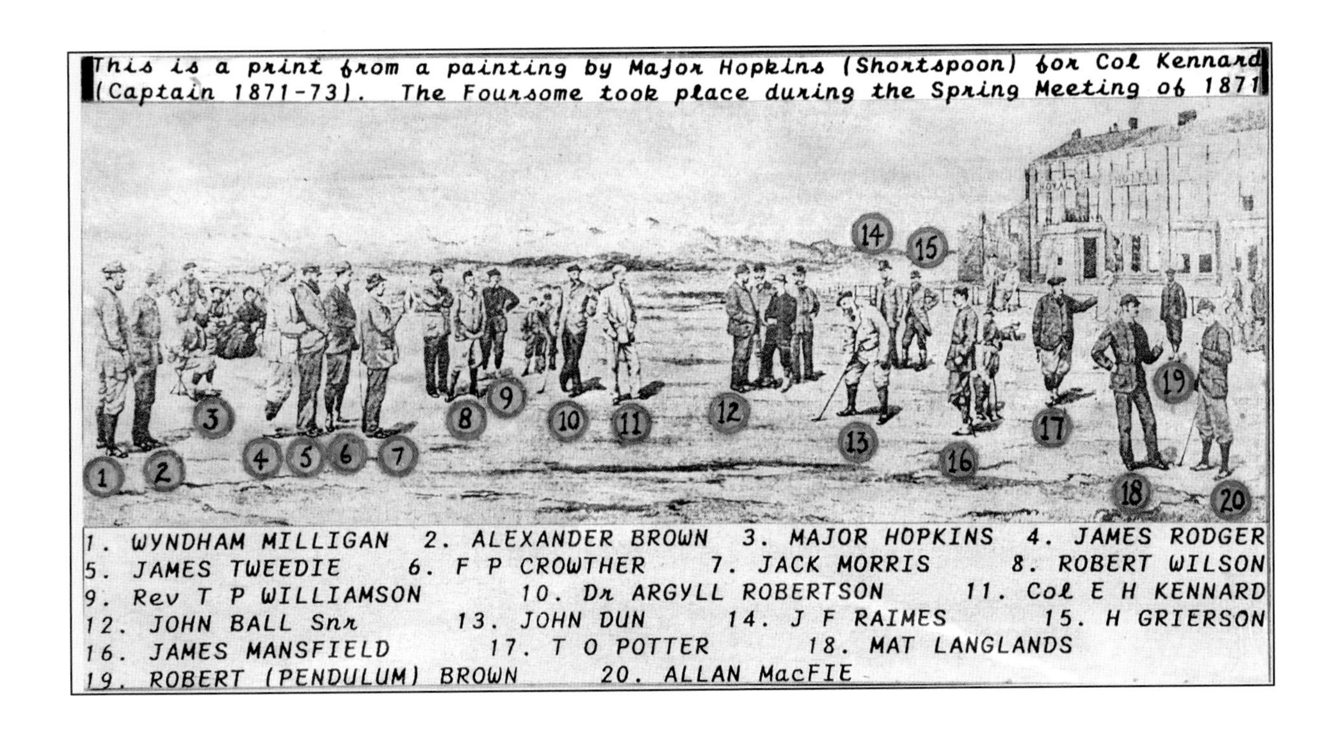

down at high water into the river Dee, in the broad channel; and the opposite shores of Wales and her mountains are sufficiently, if not sublimely picturesque." On this occasion there were 40 other people staying at the hotel, which she described as "certainly the resort of genteel people. Though a knot of young men of fortune, whose gigs, phaetons and horses cover the downs often during the day. During the evening there was singing and dancing, but little of the mind."

Nevertheless, she did enjoy her visit, commenting on her return home: "my health has certainly benefited from my excursion; from my nineteen oceanic immersions and for the exquisitely pure air of the High Lake and downs".

In 1841, WE Gladstone (a future prime minister) visited Hoylake and was impressed by the scenery: "Paestum without the temples" observed the well-read premier.

Today, Wirral is still a destination for those in pursuit of recreation. It is a sporting haven. In an area 10 miles by six miles there are 14 golf clubs, seven sailing clubs, 23 cricket clubs, 15 rugby clubs and innumerable football clubs.

The unique geography creates a wonderfully mild climate, and the annual average temperature is two degrees above that of Cannes in the south of France.

Liverpool and Manchester airports are within an hour and the Roman city of Chester 30 minutes away. Within an hour and a half you can be walking in the beautiful Lake District or the rugged magnificence of Snowdonia.

Lord (WF) Deedes on a visit to Hoylake commented on the surrounds and surmised that the "professional classes" live a lot better than their counterparts in the south of England. A couple of days with friends at Hoylake convinced him.

"You can work in Liverpool and be home in a quarter of the time it takes many to travel a similar distance in London. The gardens are bigger, the houses, many of them built in the Liverpool heyday, are spacious and cheaper. Dogs get better walks. At this time of year (August 1996) the light that shines on the Welsh hills across the Dee estuary fills me with awe. There is nothing more tantalising than to stare across the sands of Dee, reflecting on her fate and being filled with melancholy – until your golfing partner calls you to order. I usually play the next hole badly.

"The only other golf course I know with a comparably romantic view is Newcastle, County Down.

"Give yourself a chance to smell the flowers, the old American golf champion Walter Hagen used to say. When you play at Hoylake, you are reminded what good advice that was."

We have always kept that information to ourselves. However, the great landscape artist JMW Turner made frequent visits to Hoylake and the adjoining town of West Kirby

Opposite: Liverpool's majestic waterfront – now a UNESCO World Heritage Site – the departure point for 9.5 million people who emigrated to New York between 1850 and 1900

to gain inspiration for the sunsets he was noted for. There is little doubt that when the sun sets in the summer months, the long, lingering evenings as it disappears between Hilbre island and the Welsh coast fill one with inspiration and an indelible image of God's beauty.

With the silting up of 'The Lake' from which Hoylake drew its name, it became an insignificant fishing village surrounded by sand dunes, an area of little value. In 1809 a gentleman by the name of Samuel Baxter of Hinderton (10 miles from Hoylake) had bought the Manor House of Hoylake and the town itself. He was forced to sell a part of the estate to set up his daughter in marriage.

The sum of £90 was agreed between Baxter and a fisherman called Eccles. Baxter required a little more money and offered to sell the whole of the township for an extra £10. Eccles was more than willing but on consulting his wife, a judicious woman, she saw no reason for the purchase of a sandy wasteland and advised against.

To this day the Eccles connection continues as David Eccles, the great great grandson of the fisherman Eccles, is a member of the Club.

By 1846 the Liverpool Hunt Club laid out a racecourse on the warren over both The Flat and Steeplechase codes. Many mighty days of sport took place on what was regarded as perfect turf for horse racing.

It was observed that, "the weather was everything that pleasure-seekers could wish for. A cloudless sky, a warm, genial spring sun, and a bracing atmosphere, are great essentials to outdoor amusement, and on Saturday the requisite conditions were fulfilled," reported the *Liverpool Daily Post*.

"A large crowd from the surrounding neighbourhoods were congregated on various parts of the course, while the grandstand and enclosures were thronged during the entire afternoon by a mixture of gentlemen, yeomen, tradesmen and noisily-conspicuous betting men 'from Manchester' who shouted themselves hoarse in proclaiming the odds in different races." Some things don't change.

Opposite: Hilbre island through the haze, with the reed beds which are home to the rare Natterjack toad

Below: The former racecourse on the site of the Club, which operated between 1846 and 1876

Overleaf: Three stalwart members of the local 'Village Play' golfing fraternity: from left, John Dalton, Captain; Jim McVey, Chairman and Peter Williams, Secretary

The legendary John Ball Junior, right, with his father John Ball Senior, who ran the original Royal Hotel

The race meetings brought much-needed extra income to the local fishermen as the local fishing grounds were disappearing with the silting up of the Dee. This meant sailing out into deeper and more dangerous waters.

There are some records to suggest that a number of Scottish gentlemen formed a nine-hole course beside the parish church in West Kirby as early as 1852. Also on the warren at the West Kirby end of the Hoylake course, nine holes of sorts were laid out. But by 1869 the appetite was for something far more substantial.

J Muir Dowie lived in West Kirby and, when his father-in-law Robert Chambers visited, they spent some time in the area looking for suitable ground to play the ancient game. Chambers being a self-made man and a golfer of note had all the attributes to help his son-in-law create a golf links. Not only had he won the first attempt at an amateur championship at St Andrews in 1858 (a tournament that foundered) but in Old Tom Morris's brother George he also retained a personal professional.

With J Muir Dowie living in West Kirby it would appear obvious that the area around where the present eighth green and ninth tee is today, would be a perfect place for the course to begin. This was rejected and, with a view to locating the perfect clubhouse, they travelled by horse and cart round to Hoylake where they approached the owner of the Royal Hotel, Mr John Ball Snr, and suggested that they play from the land adjacent to his premises. This was known as the rabbit warren, but though the area was covered with rabbit holes the ground must have had some fine terrain as proved by the success of horse racing there since 1846.

Mr Ball, being an astute man and aware of a dwindling number of patrons at the hotel, saw a money-making opportunity. He welcomed them with open arms when they suggested that the hotel could be used by the members of the proposed new golf club.

Not only did he welcome them, he made available a room for their comfort. It was ideal. A meeting room and ample opportunity to partake of suitable refreshment.

John Ball Snr was nobody's fool. They were welcome, but on his terms. Despite the social mores dictated by Victorian society he was invited to become a founder member. So the perceived standoffishness of the great Victorian merchants and noblemen could be called into question. Why associate with a publican? Why mix with such folk? But these merchants had made a living out of finding solutions to problems. They needed John Ball and he needed them. It was early in 1869 when J Muir Dowie sent the following letter to a selected group:

> It has been suggested that Hoylake offers a suitable and convenient ground for playing Golf, and some friends have asked me to endeavour to organize a Golf Club. Your name has been mentioned as a probable member, and I take this liberty of asking you to join.
> The proposed subscription was ten shillings (50p). A meeting will be held on SATURDAY, the 15th of May, at the ROYAL HOTEL, HOYLAKE, at 4.15 p.m.
> Your reply before then will oblige.
> Your obedient servant.
> J.Muir.Dowie.
> 13th May 1869.

Two days later the following attended this meeting: A Balfour, John Ball Jnr, FL Buckle, J Muir Dowie, J Dun, J Forman, RH Forman, RB Forman, J Greenshields, M Houstoun, W Houstoun, W Johnstone, G Leslie, WD Robertson, WCA Milligan, GS Robertson, HJ Simpson, A Stoddart, L Stoddart, JL Walker, J Tweedie.

J Muir Dowie, the first Captain of the Liverpool Golf Club, 1869-71

Above top and below: 1894 Amateur Championship

Opposite: A perspective of Hoylake's oldest green, the 2nd

That evening the Hoylake sky was a mass of exhilarating colours. Locals believed a huge comet had passed over and that this was the tail they witnessed. They were so awestruck by the event they considered it a great portent. In this they were right.

At the meeting they resolved: "That it is desirable to establish a golf club at Hoylake." After some discussion it was decided that the council should consist of the Secretary, the Treasurer, GS Robertson, JL Walker, RH Forman, J Dun, John Ball. Mr J Muir Dowie was elected Captain, Mr G Leslie, Secretary, and Mr J Tweedie, Treasurer.

Gladstone was the Prime Minister at the time; on this day he had arrived by train at Hawarden (25 minutes away) for a short break. In the *Liverpool Daily Post* that day there was an advertisement offering passengers a return sea voyage from Liverpool to Glasgow with a cabin for £1.

The first nine holes were laid out by Chambers and his personal professional, Morris. The Captain resolved to present a cup, for a competition between the members. This was held on 13 October 1869 and was named The Dowie Challenge Cup for the best scratch score. This was won by John Dun with a score of 103. The Captain scored 189 and a certain W Kirkwood went round in 205. For nine holes! These scores may sound extreme to the modern golfer but please note that there were no fairways and no greens as we know them today. Most players only had two or three clubs and they had to contend with rabbit holes, rushes, briars and gorse. If the ball could be seen it had to be played from where it lay – no identification permitted, just whack it until it moved. John Ball Senior won the handicap competition.

After the golf had been completed the members retired to the Royal Hotel. There were various contributions to the feast. The Captain produced a large basket of Muscatel wine and grapes from his extensive

graperies and cellar at "mild and balmy" West Kirby. Mr Dun contributed a haunch of venison and Mr Simpson two bottles of whisky from McKenchnie's famous distillery at Girvan. A fine evening's entertainment was reported in the words of a chronicler: "When the list of toasts were exhausted, sundry songs, chiefly Burns's, were capitally sung, particularly 'Willie brewed a peck o'mawt'. As the parting hour of ten o' clock approached 'Auld Lang Syne' was enthusiastically sung with linked hands all around by not a few Scottish members in orthodox Highland style, and then a verse of our English national anthem, fervently and right royally sung, closed the proceedings."

The Club had got off to a cracking start.

It grew quickly once the first nine holes had being laid out. It was not exactly scientific as the green was a piece of flattish ground and a hole was cut with a penknife. The new professional, Jack Morris, had on three occasions done the nine holes in 47 strokes, which was regarded as good scoring.

But why the great interest in this foreign game from Scotia? Since 1850 Liverpool had become the centre of world trade, which attracted ambitious Scottish gentlemen to move south. Further, Liverpool was the European gateway to the New World – the United States of America. Between 1850 and 1900 over nine million people sailed from Liverpool to Ellis Island in New York. They were from all parts of Europe: from persecuted refugees to those who were simply very poor; from those with adventure in their souls to those who had heard of gold rushes and the land of opportunity.

HOYLAKE, 1869. ENTER GOLF, EXIT RACING.

Many American families have some contact with Liverpool. Relations of the presidential families sailed from the port: the Kennedys, Clintons, Carters, Fords, Nixons and most of the great families that developed the United States of America into the most influential country on this earth.

Many of the Scots and Irish on their way to the Americas found business chances around the Liverpool area and so stopped the journey and built up their fortunes here.

On 7 June 1869, the *Liverpool Courier* reported: "On Saturday the usual quietude of Hoylake was broken by two events out of the common run of amusements. These were amateur horse and pony races, and, what is likely to prove of much more abiding interest, the Scottish national game of golf was played on ground which, should the Club prosper, will become the central attraction of our townsmen from North of the Tweed."

The account goes on to describe how the Links area might have been made for the purpose. The reporter who wrote the article little knew what a true prophet he was to prove.

The new council at the Club were busy with all sorts of initiatives. By spring the following year a special meeting was called to approve the Rules and Regulations and to pass them as permanent rules for the governance of the Club.

The Club Gold Medal had been purchased and is still played for on the first day of the spring meeting. It can be seen in the Club display cabinet together with many of the original medals.

One trophy that cannot be seen is the Challenge Belt which was played for under the following conditions: "To remain in the possession of the holder as long as they could hold it, being obliged to accept any challenge by members of the Club in writing within one month after winning, or to lose the Belt; it being at the holder's option to accept more than one challenge during the month." There was no rule as to the method of challenging, except that it should be in writing so any holder could carefully pick the weakest challenge received during the month. It appears to have languished then disappeared shortly after its inauguration and no sight has been had of the Belt for over 100 years.

At a special meeting a revolutionary change was made. The name of the Club was changed to West Lancashire and Cheshire Golf Club. Thankfully at the first general meeting that followed, the new name was vetoed and The Liverpool Golf Club was restored. How strange life can be. A quirk of fate could have changed many events that followed. It was also reported that after the first year there was a balance of £1 11s and 7d (£1.58), which was highly satisfactory. The next year's income was put at £150.

After such a short time the Club was now firmly established. They must have had some dynamic characters so we must pay thanks to the Council of the time led by Dowie, together with the Secretary Leslie and Tweedie. The members were so full of positive

optimism that they wanted a uniform and it was decided that this should be "A red cloth coat with green cloth collar." The same as the Captains wear on important occasions today.

Events were moving fast and members were pouring in. A room was hired at the Royal Hotel, for use as a locker room; caddies were available; the charge was three pence a round. Golf rules were drawn up, one being that: "No ball shall be teed less than six clubs' lengths or more than ten clubs' lengths from the hole." In all probability it was the duty of the first couple out to place a feather or some object in the hole to mark the position for the golfers following behind.

Jack Morris was appointed professional, a position he took with some reluctance as he was only 20 years of age and far from confident. His father George Morris had brought him from Scotland and, feeling that there was not much chance of his son doing well, suggested that he should return home. He told his father he would give it a week to see if he liked it. Jack stayed for 60 years, a record for service from a club professional. This made him a friend of all the members of the Club. "Himself not least, but honoured of them all."

Jack was given an old horsebox at the back of his stables as his first shop.

A year later the course was extended to 18 holes and in 1871 Prince Arthur consented to become Honorary President of the Club and from that date the Club assumed the designation of The Royal Liverpool Golf Club. Immediately, Lord Stanley of Alderley (the lord of the manor) accepted the office of Honorary Vice President. Our north American friends will be interested that it was the same Lord Stanley who gave his name to the major ice hockey tournament that is still played today. The leading force in securing the Royal prefix was Lieutenant Colonel Kennard, who was to become the second Captain of the Club the following year. His portrait can be seen on the upper landing of the clubhouse.

The club was now moving at great speed. The first professional golf tournament was held in 1872 as outlined earlier. In the very short period of three years the Club had made great strides and it must be accepted that it was the drive of these early members who established the game of golf in England.

Geographically, Hoylake was well placed between Scotland and the clubs in the south of England, Blackheath and Westward Ho! This must have helped the progress, but it was the determination and the will of those far-sighted men which made things happen.

By 1875, young John Ball had made a huge impression on the golfing fraternity, to such an extent that a match was arranged pitting he and hero Young Tom against Davie Strath and Captain Moldsworth of the Westward Ho! club. But the early death of Young Tom prevented the event taking place. Earlier in the year Young Tom had been playing at North Berwick with his father when he was notified that his wife was extremely ill giving birth. Without a second thought he headed for St Andrews across the Firth of Forth by boat,

Left: Lieutenant Colonel EH Kennard, the second Captain of the RLGC, 1871-73. He was responsible for the Royal prefix being bestowed on the Club. From an original painting by TC Gotch but before leaving harbour he was told that his wife and son had died in childbirth. He was shattered and never recovered. He died of a broken heart six months later on Christmas Day 1875.

Young Tom is buried in the graveyard at St Andrews' cathedral. The first of the golfing greats had died at the age of 25. He was a genius who accomplished much but what more could he have achieved had his life not been so short? He was the first golfing great and would surely find a place in the pantheon of the greatest golfers who ever lived.

With the Royal designation, HRH the Duke of Connaught was invited to a function at the Club in 1876 and accepted. It was thought that even though he was patron for 72 years he never set foot in the Club. I am delighted to record through ponderous research we have found out that he did so. The visit was a tremendous success and a great party was held. A marquee was erected opposite the Royal Hotel to house the celebrations. After a fine luncheon of local shrimps and a hack of venison an exhibition match was played. Mr John Dun and Davie Strath played Tom and Jack Morris, the latter pair winning by one hole. There is no indication that the Duke played the game but he was the Patron until his death in 1942. This is the longest period any royal patron has held such a position.

In this year, at the tender age of 15, John Ball Tertius played in The Open at St Andrews and finished sixth. His journey to Scotland must have been quite an adventure for a boy of his age. There were still no cars, just the stagecoach and in John's case the train. His prize for finishing in such a high position was £1 cash. His caddy advised him to pocket the money, which he duly did. This was going to cause problems in later years as he was playing as an amateur, a status he kept the whole of his golfing life.

By 1879 the hotel proved too small for the membership as well as the general public who enjoyed the beer in the bars. What was to be done? The club approached Mr Ball and told him of their problem. Seizing the opportunity he offered to build an extension to the hotel. A special general meeting was called to consider, and pass, a proposed extension of the Royal Hotel, which was in future going to make a more fitting home for the golfers of Hoylake.

Guy Farrar writes: "This extension included a clubroom, and other accommodation, and also caddies' quarters. The rent paid to Mr John Ball was fifty pounds a year, and the lease was signed for fifteen years. In the illustration of the Royal Hotel this addition can be seen as part of the building on the right of the down spout, as well as the low building beyond. Lockers were fixed all around the clubroom" (similar to the ones at Royal North Norfolk golf club at Brancaster). He continues: "and they are there to this day, some of them full of old clubs – ghostly relics covered with the dust of years – once the pride of their original owner." Oh, to be able to see them now.

"Dinners now took place in the new Clubroom, the golfers of 1880 being very proud of their spacious and commodious home. The cost of the improvement made it necessary to increase the subscription, and at the next annual meeting it was raised by one pound to thirty shillings (£1.50), after an unsuccessful protest on the part of 'The Chieftain' – Mr Robert Wilson. There was great excitement at the spring and autumn meetings as members from around the country alighted on the Royal Hotel. One can imagine the bar parlour at that moment – all the chaff, and the challenges thrown out for the next day, and all the craft and humility used to gain the best of the handicap; and Mr Ball's universal challenge, 'me and my son will play any two' – a challenge by the way that was very seldom accepted. Great days, great golf, and great friendliness and fun were the outstanding characteristics of those meetings that took place so many years ago."

The position of Secretary was held by a number of members in the early years but in 1882 one of the most important appointments that the Club ever made was that of Thomas Owen Potter. He was a former county cricketer and a man of financial means, an extraordinary character who lived in the Royal Hotel that was under the managership of John Ball Junior.

Potter, who was known as Tosper, was a fine administrator. He was also a drinker of fine wines, notably Claret, and had a love of shrimps. It was an unwritten custom at the Club that all new members would give him a bottle of his favourite tipple. One month 18 new members joined the Club.

He always played with John Ball Snr in the Club competitions. On many occasions they arranged for a hamper to be taken to the furthest extremity of the course next to the present 8th green. On arriving they tucked into the hamper with great gusto and then headed for home "like giants refreshed".

Clarets

Pure Bordeaux Wines of the celebrated
1864 and 1865 vintages
13/-, 16/-, 20/-, and 24/- per dozen

R & H Fair Wine Merchants,
12 Dale Street, Liverpool

OPEN AM
EUR CHAM

Chapter Three

1885-1900

Thomas Owen Potter was a visionary as well as an administrator. He was instrumental in the inaugural Amateur Championship. This took place in 1885 and the winner was AF Macfie, a club member. In those far-off days the administration of the R & A was, to say the least, haphazard and not of the professional standard we have come to expect today.

There had been amateur events of sorts before but they were never sustained. It required the dynamism of an individual like Potter to establish such an important event. The year after, St Andrews hosted the Amateur Championship and claimed it as their innovation. The debate raged as to which club did host the first Championship until a few years later the R & A acquiesced and quietly accepted that the first Amateur was held at Hoylake.

For the first 30 years it was mainly played at Hoylake or St Andrews with the odd visit to Prestwick, St George's and Muirfield. For the event to be played over the original greens would have been perfectly acceptable to Potter and the members of Hoylake.

Over the 16 years from 1895, apart from the visit of the Duke of Connaught, the Club hosted many other visitors, a tradition I am delighted to say is upheld to this day. Guests from all over the British Isles and many from the United States of America and the rest of the world are made most welcome and long may that remain so. Another guest was Charles Blair MacDonald from Chicago. He had studied at the university of St Andrews and became entranced with the game. An obvious stopping place was Hoylake as all transatlantic traffic began and ended at the great port of Liverpool. In fact, he was a member for 30 years, well before golf started in America. He was the USA's major golfing administrator up to his death. He was also a fine golfer in his own right, the first winner of the US Amateur in 1895 at Newport RI.

But was he? The previous year, in 1894, what was thought to be the first United States Amateur was won by a gentleman called WG Lawrence, a member of Newport Golf Club, who took 188 shots over the 36 holes and beat CB MacDonald by a shot. MacDonald was not a sporting loser.

Despite agreeing to the conditions of entry he claimed, after he had lost, that it could not be a proper championship as all amateur events had to be decided by matchplay. There was the most frightful brouhaha, until the St Andrews club of New York, the oldest club in America, helped solve the issue.

They organised another event at their own club some weeks later. On this occasion LB Stoddart of The Royal Liverpool Golf Club, who was over in America on business, entered and played the much-fancied MacDonald in the final.

The night before the final MacDonald was entertained at dinner by some friends and supporters. Fine wines flowed and he did not make his bed till 5 am.

The final was played in torrential rain and the course was a quagmire. Stoddart took a three-hole lead but was pegged back to all square with one hole to play. However, the late night caught up with him and, hampered by the weather, he made a mess of the last hole. Stoddart became champion with an immaculate four at the last.

Once again MacDonald was dissatisfied at his defeat. Probably correctly he thought he was the better golfer. He sourly complained that it should not have been called the US Amateur; his excuse this time was that no national organisation had sponsored it.

This was upheld and by the next event the United States Golf Association was formed and, under its auspices, the Amateur was held at Newport Country Club. Stoddart entered but was knocked out in the first round. Needless to say, and at last, Charles Blair MacDonald won the first ever US Amateur Championship!

Trade between Liverpool and America was booming, not only cotton but also sugar and many other commodities. Liverpool was regarded as the gateway to the New World, a place where an extraordinary cross-section of Europeans came to make the journey to Ellis Island in New York. The millions who left Liverpool between 1850 and 1900 went for numerous reasons, mainly to escape from poverty. Of those who took to Liverpool and stayed, the 1851 census recorded 3,000 Scots registered in Liverpool. By 1901 it was over 10,000. Liverpool has always been regarded as the second home of Irishmen and north Walians.

In golf, though, the Scots were prominent. In the early days of Hoylake the names came rolling off the tongue: the Muirs, Browns, Blyths, Grahams, Leslies, Tweedies and Stewarts.

The next Amateur was held at St Andrews and the winner was another member – and future Captain – of both The Royal Liverpool and the R & A: Horace G Hutchinson.

He was a man who learned his golf at Westward Ho! and Oxford University but had very close connections with Hoylake. He was a great golfing administrator as well as the first great golf writer. Further, he defended his title the next year at Hoylake, defeating a man

Preceding page: A close-up view of the Hoylake honours board

Opposite: In the bleak midwinter on the 4th green – a rare shot of snow on the course

Above: Two examples of the splendid watercolours by Major Hopkins, which are on display in the clubhouse

who was by then regarded as invincible on the Hoylake links – Johnny Ball. Horace won the match on the final hole. The Amateur was now firmly established in the golfing calendar. So was Johnny Ball.

Great events were to follow.

The 1890 Amateur took place at Hoylake for the third time. Despite the Olympian reputation that Ball had acquired there was still a field of 44 golfers. He breezed through the first round and beat the new Hoylake prospect, Harold Hilton, in the second round after being two down at the turn. This proved his hardest match until he met the great Scottish golfer Johnnie Laidlay. They were the two top amateur golfers at the time and the international rivalry was greatly anticipated.

"Never in the final of a championship has a more brilliant start been made," wrote Harold Hilton, as Ball was six up after eight holes. Laidlay fought back but succumbed on the 15th. What a match it was, and greatly appreciated by a large crowd.

Prestwick, the home of The Open, was holding the event in 1890.

Johnny loved this magnificent course and, today, anybody who loves to play on a traditional links will adore this majestic terrain, beautifully presented on land the good lord had no other intention for than its use for the Royal and Ancient game. Prestwick is to this day one of the great golfing experiences.

Johnny was 28 years of age at the time of the event. As he progressed there was the greatest excitement. Horace Hutchinson wrote of the end to his final round: "He was going to do the most terrible thing that had ever yet been done in golf – he, as an amateur, was going to win The Open Championship. Dr Purves was hurrying along at my elbow as we went with the gallery towards the 16th hole. 'Horace' he said to me, in a voice of much solemnity, 'this is a great day for golf.'

"And so it was; and also a great day for Hoylake."

Johnny, not wanting "too much of a fuss" alighted from the train returning him to Hoylake a stop early so as to miss the great crowd waiting for him.

He walked home along the beach and up to the Royal Hotel, where he unpacked and revealed The Open Championship Trophy (Claret Jug) for its first sighting in England.

This was the first time an Englishman, not to mention an amateur, had won The Open. In the history of golf only one amateur would ever emulate this feat: Bobby Jones, 40 years later.

Johnny Ball prepared himself in his normal manner by working hard on his farm. He never sacrificed his business for the sake of a match. Probably on this account he played all the better. Always an early riser his fitness must have been exceptional and he was a natural athlete.

He also had other sporting skills: he excelled at shooting, as the rabbits on the Hoylake course could testify. A fine horse rider and ice skater, he also played rugby for the Hoylake club. A notable runner, he could give a yard or two over 100 and still beat any local over hurdles or on the flat.

The two major championships of 1891 were to take place at St Andrews. In the amateur event Johnny lost to RB Sharp of Dundee, but local interest was continued to the end when Harold Hilton lost on the last hole of the final to Laidlay.

John Behrend, in his marvellous book *John Ball of Hoylake* tells "that The Open for 1891 was to be held on 6 October but this was not announced by the R & A until the beginning of September, a mere month's notice, which elicited the following letter from Thomas Potter, The Royal Liverpool Secretary", to the Secretary of the R & A Mr Grace.

Above: Further examples of Major Hopkins' watercolours.
The lower painting shows the rails of the racecourse interfering with a golfer's back-swing

Preceding page: The clubhouse looking out over the 1st

4th September 1891.
My Dear Grace,
I see by yesterday's *Scotsman* that The Open Championship is fixed for the 6th October... It was fully John Ball Junior's intention to have another battle for the Championship honours but you having clashed with our Autumn Meeting week, it is very doubtful if you will see him at St Andrews this year; do not you think these important fixtures could be settled earlier in the year and advertised so that other clubs could make arrangements accordingly?
With kind regards,
TO Potter

The Royal Liverpool Autumn Meeting dates of 7 and 9 October had been advertised since the beginning of the year. Grace obviously replied in conciliatory terms and a further letter was dispatched to Grace on 9 September.

My Dear Grace,
Thank you very much for your letter of yesterday just received; I think if the date could be altered it would certainly be desirable. The 26th September will suit John Ball Jnr. And to this effect I wired you this afternoon guessing that my letter would not reach you in time for your meeting tomorrow, the result of which you will kindly let me know.
If at your meeting tomorrow, the 26th September be accepted you can easily telegraph the alteration to The Field Magazine etc...
I will send you the cup next week under advice and thanking you for the trouble you have taken in this matter, believe me.
Yours sincerely,
TO Potter

"In the event the meeting confirmed the original date, so sadly it is not possible to record that the date of The Open Championship was altered to avoid a clash with The Royal Liverpool Club Medal."

Such wonderful communication is certainly that of another century, the words of autocratic administrators, men of independent means, men who took few prisoners. Perhaps they were pompous, but if they wanted action there was no room for pussy footing around and less room still for political correctness. They got the job done.

John Behrend continues: "Johnny had no intention of missing the first day of the Hoylake Autumn Meeting the following day and so, after completing his second round, he headed south with Harold Hilton. But a hasty start after the event had to be taken." John Behrend plotted Ball's journey:

St Andrews *Depart* 7.15 pm
Leuchars *Arrive* 7.27
Leuchars *Depart* 7.41
Edinburgh *Arrive* 9.05 *Change*
Edinburgh *Depart* 9.30
York *Arrive* 2.15 am *Change*
York *Depart* 3.55
Leeds-New *Arrive* 4.35
Change stations
Leeds-Central *Depart* 5.00
Manchester *Arrive* 6.40 *Change*
Manchester *Depart* 6.50
Liverpool Exchange *Arrive* 8.45 *Change*
Liverpool James St *Depart* 9.05
Hoylake *Arrive* 9.38

The good news was that the strong wind at Hoylake in the morning moderated as the day advanced and, with late starting times, the weary travellers took the scratch cups. Johnny won the Dowie Cup with an 81 and Harold the Hall Blyth with an 87.

Now that was a mighty effort. Reading of their determination fills one with total admiration for these Victorian iron men. Just to show that Hoylake now had two major golfers, Harold Hilton won The Open at Muirfield the next year. It was the first time that the event took place on those links and it was the first time The Open was played over 72 holes. So Harold's win was all the more meritorious.

Suggestions Book October 1889

The members be asked not to take the newspapers with them to the lavatories. The Scotsman was several times asked for this morning and was ultimately found to have been left in a WC.

Suggestions Book 1898

That all tastes should be studied
it is admitted by all who know,
that Champagne "natural" otherwise "brut"
is THE Champagne to drink and
I would suggest that to improve the average
in the Club Wine List
as regards Champagne a purchase be made
of Pommery 1893 "Natural" in
Quarts, IMPERIAL Pints and Pints.

Suggestions Book 1900

That the labels on the water taps should correspond more nearly with the temperature of the water.

The 1894 Amateur is well chronicled. When some hitherto unknown photographs were discovered a wonderful book was produced by two Hoylake members: Doctors David Hamilton and Blyth Bell. It is still in print and through the good offices of the authors we reproduce some of the wonderful images in this book.

The winner needless to say was Johnny Ball, who beat S Mure Fergusson in the final.

This was also a year of major and far-reaching decisions for The Royal Liverpool Golf Club. The lease was expiring on the rooms in the Royal Hotel. The club had grown to such dimensions that further expansion was necessary.

Two schemes were considered. One was to increase the rooms at the Royal Hotel. The other was to move home and build afresh. A sub-committee was formed and after great deliberation it was decided to build a completely new clubhouse, one in keeping with the fast-approaching 20th century.

After investigations, a site was found on the Hoylake roundabout on the corner of Meols Drive and King's Gap. A prize was offered for the best design and the one finally chosen was by Messrs Woolfall and Eccles. The cost was to be £6,500, with the furniture a further £1,500. To meet this expenditure debentures of £50 each bearing 4% were raised and £1,000 from the reserve fund. Subscriptions were increased from one pound and 10 shillings to two guineas and those of three pounds to three guineas.*

Later, the site was moved from its proposed plot to where the Club stands today.

There have been singularly few alterations to the clubhouse over the years until very recent times. Originally

Opposite: The clubhouse in 2006, showing the new extension on the left

* £1 sterling was divided into 20 shillings, a guinea was £1 plus a shilling.

Above and below: 1897 Open Championship

Jack Morris's professional shop was where the ladies' lounge used to be. It was a hive of activity. Many of the older members of today remember the clubs being made, but in those late Victorian days they were still making the 'gutty' balls. The shop was a popular place for members to drop in and view the skills of ancient craftsmen applying their trade in front of their very eyes. Guy Farrar tells us that "after heating the gutta percha between two small moulds the smell was fascinating, whether the pitch or the glue". It thrilled him to the day he died.

The shop stayed there until ladies became members and the room was taken over by them, with the professional shop moving to the north end of the Club, where it is situated today.

Back then, as now, the Club was served by wonderful staff. In those days they were 'stewards of excellence'. 'Smith' was the presiding genius who produced the most marvellous Blue Cheshire cheeses and the most succulent of shellfish. Those local shrimps used to send Bernard Darwin into raptures.

We have continued in an up-and-down way to this very day, when the best steward in living memory, Signor Alexandro Rossi, is now in charge. He will still serve you with those tasty crustaceans as you spend your luncheon viewing the flat landscape that leads you across the Dee and over into Wales.

Further across to the right was the 'home' of our first clubhouse, where the four two-storey houses are today.

But on that spot in that single room that combined clubroom, locker room and dining room, the foundations of our club were born and nourished. Twenty-six years of activity, of ever-improving golf, of the unveiling of mighty champions, of sheltering from mighty wind, of revelry, of humour, of welcoming and meeting golfers from throughout the kingdom, from throughout the world, friendships that were forged for life. Outrageous wagers, deeds throughout the day and deeds through the night that, thanks to the writings of Guy Farrar, will be remembered forever and until golfers cease to tell of their fortune or misfortune under the glorious ever-changing Hoylake sky. For that Guy, we give you the greatest of thanks.

The Hoylake progress continued further with the staging of The Open in 1897. The new breed of all-conquering professional had appeared after the breakthrough of Ball and Hilton, winning The Open for England and breaking the Scottish dominance. Vardon, Taylor and Braid, the new Turks of professional golf; surely the winner had to come from the new triumvirate? But could they defeat Johnny Ball on his native links – and what of Hilton? Surely the 72-hole format must be in favour of the full-time player?

In reasonable weather the tournament threw up few early shocks and though Johnny had faded somewhat with a poor third round, Hilton was still in the fight.

As Harold walked to the first tee for his final round, Jack Morris told him firmly a 75 would do – "not more mind you". Prophetically, that was the score he posted. But only just. On the 18th he was on the green in two, but as Hilton later wrote: "My first putt was not bold and a spectator called it a drunken effort, and he was not far wrong. Putt number two dobbled about and eventually made its entry into the hole at the back door, but it got there and that was everything. I can see that ball now hesitating on the lip of the hole like a helpless derelict."

Poor man. He had gone out two hours before Braid, his closest contender, and suffered the agonies of waiting. He smoked, well, he always smoked! He played billiards until it was revealed that Braid required a three on the last hole to tie and enforce a play-off. Harold ran from the clubhouse, but slowed as he neared the 18th green. A serenity came over him as he saw Braid play one of the finest approach shots ever seen, the ball landing short, passing the pin by inches and coming to rest just 20 feet from the flag. A huge crowd had gathered, a crowd that fell silent as Braid stroked the putt holewards to tie the match. The ball ran and ran and fell but inches short.

Harold had won the first Hoylake Open. He was carried to the clubhouse to collect the Championship trophy for the second time.

During this time of Hoylake's growing importance to the world of golf, Tosper apart, there were powerful characters emerging to take the roll of Captain. The first Graham, John in 1887, the autocratic Charles Hutchins in 1891, Horace Hutchinson three years later and his successor, Helenus R Robertson, who was also a formidable man in the Liverpool cotton trade. They were the men who determined that leisure should become an important ingredient in the lives of latter-day Victorians. Though the politicians still grabbed the headlines, these men changed our lives.

If 1897 was most certainly the year for Hoylake, the following year was dominated by Lieutenant Frederick Guthrie Tait, who was to win the Amateur. He was the idol of the Scottish crowds. His record was impressive: third in the 1896 and '97 Open Championships followed by fifth in 1898. He had won the Amateur Championship in 1896 and made the semi-finals in 1893, '94 and '95.

In his writings, another Hoylake Graham and Captain in 1956, John (Jnr), wrote: "I imagine Tait to have been a swashbuckling type of person, afraid of no one and certainly not afraid to stay to the end of a party even in the middle of a championship. He played the bagpipes and played them often. He certainly played them during the 1898 Amateur Championship at Hoylake."

After he had defeated John Low in the semi-final in a gruelling match which went to the 22nd hole he repaired to the clubhouse, where he stayed for some hours celebrating with his many Hoylake friends. From time to time the strains of the Highland tunes could be heard coming from the pipes. It was getting late and the time came for him to return to his host's house. He was staying with my grandfather at The Croft on Stanley Road. Instead of crossing the links, which was by far the shortest way, he insisted on travelling the long way round by road, playing his pipes and followed by a merry posse.

Right: Unbelievably this aeroplane landed on the golf links in 1910

Opposite: Jim McVey, a starter at the Club – and a member of 'Village Play' – outside the old starter's hut, which was used from the 1930s right through to the 1990s

On arrival at my grandfather's house the merriment continued. He mounted the table and continued to play, leaving tell-tale marks from his nailed shoes on it. Some time later, in 1936, the Tait family contacted my aunts, who confirmed that Freddie's nail marks were still very evident. The next morning he dressed up in his full Highland uniform and marched to the Club, again playing his pipes, and went on to win the Championship by six and five in what his nephew 'Pedro' Tait described as "a haze of good will". "It was," said Pedro "a slightly bibulous Championship."

In the Championship the next year, Tait lost to Johnny Ball on the 37th hole of the final at Prestwick, described by Bernard Darwin as the greatest final of them all. Shortly afterwards he went to South Africa as a Lieutenant to fight in the Boer War. Leading his company of The Black Watch he was killed, just four months after the epic of Prestwick. The whole of Scotland mourned their beloved son. What a man, what a man.

Johnny Ball, although 39, volunteered for the Boer War with the Denbighshire Yeomanry and managed to convince the authorities that he was suitable material. Dr Frank Stableford also fought in the Boer War. Before he left, the Club hosted the annual St Andrews dinner in his honour – and what a dinner! His friends collected enough money to buy him a Charger.

Right: The 7th green covered in sand, 1894

Overleaf: The rather remarkable parasol cap mushroom, which grows in clusters on the seaward side of the Royal Liverpool course

But why did he go? One cannot help thinking that Freddie Tait had told him it would be "capital fun" and a great adventure. It most certainly was, confirmed by a letter sent home by Trooper Hinde from Rock Ferry, just six miles from Hoylake. "In the gallop from the breakwater one man's horse came down, and John Ball immediately pulled up and went to his assistance, getting the horse up from the poor beggar's leg – all this of course under heavy crossfire ... Ball is too modest to speak about himself in any such connection and won't have his name in the papers if he can possibly help it."

The war was hardly over for Johnny. Trooper Hind wrote home again, describing that they had occupied a Kraal for 40 minutes with bullets hailing around. "John Ball had a little Basuto pony of which he is very proud, and I saw him lying in the open with his reins over one arm blazing away for dear life. He told me after several bullets passed between his arm and the horse. He seemed more concerned about the beloved pony than his own safety. One bullet left a scar on his neck."

A few days later the Denbighshire Yeomanry were called home, so in early July 1901 Johnny arrived in Hoylake amidst scenes similar to those of his returning from another famous Championship victory, but this time the fishermen had their way. As Hoylake's hero alighted from the train, bronzed, upright, khaki-clad, a great shout of welcome went up. Johnny took his sister's arm and led the way to the carriage, followed by his father. They had no sooner taken their seats than the horse was detached from the carriage and Hoylake fishermen seized the shaft and bore the party off to their home at the Royal Hotel.

As the century came to its conclusion a suitable honour for Johnny would have been appropriate. Here was a man who should have added a VC to his many golfing honours. In the words of Guy Farrar: "He was the greatest Roman of them all."

The annual match against the Tantallon Golf Club was played regularly up to 1900.

Since then only two matches have been played, albeit on a regular basis, once every 50 years.

When we visited that magnificent course at North Berwick in 2001 it was the intention of Johnny Turner and myself to find the North Berwick Tee Repair Centre.

After dedicated research we regret to report that this establishment no longer practises this skilful trade, in fact there was absolutely no sign of the company.

With the modern longer tee, perhaps there is an opening for some enterprising craftsman?

Chapter Four

Johnny Ball: Essay to a Champion

Johnny Ball, Hoylake born and bred, was the finest amateur golfer England has ever produced. He bestrode the game like a colossus, winning eight British Amateur Championships and one Open Championship.

He possessed a golf game that was both extraordinarily graceful and powerfully effective. He was worshipped in the manner of a Palmer or a Woods.

And for all this, for all the gifts, for all the triumphs, for all the adoration, he was a man consumed by shyness. A man who hid from fame in the bubble of concentration that focused eye, mind and limb on ball and hole.

Guy Farrar summed him up best: "No man has ever aspired to greater hero worship – and no one has ever courted it less."

We are all, to a greater or lesser degree, a product of our surroundings. Johnny Ball was born on Christmas Eve 1861, the son of John Ball, owner of the Royal Hotel which stood for years just a few yards from Royal Liverpool's 17th green. If the place was right then, so was the time and, in 1869, with Ball just a small boy, the golf links that form today's mighty course were laid out on his doorstep.

He took to the game as if it had been invented for him and at 11 he was winning the Boys' Medal at the Club and at 16 he had finished fifth in the 1878 Open at Prestwick.

As the importance of the Amateur Championship grew, then so did the reputation of Hoylake's Ball. In 1888 he won it for the first time, beating JE Laidlay at Prestwick by 5 and 4 in the final. He won it again in 1890, the year he did the supposedly "impossible" by winning The Open Championship too.

Seven further Amateur Championships were to follow: at Hoylake in 1890, 1894 and 1910; Sandwich 1892; back at Prestwick in 1899; St Andrews 1907; Westward Ho! 1912.

Elsewhere in this book, pages are devoted to the titanic struggles with men like Laidlay, Freddie Tait and Horace Hutchinson as a picture forms of a man who played sublimely, who never knew when he was beaten, but could always be counted upon to accept defeat with the same good grace and humility that he accepted victory.

It is likely that had Johnny Ball played today his spirit and will to perform would have been tested but never broken by the glare of 24/7 media attention. Simply, he would have hated it but he would have coped. Here is a man who defied his age and expectations to win the Amateur at Westward Ho! in 1912. As was custom his Hoylake friends and admirers gathered in their droves at Hoylake station to welcome the hero home.

Shy? Certainly. Dour? Perhaps. Humourless? Never. He was a man who chose his words carefully, but often brilliantly and often to prick the balloon of pomposity. In the final of the Irish Championship at Portmarnock he was pitched against a Scot with a notoriously bad temper. The night before, the Secretary told Ball not to turn up for the scheduled start time of 10 am, but to be ready to start at 10.30 as a professional competition would now be going out ahead of them.

Unfortunately, the Secretary forgot to tell Johnny's opponent and when Johnny turned up for the 10.30 start the Scot was already in the full flow of rage demanding Johnny be disqualified. Johnny naturally remonstrated, saying he had turned up when requested by the organisers and, anyway, what was the problem? They had all day to play 36 holes.

Preceding page: Johnny Ball (Junior) from a painting by RE Morrison

Right: Johnny Ball (Junior) driving the 8th

Opposite: Red Rocks marsh, which butts onto the westerly tip of the Royal Liverpool course, is home to the Natterjack toad

Above: Johnny Ball (Junior) driving the 8th

Below: Johnny Ball (Junior) without moustache. He had worn facial hair on his upper lip for over 30 years but after acquiring a motorcycle in 1911 his 'tash' tended to ice up. It had to go

"Oh no," replied his opponent. "I want to get the match over early so I can catch the evening boat back to Scotland."

"All right. I won't keep you long," said Johnny. "Just let me change into my golf shoes." Johnny then won 13 up and 11 to play, made his opponent a little bow and said: "Now sir, you can catch your boat."

To get on the wrong side of Johnny was a sure route to defeat. As Darwin said: "To make him angry is to make him win." Yet, he was capable of extraordinary kindness. In one mismatch his opponent, witless through nerves, had indicated his intention not to turn up. Johnny sought out the man's wife and persuaded her to convince him to play. The next day Johnny won on the last green, the crowd perplexed by the number of times the great man seemed to find a bunker when well placed.

There you have then a little of Ball the man, and a little was all he chose to give, despite his deeds on the course and some distinguished service for his country in the Boer War, where in one bullet-strewn exchange he pulled a comrade to safety from under the haunches of a fallen horse.

Ball the golfer was renowned for enormous accuracy with his woods and long irons. His short game appears to have been more functional and, as befits a true son of Hoylake, from 100 yards in he favoured the bump-and-run delivered with a half-shot from a closed face. Rarely would he play an open-faced shot and once famously referred to what we now call a sand wedge as "that damned spade".

His grip was his single biggest peculiarity: right hand underneath, knuckles pointing at the target in a manner it was suggested he copied from the best of the Scottish professionals he encountered while playing challenge matches as a teenager at Hoylake.

His weakness was a poor putting stroke on the shorter stuff, described once as a tendency to try to draw the ball into the cup off the toe of the putter or to push it in off the heel. It may, though, have cost him many more triumphs.

How good was he then? Comparisons are dreadful things.

In a world where technology moves forward by the day it is neither right nor useful to ask if Nicklaus was better than Woods; if Palmer was better than Els; if Ball was better than Vardon. What we do know is that in his pomp, believed by the best judges to have been in his early days between 1887 and 1892, he took golf onto another plane; to a different level in the same way that Nicklaus did in his day, and Woods in his. Nicklaus astonished golf lovers with a power and accuracy of long game that had never been seen before. Woods mystified the previous generation by driving the ball to places never before visited in a single shot and then demonstrating as velvety a touch as anyone on and around the greens.

Above: Johnny Ball (Junior) chatting with Harry Vardon, right, 1936 Open Championship

Opposite: The painted wooden pineapples in front of the clubhouse were on the posts at the entrance of the winners' enclosure when horse racing was held between 1846 and 1876

Overleaf: The front of the clubhouse, winter 2006

And Ball? He too played shots that the rest could neither replicate nor comprehend. A fellow golfer once talked about Johnny's uncanny ability to draw the ball from a divot, when the best of the rest could manage no more than a controlled fade.

Had Johnny written an instruction book, then that chapter might have begun, "Don't try this at home ..."

Home for Johnny, as he grew old, became rural north Wales where he married his housekeeper and lived peacefully, golfing occasionally, until his death in 1940. Why did he leave the Wirral? No one really knows, but perhaps even Hoylake became a trifle too loud and brash for a quiet man.

Harry Beswick wrote a feature about Johnny in the *Despatch* of 5 June 1906. "Johnny Ball" it read, "is the Emperor of Hoylake. He is also its golfing Pope, Chief Magistrate, Verger, Chancellor of the Exchequer, Archdeacon, Coroner, Presiding Barrister, Groom of the Backstairs and Lord High Everything Else.

"For a man to ask in Hoylake who is Johnny Ball, is to court instantaneous death as a supposed criminal lunatic. Hoylake people live but to bask in the light of Johnny's flashing cleek. Strong men bend the knee and salaam when he passes, and beauteous maidens strew his path with roses."

Bernard Darwin was not only a great golf writer but also covered other sports for *The Times* including cricket and the 1936 Olympics in Berlin when Jesse Owens was supreme.

However in his 1944 book *Golf between the wars* he wrote "the beauty of any particular player's style, like his exact place in the golfing firmament, be a matter for individual feeling, and I can only say that I have derived greater aesthetic and emotional pleasure from watching Mr Ball than any other spectacle in any game".

How Johnny would have hated it.

The Tempest and Hilton's Second Triumph

When Johnny Ball became the first Englishman and the first amateur to win The Open at Prestwick in 1890, well, the alarm bells rang throughout the links of Scotland.

On his return to Hoylake there was tremendous excitement. A great crowd gathered to welcome him home, including members of RLGC but, particularly, a great many of the local fishermen, as always wearing their dark blue jerseys. To use modern vernacular they were "his fan club".

No-one ever-inspired greater hero worship – and no-one ever courted it less – than Johnny Ball. So, hearing about the welcome in advance he alighted from the train a station early and walked home along the beach to the Royal Hotel; his father was the owner and in those days it was also the clubhouse for RLGC. This modest action was a great disappointment to his followers, who had a trap, minus the horse, ready to usher him home.

Although the very greatest of friends, Harold Hilton was of a different personality. He loved the atmosphere of the big occasion: "the dust of the arena". He wallowed in the appreciation that came in his direction. Further, this acted as a great incentive to Hilton, who was determined more than ever to emulate Johnny Ball.

However, he was not from a wealthy family, although the locals regarded him as part of the establishment ... one of the toffs. Johnny Ball was their man.

Hilton worked in Liverpool and spent most of his free time either playing rugby football or, in the main, practising his golf. One of the local boys, Joe Lloyd, known as 'The General', helped him a great deal with thoughts about and ways of playing a golf course. He was also accepted as just about the best caddy in the parish. Joe Lloyd later became a professional golfer, moving to Pau in the south of France for medical reasons and in the summer working at the Essex County Club in Boston.

In 1892 The Open was played at Muirfield for the first time. A few weeks before, Hilton had no intention of making the journey. However, at the last moment a friend invited him to stay. He knew that the parental wishes were against such a proceeding, and the parental wishes in those days coincided with those of his employer.

Eventually he summoned up the courage to suggest he should go – this being about 4 pm on the Monday afternoon and the Championship began on Wednesday. His father was not keen, "well, go if you want to go ... but I cannot see much use in your going". As he wanted to go so badly he wasted no time and was off on the midnight train. With just one day's practice he managed to play three rounds. Austere training, on top of an all-night train journey!

This was the first time the Championship had been played over four rounds, making his victory even more astounding. After a tense affair and against all the odds Hilton won the Claret Jug (The Open Championship trophy). The runner-up was Johnny Ball.

Approaching the train station at Hoylake he was anticipating a huge welcome, only to find that there was his father and a few members. He did not show his disappointment, but he wouldn't ... would he? But he did enjoy a jolly good hot meal at the Royal Hotel with the members.

They continued their friendly rivalry, with Ball on top in matchplay but Hilton holding his own on medal days. When the news came that Hoylake was to hold The Open in 1897 for the first time this created great excitement amongst the local community and members alike.

The early days of resentment were still there, particularly as the local fishing grounds were silting up and the fishermen had to go further afield to make a living. Times were hard.

Shortly before Christmas in 1896 there blew up a terrible tempest; the Hoylake fleet was in grave danger. Word spread to the Royal Hotel and most able-bodied men and women sped down to the sea front to see if they could help.

Johnny and Harold were to the fore but they could not prevent a terrible tragedy and 38 fishermen lost their lives. There was a most dreadful sense of loss; the Club rallied round and raised a great deal of money and the fishermen's families and the local community, especially, appreciated this.

The following summer The Open was held at Hoylake, but before the event word came through that the man who had caddied for Harold Hilton years previously – Joe Lloyd, 'The General' – had won the third playing of the US Open in Chicago.

When The Open started the men to beat were the new breed of young professionals, notably Harry Vardon, JH Taylor and James Braid. Could the local heroes overcome these odds? To add to the occasion RLGC had built a new clubhouse, the one we have today.

On the last afternoon Hilton had posted a score that would take some catching. In those days the players went off willy-nilly and not as today, with the leaders of the previous rounds bringing up the field.

Consequently, he had two hours to wait before the last players finished their rounds. These hours were spent in nervous anticipation playing billiards and smoking furiously – he was rarely seen without a cigarette on the go. Word came that James Braid required par figures for the last three holes to force a play-off. Harold Hilton rushed to the window in the clubroom overlooking the course and witnessed on the 16th green "the enemy taking a six". He returned for a bit of aimless billiards.

Then the word spread that James Braid required a three on the last hole to force a play-off. In his book Hilton recalls that he collected his thoughts and realised that it was most unlikely that anyone would score a three on the final hole ... it was time to witness the event. He braced himself and calmly walked to the 18th green to see James Braid in the middle of the fairway about to play his approach to the home green.

Braid hit the ball into a silent sky, it landed short of the green and rolled threateningly, passing but inches from its intended destination and coming to rest 15 feet beyond the flag. Nervous chatter filled the air. A man next to Hilton remarked: "You must be in a blue funk." He assured him that that was far from the case as he felt in a "much more composed state than I had done for some considerable time".

Then, total silence as he prepared for the putt. Braid stroked it beautifully, the ball was dead on line, and there was a huge gasp from the crowd when the ball fell but inches from the hole. A great roar erupted and everybody congratulated Hilton.

He recalled that he felt most strange, not quite with it, and strolled in the direction of the clubhouse where the presentation was to take place. But there was a rumble behind him, the great crowd became animated and then, to his astonishment, a phalanx of blue jerseys approached him. Without a word they gathered round and rushed him shoulder high to the clubhouse. "Let me go," he shouted, half hoping they would not hear. The Hoylake fishermen escorted Hilton to the presentation ceremony, where he received The Open trophy for the second time.

Although he never replaced Johnny Ball in the affection of the fishermen, they showed their appreciation for his heroics on that dreadful day before Christmas when the Hoylake fishing fleet was shattered.

Left: Harold Hilton driving off at St Andrews watched by Old Tom Morris and John Low

Chapter Five

1901-1914

by Roger Greenway

Members, visitors and guests climbing the main stairs of Royal Liverpool's clubhouse invariably find their eyes drawn to the imposing portraits which dominate the staircase. The gallery is dominated by the paintings of Hoylake's John Ball and Harold Hilton, which hang alongside each other, and of Bobby Jones.

Directly across the staircase landing is a recently renovated oil painting of a distinguished figure in a bold black-and-white check suit, seemingly watching and admiring the golfing greats opposite. This portrait is of Harold Janion, who became a Royal Liverpool member in 1889 and was Club Secretary from 1900 until his death in 1922.

Although he was an indifferent golfer, the positioning of Janion's painting amongst legendary golfers recognises his outstanding contribution to the Club and the game during that period. Known to his many friends as 'Jane' even in those rather correct days, Janion was a fine organiser of events and people and was highly regarded for his enthusiasm, astuteness and wide-ranging views. That said, there was a bluntness of approach that enabled him to walk out on a meandering Green Committee meeting and leave the members to lock up.

The years from the turn of the century to the outbreak of World War I were especially important both for Royal Liverpool and the game of golf. During this period Harold Janion's organisational skills were much needed as The Open and Amateur Championships were each played three times on the Hoylake links.

The playing standards of professionals were becoming noticeably greater than the amateurs and the professional Triumvirate of Braid, Taylor and Vardon now dominated The Open. Prize money was to be won at an increasing number of events, particularly in the United States where the game was growing dramatically. The technology of equipment and particularly the ball were also changing the way in which the game was to be played.

1902 was arguably the most remarkable year in Royal Liverpool's distinguished and proud history as between late April and

Preceding page: Harold (Jane) Janion, Secretary The Royal Liverpool Golf Club 1900-1922, from a painting by John AA Berrie

Right: RW Pendulum Brown, first Captain of the Wallasey Golf Club

early June the Club hosted both The Open and Amateur Championships and also staged the first international match between England and Scotland.

Golf had been played in Scotland for 400 years and in England since the reign of James 1, yet it was not until 1902 that the first match between the countries was played. After much Press comment and speculation and discontent about the R & A's unwillingness to take the lead, it was Royal Liverpool that both instigated and organised the first match with the credit for the initiative being given to Harold Janion.

The format for the inaugural match was 10 singles matches over 36 holes with the winning country being decided unusually, by modern standards, by the team with the most holes won. Controversy also arose over the exclusion of professionals and about the ball. Some players chose the new rubber dimpled Haskell ball which had been patented in the United States in 1899 and was soon to became established as a replacement for the gutty on both sides of the Atlantic.

The Royal Liverpool Club had four players in the English team including John Ball and Harold Hilton and, amid yet more controversy, Jack Graham Junior was one of two local members selected for the Scots side. Although born in Scotland he was regarded by most as an English golfer!

Press reports of the match gave an interesting insight into the condition of the links for this event including comments such as: "looking at its best ... through the green lies are excellent ... a good deal of coarse weed ... and on some of the greens notably the Cop there were a great many daisy heads half open".

A strong east wind did not deter a crowd of at least 3,000 people, with many arriving on special trains from Liverpool. Harold Hilton, writing in the *Sporting Chronicle*, described the badly behaved crowd as "quite a disorganised rabble" and had his concentration broken by "camera fiends".

The match was played on Saturday, 26 April 1902 and the opening shot was played at 10 o'clock by Robert Maxwell, the Captain of the Tantallon Golf Club, and his opponent was Royal Liverpool's John Ball. This scene became the subject of one of a famous series of paintings by Michael Brown and a reproduction now hangs above the fireplace in the clubhouse bar.

After the morning's play, the match was evenly poised with the favourites Scotland leading by just one hole. In the afternoon Scotland extended their lead to win by 28 holes to 21. With this seven-hole winning margin, Jack Graham's role proved pivotal.

He won his game against fellow club member Horace Hutchinson by nine holes thus clinching the match and leading to the Press and public questioning both his eligibility and now his loyalty!

That evening, the Club hosted a grand six-course dinner for the players. Hutchinson led the speeches of thanks to Harold Janion and the Scot John Low in his speech, expressing the view that "he did not want in the international match to perpetuate Bannockburn but still it was as well to avenge Flodden".

The international match was next played in 1903 at Muirfield and became established as an annual event in amateur golf, although partly because of Scottish dominance the series was to be temporarily discontinued after the 1912 match at Westward Ho!. Later the match was to become an integral part of the Home Internationals matches and this it remains today.

In 2002, the centenary of that first International between England and Scotland was celebrated at Hoylake 100 years to the very day. The first match was recreated with a commemorative encounter between teams of distinguished former English and Scottish internationals

Saddling bell from the former racecourse days

who were to be marvellously acclaimed by Royal Liverpool Captain Joe Pinnington as "the best players of the last era of true amateur international golf".

Sir Michael Bonallack, regarded by many as his country's leading amateur player of all time, captained the England team which included home club former England players Brian Chapman and Mike Pearson. Scotland's most capped player, Charlie Green, led the Scottish team. The match was preceded by a singles match between players representing the British Golf Collectors' Society who were dressed, as were their caddies, in period clothes. They played with clubs of the era.

The result was decided as in 1902 by the team with the most holes won and the Scots were again decisive winners. The competitive English team, though, made it clear the concession of an average seven years per player was a rather demanding handicap.

After the match, Royal Liverpool hosted a dinner for players, guests and members, with the menu for the dinner closely following that of the meal after the first match.

Charlie Green spoke with both great humour and affection of his recollections of past matches and Sir Michael Bonallack – an honorary member of Royal Liverpool – graciously and kindly recognised the Club's place in golf history and its inauguration of the first International.

Back in 1902, three days after Robert Maxwell and John Ball had played for their countries in the leading match of the first International, they stood on Hoylake's first tee now as opponents in the second round of the 1902 Amateur. Maxwell avenged his earlier defeat but the Championship was to be won by home club member Charles Hutchings. England's most convincing win in the International had come from the tough Hutchings and he was clearly a man in form. But in many other respects he was the most unlikely of champions.

Hutchings, the 1890 Royal Liverpool Captain and known to his member friends as 'The Marquis' had retired from his Warrington tannery at the age of just 27. With wealth and several directorships he took up golf only after he had passed the age of 30. He sometimes suffered from chronic sciatica, and was now a 53-year-old grandfather, as adept with billiard cues, fishing rods and hunting guns as with golf clubs.

His opponent in the Amateur final was Sidney Fry from the Mid-Surrey club, who himself had only played the game for six years and had been seen as an unexpected selection for the English international team – and coincidentally had earlier won the Amateur Championship at billiards. During a distinctly wet morning the Hoylake player had seemingly taken control of his final against the chain-smoking Fry and his commanding eight-hole lead at lunchtime still remained after the opening six afternoon holes. A Hoylake custom had been established of 'chairing' the champion shoulder high back to the

Above: Harry Vardon by the front door, 1897

Overleaf: Hoylake from the air with Hilbre island and the rolling Welsh hills

clubhouse and the supporters of the Marquis had been so confident of an early win they carried the chair out to the far end of the course. However, the chair had to be carried all the way to the final green. Fry began to play some fine golf starting with a two at the Dowie as the weary Hutchings, apparently struggling with his age and his sciatica after the morning's damp conditions, began to falter with his normally excellent short game becoming susceptible.

By the final hole the lead had dwindled to just one but two putts on the final green – the second a nerve-jangling nine-footer – and the veteran was a popular Amateur Champion who was never again to enter the Championship. The much-travelled chair was used only for the 200 yards back to the clubhouse!

By early June, the golfing Press was previewing the 1902 Open which Royal Liverpool was hosting for the second time. Many newspaper articles speculated that the champion would almost inevitably come from amongst the great professional Triumvirate. Some columnists continued to comment on the merits or otherwise of the Haskell ball, which in the United States was now being known as the 'Bounding Billy', and about which both Hilton and Harry Vardon were sceptical.

The 1902 Open attracted a record entry of 112 players and the most significant practice round was that involving the Huddersfield professional Sandy Herd and John Ball. Herd had learnt his golf at St Andrews and held several club professional positions before settling in Yorkshire. The Scot had a number of very good finishes to his name in previous Opens, but modestly did not regard himself as a leading contender or as a potential Open champion. During their practice round, Johnny lent his playing partner a Haskell ball and immediately afterwards Herd visited the shop on the first floor of the clubhouse. There, Jack Morris was rationing the Haskell and provided just four balls to Herd. But with these, and wearing a new Shetland golfing coat, he was to become the 1902 champion.

After an opening round in warm conditions, Vardon led the field with a wonderful 72 which equalled the competition course record, and this despite two penalty shots for twice being out-of-bounds at the opening hole.

Excellent organisation by Janion and the speed of play enabled two rounds to be completed comfortably within a fine early summer's day. With Vardon leading by four shots on 149 and with Braid and Taylor in the leading four players, the predictions of the Triumvirate's dominance looked to be justified. But Herd, with steady rounds of 77 and 76, was again very much in contention.

On the second and final day Johnny Ball was drawn to play with Herd and this was a great help as they had struck up a genuine affinity during their practice round.

Herd, despite a strong westerly wind, returned a fine 73 in the morning, but he threw away a fine afternoon start to limp in with an 81. His final hole included recovering from railings and a gateway behind the green.

Both Vardon and Braid, playing in different matches and behind Herd, had opportunities to clinch the Championship but Vardon took three disastrous putts on the final green to finish on 308 – one outside Herd – and Braid could not quite secure a tie when he needed a three at the last. Neither was to win an Open at Hoylake although JH Taylor was later to be the champion golfer at Royal Liverpool's last Open before the Great War.

The final results of the 1902 Open provided evidence that Open Championships played on demanding seaside links almost always conclude with the best golfers in most of the leading places. The great Triumvirate were all in the top seven – and between them collected winnings of £57 and 10 shillings – while Hilton tied with Taylor and the other leading amateur Robert Maxwell finished remarkably with all four rounds under 80.

The real glory however belonged to Herd in winning what was to be his solitary Championship Medal and the prize of £50. The Press had not anticipated it but praised his victory and while Herd was sometimes renowned for his frequent club waggling when addressing the ball the *Athletic News* memorably and curiously described his swing as "sufficiently slashing to satisfy the desire for style". Interestingly and perceptively several golf columnists, including Hilton, commented on the promise and quality of play of a French professional by the name of Arnaud Massy who just five years later was to make Open history of his own on the Hoylake links.

The 1902 national and international golf scene moved on after The Open and The Royal Liverpool Club Captain Adam Rankine and Secretary Janion were left to reflect proudly on the unprecedented period from April to June. Those same members, visitors and

guests reflecting on the staircase portraits will have also studied the displays in the hallways and the Honours Board on which great players and memorable Championships are recorded. How many notice that in such an illustrious history there is just a single year with three Championships and International entries? Such is the importance and uniqueness of the year 1902 in the history of Royal Liverpool and, indeed, golf.

The prominent position of the Great Triumvirate in The Open spoke for itself. But Hoylake, in Ball, Hilton and Jack Graham Junior, had a triumvirate of its own.

The Grahams have been amongst the most influential families in Hoylake's history. John Graham had moved his family from Glasgow to Liverpool with the family business in 1873, built a summer property in Stanley Road overlooking the links, and from there saw his three children Jack, Molly and Allan into famous golfers.

Jack, the elder son, was regarded as the best player never to win the Amateur Championship and many observers and historians have been critical of his matchplay record. Yet in 10 years of representative golf for Scotland he lost just two matches and reached five Amateur Championship semi-finals. Suspect putting and a lack of stamina and killer instinct were said by some to be his main failings – yet he was also five times the leading Amateur in The Open Championship, the winner of 25 Royal Liverpool gold medals and in 1910, astoundingly for that time, scored a 66 on the Hoylake course. The more astute observation about his record came from those, Guy Farrar included, who felt Jack was too reserved and unassuming and preferred congenial games with his friends or playing alone with just his pipe and black retriever to playing in championships.

Jack Graham showed an interest in course architecture and by 1913 had developed plans for significant changes to the links but these were never

The Ancient Hoylake Golfer

Over the gorse the wet wind blows,
I'm starting to slice and there's cold in my nose.

The rain comes splattering out of the sky,
Now I hook I don't know why?

The mist creeps over the red sandstone,
As for my putting I'm left alone!

When I am old with only one eye,
I'll walk the links and look at the sky.

carried out due to the outbreak of the Great War. The war was, however, to cost Jack more than his course plans – as his golfing career and his life were to end soon after the outbreak when he was tragically killed near Ypres, aged 37, leading his company of the Liverpool Scottish.

Bernard Darwin captured the real talents of Jack Graham Junior by simply and eloquently describing him as "a player of unquestioned genius" and on his death added in the many published obituaries the words: "he could not have left a more unforgettable or pleasanter memory".

The Royal Liverpool club remembered their fallen friend and legend with a posthumous portrait by RE Morrison, the costs of which were heavily over-subscribed by members' contributions. To this day Jack Graham Jnr's portrait hangs on the clubhouse staircase with Ball, Hilton, Bobby Jones and watched over by Harold Janion.

After the momentous events of 1902 there were no further championships at Hoylake until the 1906 Amateur and in the intervening years there were no significant championship wins for Royal Liverpool members and several of its best players were at Lord's in golfers' cricket matches that year. The by-now established golf matches against other domestic clubs took on an international dimension when in 1903 a Royal Liverpool team of its best golfers played in a match at Cannes against the Grand Duke Michael of Russia's team and this was followed later by a return game at Hoylake.

The club finances for 1902 published in early 1903 made interesting comparisons both with the previous year and current-day figures. The International match, the Amateur and The Open in 1902 meant both extra income and additional costs with the result being a profit of £147 – an increase of £2 on 1901. Visitors' income doubled to £280 for the year – the cost of three green fees in the early 21st century. 1903 saw extensive additional bunkering introduced to increase the penalties for errant shots and to produce hazards to replace the natural burrowing of rabbits which by then had virtually become extinct on the links. For those who believed that amateur championships are always synonymous with good golf, the 1906 Amateur at Hoylake could politely be called the exception and it was to be commonly recognised as the poorest of all championships. Thirteen Royal Liverpool members were to make early exits and the surviving representative, Jack Graham Junior, reached the last eight then snatched defeat from the jaws of victory by playing the final two holes disastrously.

The quality of golf throughout the Championship matched the poor weather and some of the worst golf and weather came in what became known as the 'umbrella' final between James Robb and CC Lingen. As always for Hoylake finals there was a large crowd – those who travelled from Liverpool mostly travelling on the recently electrified Mersey Railway – but the usual enthusiasm was dulled by both the rain and uninspiring golf.

Robb, who had been losing finalist in two previous Amateurs, won the opening four holes in the morning round and this was eventually to be his winning margin. The opening holes of the afternoon round summed up the weather and the golf – the Briars hole was halved in nine.

The annual match between Oxford and Cambridge universities and the Army Championships have both been played regularly at Hoylake. The universities first met at Hoylake in 1906 and the following year the Army event began with a team championship between the Black Watch and the Argyll and Sutherland Highlanders.

Despite the wet weather during the Amateur the previous summer the Club installed piped watering to part of the links during the winter of 1906-07 and electric lights and a new telephone system were fitted in the clubhouse before the Club hosted the 1907 Open. The funding for these came partly from selective increases in membership. This period coincided with one of the great periods in the life of the city of Liverpool and the new members were representative of the traders, manufacturers, financiers, lawyers and businessmen who had brought Liverpool to the position of one of the world's most important trading cities. This international trading in Liverpool and the growth and expansion of The Open seemed to set the background in 1907 for another two Hoylake firsts – the first Open won by a player from outside Britain and the first Open with qualifying rounds.

The 1904 Amateur had been won by an American and now British domination of The Open ended with a championship win by Arnaud Massy from France. The Royal Liverpool Council minutes showed that much time in the year before this Open had been spent consulting with other host clubs in coping with the ever-increasing number of entries for The Open.

For 1907 the schedule was altered to a demanding format involving half the entrants playing 36 holes on Tuesday and the rest on Wednesday with the leading players on each day qualifying for the four Championship rounds on Thursday and Friday. There was no need for the new irrigation pipes as rain lashed the first-ever Open qualifying round and gales blew all the following day. The first Championship day had what *Golf Illustrated* described as "hurricane winds interspersed with torrential rains".

Arnaud Massy was a cheery Basque from Biarritz and his working life began as a sardine fisherman. When not at sea, he played the local game of pelota on the courts of south west France and caddied for golfing visitors to the fine courses in this fashionable region. With his open stance and pre-Vardon two-handed grip, Massy, after the first two rounds of the Championship proper, had a single-shot advantage but after the third round JH Taylor had reversed this lead. The decisive fluctuation came in the opening three holes of the final round when Taylor's long game unexpectedly deserted him and allowed Massy with a final round of 77 and a total of 312 to become a popular champion.

During The Open, his Scottish-born wife gave birth to a daughter and soon after the event finished he rushed back home to name his new-born 'Mademoiselle Hoylake Massy'.

Left: 1907, Arnaud Massy, the cheery Basque

If the 1906 Amateur was remembered for the wrong reasons the 1910 event would be recalled for the quality of golf and a seventh Amateur Championship win for Johnny Ball. Jack Graham played masterful golf until losing to Hilton and at the semi-final stage there was every prospect of a Ball-Hilton final. This was denied by one CC Aylmer – who appears never to have been known by any Christian name. In the final, Johnny excelled in a magnificent display which clinched victory in the 36-holer by 10 and eight and was generally regarded as his finest ever golf.

Brilliant golf abounded, with low scoring needed for victory in many matches – except in the historic 19th hole of the match between two great golf writers, Horace Hutchinson and Bernard Darwin, who so often wrote passionately and eloquently about Royal Liverpool. Golf historians have described the events (including sockets) on this hole in great and lurid detail. However, when Guy Farrar recalled this hole in his history his respect and affection for this great writer was shown by a shortened version which simply said that he would "merely record that both players put an incredible number of balls out-of-bounds and the writer of the Foreword had eventually to give up through lack of ammunition!"

John Ball's previous wins had been recognised by the purchase of the clubhouse clock and the portrait now on the staircase. This 1910 victory was to be less grandly remembered. The club Council met and agreed that in future John Ball would be allocated a reserved starting time for major club competitions. That was his reward.

By the next major Championship, Royal Liverpool had purchased the Hoylake links and clubhouse site from Lord Stanley for £30,000. George Cox, Club Treasurer from 1901 to 1919, presided over these 1911 dealings and finances which involved offering life memberships to 100 members and raising a £10,000 mortgage.

Suggestions Book, 15 December 1903

Urgently suggest that rabbits be not shot.

Suggestions Book, May 1913

This morning Miss Knowles started ahead of me with one dog and Miss Getty and Miss Tarbart (sic) followed with THREE dogs. All four were a continual nuisance. I fell over one and Miss Knowles' dog stopped my best drive.

AND

JH Taylor of the characteristic jutting chin and flat-footed stance was to be the only member of the Great Triumvirate to win an Open at Hoylake and this he was to achieve in 1913, just 16 years after his first Open appearance at a course which he regarded as a second home. Yet John Henry only qualified for what was to be one of his five Open wins by a single stroke, having holed a difficult six-foot putt on a shiny final green. After the opening two rounds of the Championship, the reigning champion Ted Ray led by a single shot from Taylor but the Championship was to be decided on the morning of the final day.

In this third round, JH Taylor played what he regarded in his life story *My Life's Work* as the finest round he ever played. In an incredible gale and torrential showers Taylor scored just 77 and many of the shots, particularly on the opening six holes, were recalled in detail when that book was published 26 years later. Three full brassies and a long run-up stone dead at both the first and third holes are recalled as two of the best fives he ever scored, but much praise is reserved for an unknown gentleman who kept producing from beneath his raincoat dry towels, presumed to have been stolen from the lavatories. The final afternoon round was played in dry and less windy conditions which Taylor played in two shots more than in his morning heroics. It was still sufficient to win by eight shots.

The 1913 Open was the first at Hoylake in which an American entered and in conditions far removed from his native Atlantic City JJ McDermott was to finish a creditable equal fifth. The American influence on Open and Amateur Championships was to emerge strongly after the Great War ended

With World War I breaking out in the following year this 1913 Open was to mark the end of a wonderful era for Royal Liverpool.

Opposite: Above the front entrance to the Club, a carved stone liverbird

Chapter Six

Harold Horsfall Hilton: Essay to a Champion

Harold Hilton was born in the year of the Club's formation in 1869. He first set foot on the Hoylake green when under 10 years of age.

A natural sportsman he was soon beating his father who was one of the first members of the Club. His father, noticing the talent his son displayed, tried as all fathers do (may I say even today) and gave what he thought was helpful advice. On one occasion, Harold mentioned in his book *My Golfing Reminiscences* the time when playing with his father and becoming irritated by his imploring to "follow through" with his swing. Eventually Harold took a run at the ball and smashed it whilst on the run. "Is that enough of a follow-through father?" he asked. "Harold if you are going to act like a baby we shall go home right now." And off they went. How many fathers trying to be helpful have witnessed such ingratitude? Harold later accepted that his behaviour was hasty and duly apologised to his 'Long Suffering'.

On his way to school along Stanley Road, that runs along the 17th green and 18th tee, he would eye the Royal Hotel. On his return he would sneak out at night and hit balls over the hotel on to the home green (then the finishing hole).

The other great Hoylake golfer Johnny Ball was gaining significant notices in the golf world, hitherto dominated by the Scottish professionals. When Ball became the first Englishman and the first amateur to win The Open at Prestwick in 1890, well, the alarm bells had rung throughout the links of Scotland.

Although the very greatest of friends, Harold Hilton was of a different personality to the retiring Ball. He loved the atmosphere of the big occasion, "the dust of the arena". He wallowed in the appreciation that came in his direction. Further, this acted as a great incentive to Harold, who was determined more than ever to emulate Johnny.

However, he was not from a wealthy family, although the locals regarded him as part of the establishment ... one of the toffs. Johnny, an innkeeper's son, was nonetheless loved by everybody.

Harold worked in Liverpool and spent some of his free time playing rugby football but in the main practising his golf. One of the local boys, Joe Lloyd, a fine young golfer, known as 'The General', helped him a great deal with thoughts and ideas on playing a golf course. In other words he taught him course management.

Lloyd was also accepted as just about the best caddy in the parish and later became a professional golfer, moving to Pau in the south of France for medical reasons in the winters and spending the summers working at the Essex County Club in Boston, Massachusetts.

In 1892 The Open, for the first time, was played at Muirfield just outside Edinburgh. In his book Hilton says that "a few weeks before I had no intention of going, chiefly for the reason that I did not think it was worth the financial outlay; but a week before the meeting I received an invitation from a friend to come and stay with him during the meeting. I still could not make up my mind, chiefly for the reason that I knew the parental wishes were against such a proceeding, and the parental wishes in those days also coincided with those of the employer.

"Eventually I summoned up the courage to suggest that I should like to go – this being about four o'clock on the Monday afternoon, and the Championship began on the Wednesday. The suggestion was not received with acclamation or loud cheers, but finally the words came forth 'well, go if you want to go; but I cannot see much use in your going'. I wasted no time and was off on the midnight train."

He played three rounds on the day before the meeting – yes, dear golfers, three rounds in a day – to prepare himself. His first round was a course record, which so impressed writer and amateur golfer, Garden Smith, that he took odds of four to one on a Hilton victory. Not feeling safe, he had a wager on Willie Park and when Hilton told him he thought Johnny Ball would win, he invested again.

Preceding page: Harold Hilton from a painting by R Jack

Opposite: Heading down the 9th

Harold Hilton at Apawamis Golf Club where he won the US Amateur in 1911

Amid ridicule, he found himself in a happy position of having laid odds of six to four on three players against the field. As it happened the wager came off and he remarked that he who laughs last laughs best.

This was the first time the Championship had been played over four rounds of 18 holes, making his victory more astounding. After the first day he was eight strokes behind the leader Horace Hutchinson; on day two there was a different tale to tell. "I could hardly do any wrong. I nearly holed at the 1st hole in one and then had a succession of fours to finish the third round in 72 to be only three strokes behind Johnny Ball."

He admitted that his last round was lucky. He holed two mashie pitches and six or seven very missable putts, some of them up to 10 feet. He played the round at "a terrible pace, fairly running my poor partner, Jacky Ferguson, off his legs". He managed to chase down Johnny Ball and clinch The Open. He concluded that: "my ambition leaned towards the amateur event and could not realise that I had secured the bigger prize before the lesser".

He returned home with Johnny and as the train approached the station at Hoylake he was anticipating a huge welcome only to find that there were just a few members waiting to greet him. He did not show his disappointment, but he wouldn't, would he?

He did, though, enjoy a jolly good meal at the Royal Hotel with the members of the Club.

He and Johnny continued their friendly rivalry, with Ball on top in matchplay but Harold holding his own on medal days. When the news came that Hoylake was to hold The Open in 1897 for the first time this created great excitement amongst the local community and members alike. Harold again struggled against Johnny and the great Scottish sportsman Freddie Tait. Harold played Tait on many occasions in matchplay but never got the better of him in any of their gruelling encounters.

When The Open came to Hoylake for the first time in 1897 it began a year of "a rich and plentiful harvest". Coming up to The Open Harold agreed "that local knowledge may be a distinct asset, but I came to the conclusion that we wanted all that and a little more to get in front of JH Taylor, Alex Herd, Harry Vardon and James Braid. The lessons taught in 1895, '96 and '97 had not been lost on me, and it was evident that the professional was gradually leaving the amateur behind."

It was not until 1900 that Harold won his first Amateur Championship. How many great golfers find it more difficult to play against the man rather than the card? He won again the next year but then little was heard of him on the golf links for nearly 10 years. He suffered greatly with sciatica, an affliction that is the curse of many a sportsman.

Not being a wealthy man, in fact a man of little means, he started making a name for himself as a golf club Secretary and he held a number of positions – at West Lancashire golf club, Ashford Manor, West Hill and Fearndown, a great geographical spread. He was also the first editor of *Golf Illustrated*.

He was back as a player in 1911, winning the Amateur at Prestwick and finishing third in The Open, just one shot behind Vardon and Arnaud Massy, the former winning the Championship for the fifth time.

But what is more astonishing is that he travelled to America to play in their Amateur at Apawamis golf club on Long Island Sound. Either his finances were looking up or it was an offer he could not refuse. He won the qualifying event and breezed through to the final, where he beat Fred Herreshoff (of the boat-building family) at the first extra hole of the play-off.

A number of members spent a most enjoyable day at the Apawamis golf club in 2001 and, together with the members of the Club, unveiled a plaque to commemorate

Harold Hilton's second Open Championship Medal: Hoylake's first Open, 1897

A painting of Harold Hilton in action by JJ Inglis

'The Shot' – his second to the green at the 37th which bounced off a rock in the rough and onto the green, effectively giving Harold victory. The first hole at Apawamis is called 'Hilton's Rock' to this day.

The doyen of American golf writers, Herbert Warren Wind, said: "The effect of Hilton's victory on Americans who did not play golf was even more significant ... Americans were not pleased with the idea that a foreigner had carried one of our Championship cups out of the country, and men who had never cared a straw about golf before now wanted to know the inside story."

Furthermore, the next day he went over the newly formed National Golf Links on Long Island and won the inaugural competition. The next US Amateur was in Chicago; he travelled but failed to retain the trophy. One final, great, golfing trophy awaited Harold when he won the 1913 Amateur Championship at St Andrews.

He did enter events after the Great War but now aged over 50 and a chain smoker his days of golfing success were over. He did play a number of exhibition matches against a fine lady golfer, Miss Cecil Leitch. It made great headlines when he lost having given her a shot every other hole. The Suffragette movement loved it.

No rich man, some generous members helped him out. He moved around the country but always played golf out of The Royal Liverpool Golf Club.

In spite of his image of cigarettes, white shoes and a jaunty walk, he was a kindly man always willing to help others. He loved the game and spent hours experimenting with new grips and clubs.

For all the research I have done it was never known if he was married, then out of the blue in September 2002 I received a letter from a gentleman on the Isle of Wight:

> Dear Sir,
> I am Harold Hilton's grandson ...."

It was signed by Tom Fenwick who made a visit to Hoylake with his wife Trish. Harold had indeed married – a lady called Sarah. They had three children, the eldest, Dorice, was Tom's mother who married for the second time to a Melville Fenwick.

Tom's only recollections of his mother discussing her father was that "he never had two pennies to rub together".

I am still looking for Harold's grave, as I write. We do know that he died in Bethlehem, Westcotes, Gloucestershire on 6 March 1942.

Shortly after Harold's death Bernard Darwin wrote: "There are few people in the world that really know their subject. He knew his golf."

A group of amateur champions, 1906

Standing: Mr WJ Travis, Mr John Ball, Mr Robert Maxwell

Seated round table: Mr Leslie M Balfour Melville, Mr AG Barry, Mr Horace G Hutchinson, Mr Peter Anderson, Mr JE Laidlay, Mr C Hutchings, Mr James Robb, Mr HH Hilton

The Royal Liverpool clubroom, 1988

Tim Marshall, John Spence, Tony Colvin, Michael Marshall, Nicko Williams, Michael Pearson, David Shone, John Graham (Jnr), David Staveley-Taylor, Anthony Shone, Joe Maxwell, Bill Renison, Billy McGhee, Jock Warnock, Roger Robinson, Lytton Goodwin, Poddy Williamson, Gerry Maxwell, Bruce Thompson, Laurie Briggs, Brian Gourley, John Brocklehurst, John Rees-Roberts, Nick Wainwright, Graham Brown, John Moore, Rob Kirkpatrick, Tom Draper-Williams, Neil McBurney

The Royal Liverpool clubroom, 2006

Standing left-right: John Norbury, Barry Owen, Doug Norval, Chris Moore, Mark Brocklehurst, Duncan Fraser, Alastair Machray, Roger Greenway, Joe Pinnington, Brian Gourley, Nick Wainwright, John Heggarty, Neil McBurney, Andrew Renison

Seated left-right: John Spence, Tim Marshall, Nicko Williams, David Lowry, Johnny Turner (Captain 2005), Gerry Maxwell, Peter Smith, Anthony Shone, Davy Pain, Barry Shortall, Alan Booth, Jim Kennefick, Tony Colvin, Sean Duncan, Graham Brown, Roger Robinson

Chapter Seven

7th hole

The Course and the Clubhouse ...

As Guy Farrar said all those years ago: "Will The Royal Liverpool hold its place as one of the premier golf clubs? The answer to that question lies with 'the powers that be'."

During early May 1869 "the powers that be", Robert Chambers and George Morris, set about the construction of the first nine holes on the Hoylake warren.

Although the ground was deemed perfect for the game of golf, setting off from the Royal Hotel they had a number of obstacles to negotiate. There were no such beasts as JCBs or any mechanised ground removal apparatus. If anything had to be moved or dug it had to be accomplished by "the toil of man".

The first obstacle was a multitude of rabbit holes whose inhabitants are not appreciated by golfers. It must have been a nightmare, but, by 1894, within 20 years, Johnny Ball and his gun had established control.

The warrens were dug up and made into bunkers.

The second obstacle was that there was the racecourse running through the intended location of the golf links. As racing continued until 1876 there was a major conflict, not only with the equine fraternity but also with the local residents who favoured the sport of the horse to the one of the stick 'n' ball.

There are paintings by Major Hopkins (who wrote under the pseudonym of Wooden Spoon) showing the difficulties of playing next to the railings. The railings were still prominent well into the 1960s. They were located just before the fairway begins on the 18th hole, in line with the drive. It seems rather sad that they were ever removed as they were a last tangible link with the pre-golf days.

Within two years, the course was extended to the full complement and there is no better way of describing those holes than to reproduce the words of Guy Farrar.

The question one may ask is why was the course not played to the apex of the river Dee and Irish Sea where Red Rocks is situated? What a hole that would have been, the sea, with the wind howling on the most westerly available point. The sea in fact came onto the present course around the present 13th tee and, again, there was a lack of earth-lifting machinery, but what a shame.

Farrar writes: "What degree of alteration constitutes a reconstructed course?"

The course was ever-changing in those days, to such an extent that it was not until the Captain in 1923, John P Brocklebank, and a few far-sighted members fought long and hard for the alterations that the great Harry Colt carried out in 1924.

And what changes they were!

Briefly he moved the 8th green from the hollow on the left to the raised plateau of today; he made the same change to the 10th green from the right; with the 12th green he moved it back and up the slope."

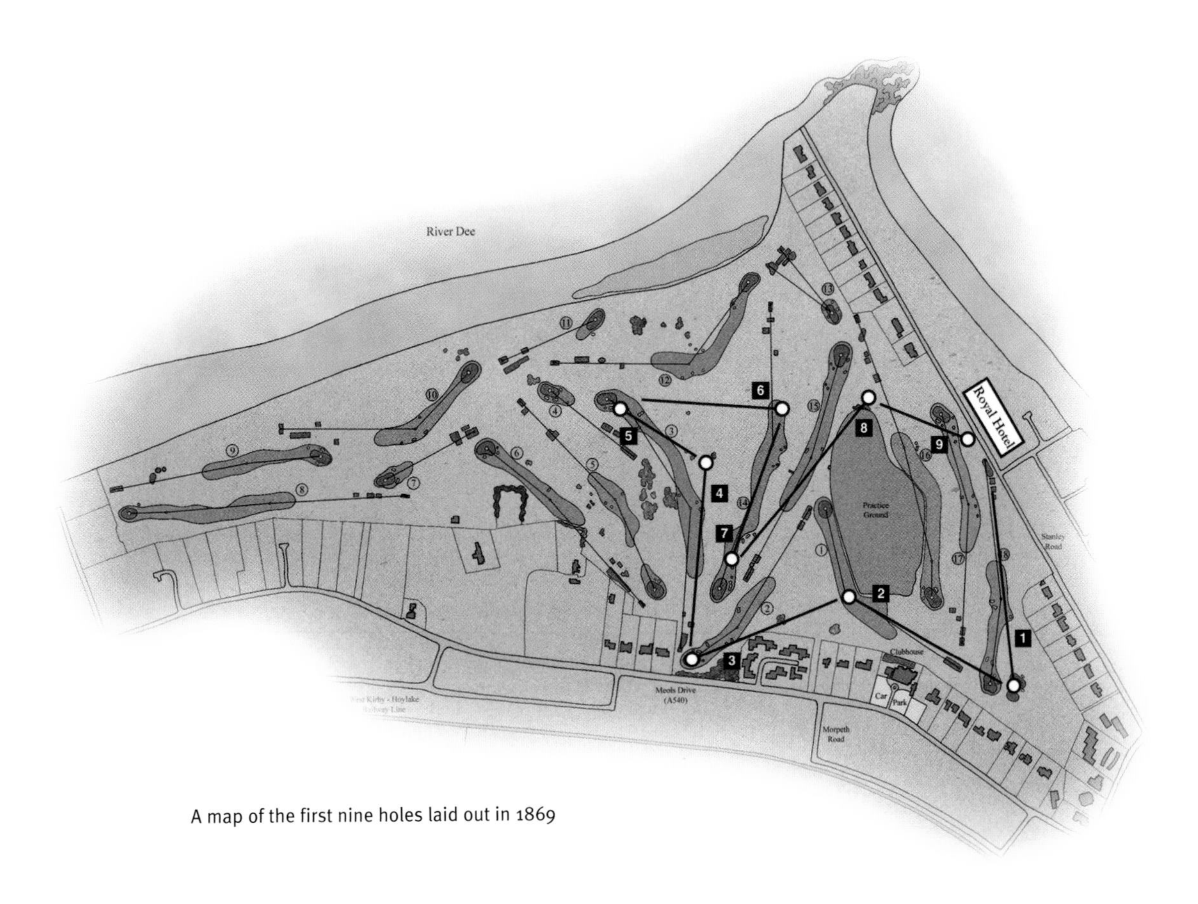

A map of the first nine holes laid out in 1869

1956

During the Open Championship an American professional Mike Souchak observed that he "rated Hoylake with Pebble Beach and Pinehurst No 2. The three courses are different, but all of them are real tests of golf".

Now, and this will shock the perceptive reader, there was the most frightful stink. Members were up in arms: "You're destroying old Hoylake ..."; "... ruining a perfectly good course" – the observations went on, and on.

But Brocklebank was determined and the results were spectacular, as we see them today. The changes to the 11th (Alps) and 17th (Royal) were particularly well received at the time.

By this time it was too late to place a hole by Red Rocks as the building of houses had taken all the available land.

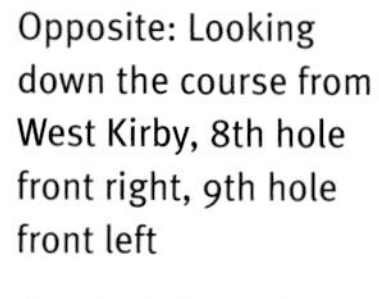

Opposite: Looking down the course from West Kirby, 8th hole front right, 9th hole front left

Overleaf: From the 10th tee

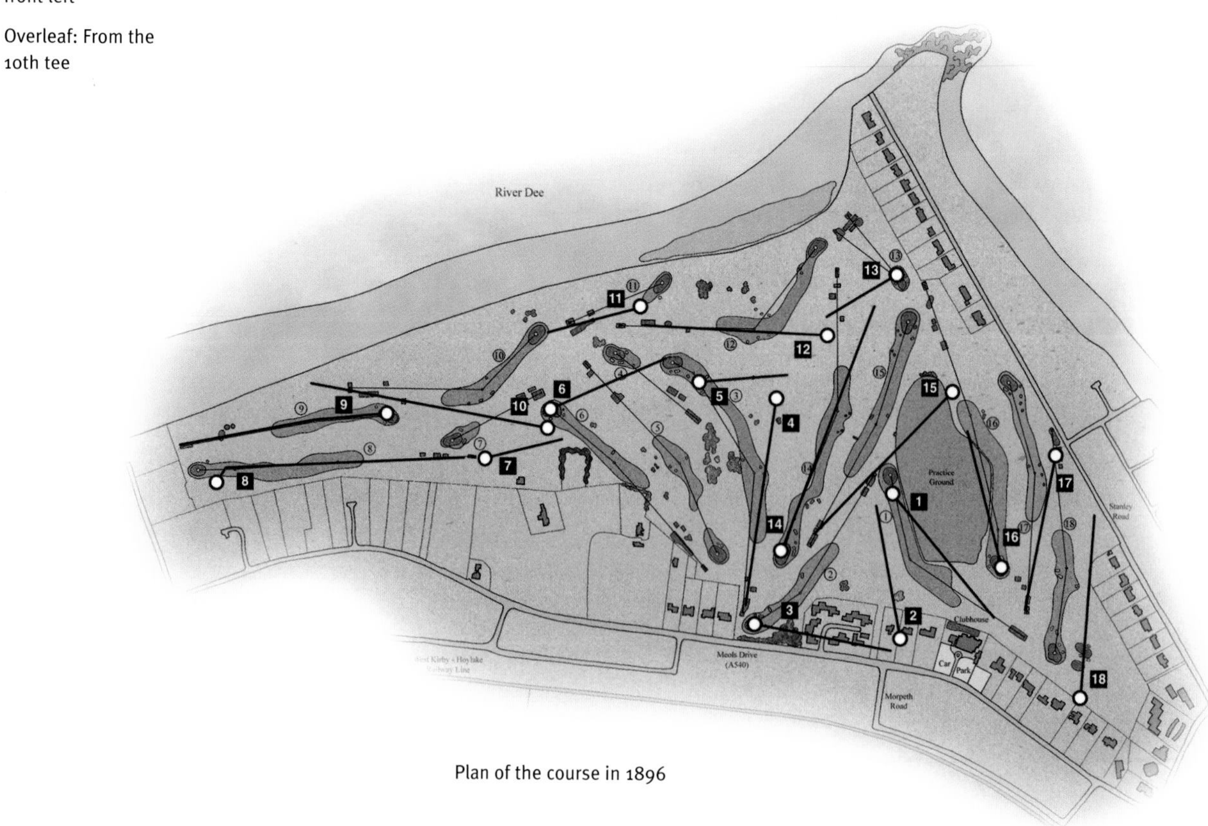

Plan of the course in 1896

The demise of the Dowie, 27th March 1993

Since the character of the Dowie will now be completely altered it is suggested that it be renamed e.g. 'Pinfold'

J.C. Armitage 1/4/93

Since 1924 there have been few changes of note. There has been a great deal of fine tuning, some of it often unnecessary, and only three changes of real significance.

In the mid-1960s the 3rd hole was made into a dog-leg left, a completely new 4th hole made and the 5th tee moved towards West Kirby. Great innovations carried out by the Club in the most desperately severe financial times.

The longest saga in Hoylake history was dealt with in 1993, when the legendary 7th hole was finally changed for all golfers. The point of contention was a cop running along the left side of the green and this was always deemed out-of-bounds, consequently a two-shot penalty.

This first became a problem in 1932 when the rules of golf changed the out-of-bounds penalty from one shot to stroke and distance. By the time of the 1967 Open the professionals would not play it as out-of-bounds. In years to come nor would the amateurs, so eventually the Club took the matter to an extraordinary general meeting and the motion was carried by a majority of three to one.

Again, there was great friction within the Club. Most of the older members were against the change, including a former Captain, Michael Marshall. When the vote was announced he slowly rose to his full height of six foot four, glanced around the room, the

Opposite: After an extraordinary general meeting the Club voted to remove the out-of-bounds at the 7th hole in March 1993

Left: 1921 Amateur final. WI Hunter driving out, Allan Graham, with caddy Campbell, behind audience in a state of anticipation. He coughed, and in his flowing, fascinating tones he pronounced: "Fine, we've had the vote, now (a long pause) ... now, let's just get on with it." There was spontaneous applause and a silent sigh of relief from the majority. If the great man said "get on with it" then we had to "get on with it". So we did, and we have lived to love the change.

However, a member, Jos Armitage (Ionicus, the man who painted the covers of the Penguin books for PG Wodehouse), made a contribution to the suggestions book that indicated a certain disenchantment.

The Club was now in full flow and there was urgency in the air. The 100th playing of the Amateur Championship took place in 1995 to the accompaniment of great compliments from the many visitors from around the world.

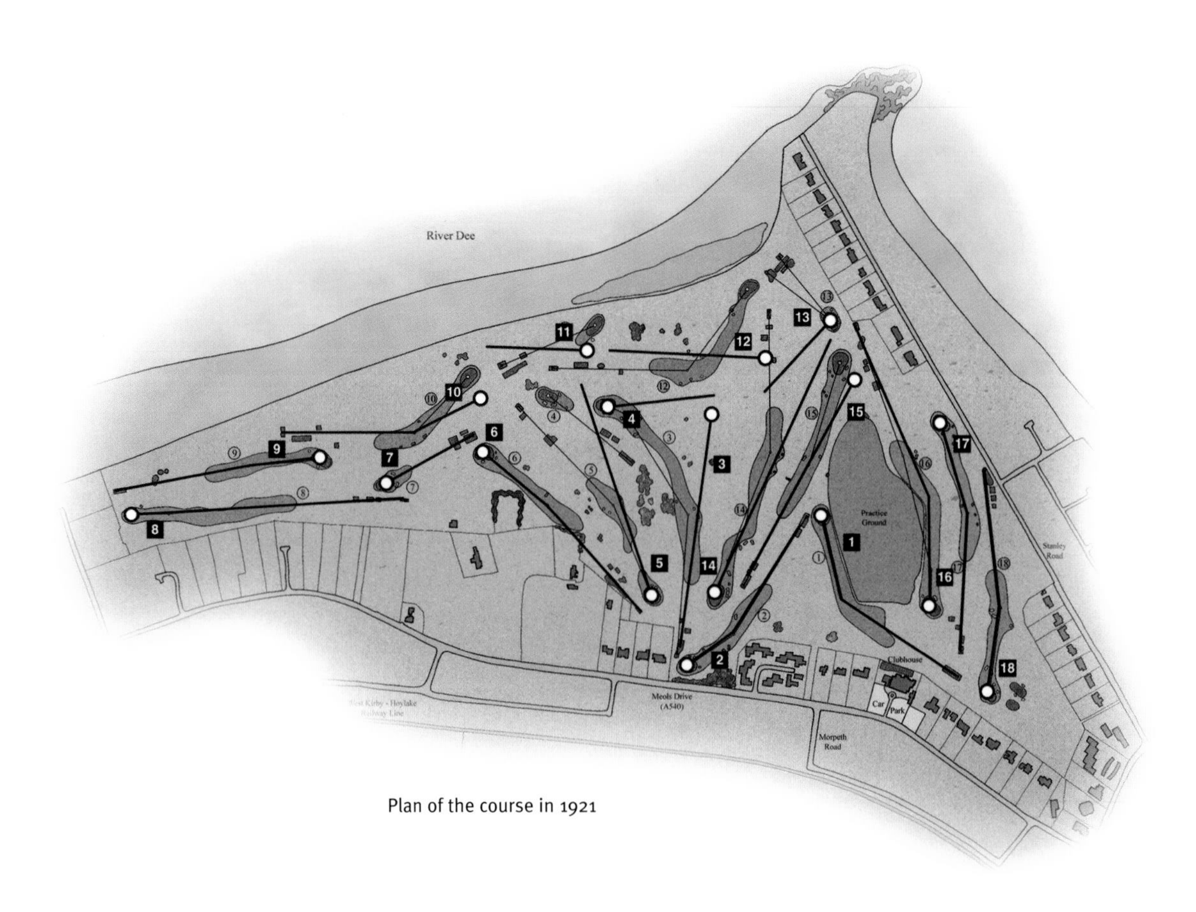

Plan of the course in 1921

The most commonly asked question was: "Why do you not have The Open back?" It was last staged in 1967.

But behind the scenes action was afoot. Constant discussions took place at St Andrews between the R & A and members of the Club, notably Anthony Shone who, in the way of the clever politician he is, began to plant the seeds of possibility into the minds of those that mattered. The golfing Press was a great ally, particularly John Hopkins of *The Times* and the late Michael Williams of *The Daily Telegraph*.

The battle to win back The Open is dealt with in detail in chapter 17, but suffice to say that the genius of greenkeeper Derek Green meant that the R & A was hugely impressed by the state of the course for the 2000 Amateur Championship and by the quality of the Hoylake administration on and off the links.

The next winter a golf course architect was appointed to make the alterations necessary for the holding of "the big one". The R & A recommended Donald Steele, who in his day was a fine amateur golfer, a writer of distinction and now a world-renowned golf architect.

After careful discussions there were to be alterations on every hole. Some small and some incredibly complex.

The three major changes were an extension of some 60 yards to the 3rd; similar work to the 17th but bringing the hole out from the road 30 yards. The 18th was altered again, for probably the sixth time in living memory. This time a few new bunkers were added and the green turned to the left with more undulation.

The whole work was carried out over the winter of 2000 and 2001 and was open for the Spring Medal on the first Saturday in May.

I am delighted to recall that the writer was the first course record holder. (I was in the first pairing out and kept that record for a full 25 minutes.)

Drawings by Jos Armitage, that hang in the clubhouse. He went under the pen name Ionicus and was responsible for the gorgeous covers of the famous PG Wodehouse series in Penguin Books

Suggestions Book, 1897

We beg to bring before the Green Committee (in view of the present state of the greens) the availability of re-stocking and preserving the rabbits.

It was announced in 2002 that The Royal Liverpool Golf Club was to be added to The Open rota. Eventually, after all the preparatory work was completed, the official announcement was made in December 2002 that, after a period of 39 years, The Open was coming back to the Hoylake links in July 2006.

After a long period of absence from the world's golfing stage the current "powers that be" had succeeded in bringing The Open Championship – the greatest golfing event on this earth – back to the flat fields of Hoylake. From those many grateful members, thank you and bravo.

Opposite: Craig Gilholm whose role as links manager is vital to the health of the greens

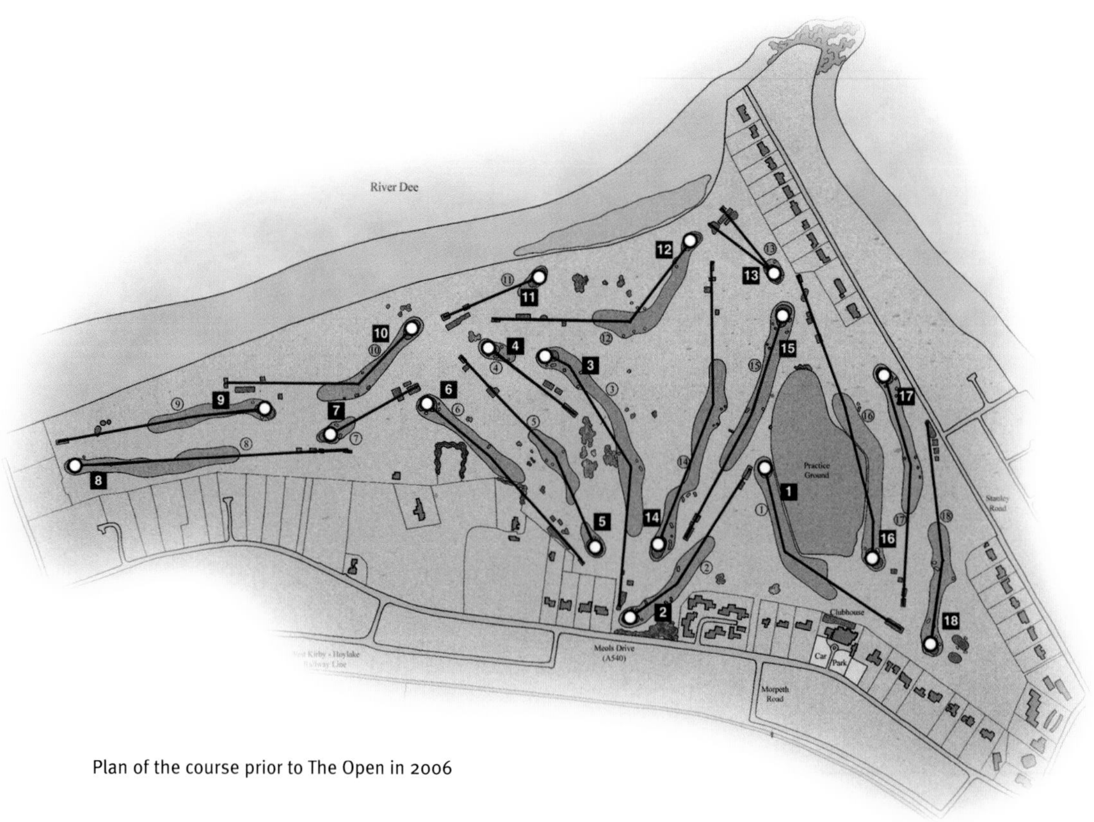

Plan of the course prior to The Open in 2006

Greentek
0113 267 7000

The Clubhouse

"What a ghastly building," remarked Peter Alliss as he walked in the direction of the 18th tee. He made this remark during the week of The Open Championship in 1956. I accept that time does play tricks with the memory and, appreciating that I was only 10 years old at the time, I am still convinced he uttered those words about the Royal Hotel.

In truth, it was a ghastly building. Within a year it was to be razed to the ground and the houses we see today would rise from its ashes. But, the history of the building?

Ah, what a history!

It was the first clubhouse of The Liverpool Golf Club, in 1869. The parties they had, the revelries and friendship, the characters from the local community! If ever a building had witnessed life this was it. But how on earth was this relic of the past situated in such a place? In 1792, Sir John Stanley built the hotel, hoping to attract holidaymakers. The roads in the early 19th century "were of frightful ruggedness" according to Anna Seward of Litchfield, who experienced the journey from Parkgate. However, she must have enjoyed her stay as she returned three years later.

The original Royal Hotel with single storey on the right: they were the rooms, or first clubhouse, of The Royal Liverpool Golf Club

The setting was spectacular. A long lawn sloping down to the sea, a sea uncontaminated and most suitable for bathing. The bliss of those long summer days was interrupted somewhat by the introduction of a golf links on the warren, a warren sometimes used as a horse-racing track.

The golfers were a determined lot and progress was swift. How they negotiated the agreement with the landlord John Ball Senior is not recorded, but a room was set aside for the members. The first mention was on 3 July 1869 when, as Guy Farrar reported: "The Secretary was authorised to get boxes made for storing clubs and have them placed round the room engaged at the Royal Hotel, according to plans and estimates."

In the picture of the hotel, the clubroom is the one to the right of the porch. The members used the dining room for meals. There was obviously a conflict between these wealthy Liverpool merchants and the local fishermen. A working relationship was established, probably helped by the reverence and adoration the blue-jerseyed fishermen held for the golfing skills of Johnny Ball, "the greatest Roman of them all".

The Club was now established. There was great fun to be had at the musical evenings in the bar parlour of the Royal Hotel. Bar parlour sounds quite ominous, but I never remember seeing a man in it who could not talk straight, nor walk straight out of it – and some of the golfers had great voices. A certain RW (Pendulum) Brown sang 'The Farmer's Boy' whilst Tosper (Thomas Owen Potter), the Hon Secretary, conducted with a beautiful ivory baton, now the Captain's wand of office.

Matches were arranged for large sums of money during these evenings. John Ball Senior keen to pair up with his son and take on anyone.

On one occasion, the aforementioned Pendulum Brown backed himself to play the five holes round the

Above top: Clubhouse 1902

Below: Clubhouse 1913

Above: The clubroom, top 1988, below 2006

Opposite: Silver cruets in serried ranks in The Royal Liverpool dining room

out-of-bounds field, 'the Circus', in a stipulated number of shots at dead of night. Not only did he win his bet but accomplished those holes in fewer strokes than he took the next day in broad daylight.

Alec Sinclair was a great humorist and George Dunlop was regarded as one of the best after-dinner speechmakers. Both Sinclair and Dunlop became captains. As for dear old Pendulum, he did not make the captaincy, but went on to found Wallasey Golf Club and became their first Captain.

From the famous lawn, members, for a wager, would play a shot over the hotel onto the home green (now the 17th) to see who could hit it closest to the flag.

Legend has it that Harold Hilton was an expert at such a challenge. John Ball Senior was not impressed with this activity, as the less-skilful member would thin the ball into the hotel. He did not hold back from reprimanding the offender.

When Johnny Ball won The Open in 1890, he was not only the first Englishman but also the first amateur to win the Championship.

As he was on his way home by train word reached him that there was a large welcoming party at Hoylake station. Some members were waiting for him, together with a great gathering of the local fishermen who had a cart minus the horse ready to draw him home.

Johnny, who loathed attention, alighted from the train before it arrived at Hoylake and walked home to the Royal Hotel along the shore. Climbing up the long lawn he was met by his father who proudly ushered him into the hotel with The Open trophy packed in his suitcase.

The first sight of the Claret Jug outside Scotland was in the Royal Hotel, where it remained for 12 months. Two years later Harold Hilton won The Open, returning it to the Hoylake clubhouse.

An agreement was eventually signed in 1879 between Mr John Ball Senior and the Club and an extension was built. A single storey that could be seen at the far end of the building. The sum of £50 per annum was charged.

In return the Club stipulated their requirements, including that "Mr Ball shall provide one thoroughly competent, efficient manservant to attend to the wants and requirements of the members of the said club." Rather strong language, but with the Victorians there was little chance of misunderstanding them.

This agreement lasted for 15 years but, when the lease had expired and the Club had grown to such dimensions that further expansion was necessary, a move was considered.

The transfer to the present clubhouse took place in 1895. At the same time, the lease of the links was also renegotiated with Lord Stanley. He must have been a busy man as he was at this time Governor General of Canada. This was one of the major events in the Club's history.

Was the move a natural progression or was it forced by the demands of John Ball Senior?

There is little doubt that the Club was expanding and a move would inevitably take place. However, John Ball Senior was a hard man. He also had a great ally in Thomas Owen Potter who lived at the hotel and, of course, was the Honorary Secretary up until the move. It seems likely that Ball's demands became excessive and, ultimately, the Club voted with its feet.

The hotel still had another 60 years of trading. John Ball Senior died in 1902. His son Johnny, the great golfer, and daughter Elizabeth took charge but Elizabeth died in 1913 and Johnny married his housekeeper Nellie and went to live in Wales.

The Royal Hotel very nearly housed royalty. In 1929 King George V was strongly advised to spend more

Opposite: Portraits of former Captains adorn the clubroom

Above: Lounge bar 1988, below 2006

Opposite: The current Secretary, Group Captain Christopher Moore CBE

Overleaf: A panoramic view of the clubhouse in 2006, prior to the return of The Open

time by the sea due to an asthmatic condition. Hoylake was recommended, but the Court at the time thought that Bognor in Sussex would be better suited for its proximity to London. Consequently it was awarded the suffix of Regis. Pity. What an address it would have been: The Royal Hotel, Hoylake Regis. Marvellous.

The hotel survived as a public house, selling fine draught ale and open all hours.

Ken Cranston, the oldest-living former England cricket Captain, told me that in the 40s golfers would climb under the fence at the 17th and nip into the hotel for a pint of draught beer. The golf club only sold bottled beer at the time.

Between the bar and the lounge bar was a huge fire servicing both rooms. A great arch housed the fireplace. It was about five feet high and one could see through to the other room. For a wager, the more daring customer would dive through the flames and somersault into the other room, often interrupting a conversation as he fell to ground. Picking himself up he made his apologies and explained that to accomplish the bet he had to make the return journey and promptly disappeared through the flames once more and out of sight.

Haunted? Was the Royal Hotel haunted? Well, of course it was.

In the years before the hotel closed, a number of the staff reported that a man dressed in a brown Norfolk jacket, knickerbockers and a tweed cap had been seen walking down the corridor from the hall to the ballroom before vanishing. When mounting the main staircase of the present clubhouse, cast an eye upwards and see for yourself if there is a resemblance between that description and the portrait of John Ball.

I am only grateful that the place was knocked down before I started calling at the Green Lodge a number of years later! Or am I?

Above: Inner hall clubhouse 1988, below 2006

We must be grateful that the Club had a natural home to walk into. Without that, visiting golfers would have had nowhere to stay and it is inconceivable that Hoylake would have flourished so quickly. What effects would that have had on the development of the game in England?

One final thought. On a summer evening, when you are playing to the 17th green, look over to the houses to your right in the direction of the sea; witness for yourself the setting sun, gently disappearing over what was once the sloping lawn of the Royal Hotel.

While we can look back with affection on the Royal Hotel there is no doubting the special place in our affections its successor enjoys, even though it was sadly neglected for far too many years.

Let me give you an example. I remember playing snooker there one night and there was the most tremendous crash! I shall never forget the moment, as I was about to pot a long black for a famous victory on the green baize. Due to this explosion, my shot was, well sort of topped sideways, and the cue ball dribbled into the centre sack.

"What's going on?" I implored, with a combination of shock and irritation, only to be informed that a further part of the roof had expired and imminent flooding was now due.

This news was given by that epitome of sartorial correctness and respectful service, 'Grimshaw'. Grimshaw was a lovely old boy, not exactly the sharpest tool in the shed, who always had problems remembering a drinks order. Perhaps his greatest misunderstanding was after being given instructions for two Haigs and water – he eventually appeared with two glasses of water, a hard-boiled egg resting in each vessel: "Two 'aigs' 'n' water ... sir?"

The roof incident illustrated why "Our Old Friend", the clubhouse – described in the early days of this century as the finest clubhouse on earth – appeared by the early 1980s to be in a poor state of repair. The roof required urgent attention.

There was talk of rebuilding.

One idea mooted was to build the clubhouse on stilts behind the 12th green. Spectacular speculation but, due to the Natterjack toad, this idea was soon quashed by a combination of Green Committee and Green lobby. However, the nettle was grasped and a new roof appeared by the end of the decade.

The first part of the refurbishment started with the clubroom. All sorts of ideas were put forward until a designer was appointed and a most satisfactory result achieved.

It was not until the early 90s that a plan was agreed for the whole clubhouse and surrounding areas. By this time the Coach House had been purchased from the Conservative Club and this, too, was incorporated into the grand plan.

There was the old Spike Bar. Oh dear! What a sight! All vinyl and junk, but I did love the photographs around the walls.

During the time when the work was carried out, the clubroom was used for the after-golf relaxation.What a great irony that now we have such a splendid players' bar, the clubroom is used less and less.

The refurbishment continued in the ladies' lounge. How easy it is to forget the sliding façade to the bar with that marvellous aerial view of the course.

Last year, the spindles on the staircase re-appeared after 40 years.

It was claimed that the reason boards covered the spindles was in deference to the ladies who were able to use the main staircase for the first time in the 1950s and needed to do so without revealing an ankle or glimpse of stocking to the male fraternity.

Suggestions Book, March 1893

We would suggest that something be done to prevent the Everton Football Club playing on the green every week and cutting the ground up very much. The foul language used even in the presence of ladies is a perfect disgrace.

Suggestions Book, October 1895

Are members supposed to wash their feet in the basins of the lavatory? I saw it done!

Suggestions Book, April 1896

Why should old golf balls be dished up as curried chicken – surely Jack Morris would have a better sale for them.

And so to 2005, and the completion of a wholesale series of large-scale improvements. These were achieved to bring the clubhouse up to date and offer a wonderful facility to future generations.

This work involved the creation of a new professionals' shop within the main building, a bag and club storage area, a golf reception area, improved locker rooms and enhanced catering and dining facilities. There has also been an update of the entire ladies' section of the Club.

As long as there is money available it is the intention to continue on similar lines.

Much has changed and I, for one, will always miss the revolving doors that led to the course. But change is inevitable and necessary and, whatever the cost, it is a small price to pay for the work that preserves "Our Old Friend".

1998

Fairbrother demanded Eccles cakes and Joan, who had been at the Club for many years, pointed out that the kitchens were closed. Fairbrother insisted that he would like some of those tasty currant cakes.

Eventually they arrived and Fairbrother asked, everything ok with chief? Joan, who was one of quick wit replied, "well there were 3 f's in the reply and Fairbrother was only mentioned once."

Opposite: Michael Groves, a well-known club member and ex-county cricketer

Left: March 2006. The renovation work was completed. A party was held to thank all involved, including architects (Owen Ellis Partnership), designers and contractors

Overleaf: Sandro Rossi, clubhouse manager, always ready with a welcome for members and guests alike

1975
WARSTEINER

WARSTEINER
GUINNESS
ORIGINAL

GRAHAM
H · GRAY
HARVEY

Chapter Eight

8th hole

1914-1939

by Barry Shortall

In 1914 the acrid mists of war replaced the soft mists of summer, blotting out the golfing scene. Those who crouched in terrible bunkers in the Somme, at Ypres and at Verdun, who faced the awful smog of gas and smoke, thought not only of loved ones back home but of the course they loved, the greens they had played in the company of those whose company they valued.

This poignant reminder of that came from 'Old Bill', a cartoon character of World War I. To a complaining comrade as they sheltered in the trenches: "If you know of a better hole go to it." "I know a better hole," was the reply, "but I can't go to it because it is not a shell hole but a hole on a golf course and the rules won't let me."

No history of The Royal Liverpool Golf Club would be complete without a remembrance of the members who perished in that awful war, who paid the ultimate price for doing their duty. The plaque in the clubroom reveres their memory.

E.W.H.Brockelhurst; A.S.Buchanan; V.J.Derbyshire;
L.F.Dunn; C.D.H.Dunlop; G.Fitzhugh; G.H.Getty;
J.Graham,Jr; A.D.H.Grayson; J.Harvey; W.Harvey;
E.Herschel; G.F.Higgins; M.Honan; A.Hughes;
P.Lancaster; D.Macleod; K.McDiarmid;
A.G.Nicholson; T.S.Paterson; K.M.Rae; D.H.Scott;
E.F.Sellars; B.Stott; F.H.Turner; A.Twentyman;
H.D.Vernon; A.N.Walker; G.D.Wilson; J.A.Wolff;
R.F.Wolstenholme.

It is impossible to distinguish between these brave men but some may particularly be remembered for their golfing prowess. One was Captain Jack Graham Junior, who gave his life leading his company in the charge of the Liverpool Scottish Battalion at Hooge. Graham was a great loss to all who knew him, one of the family of Grahams who had represented the Club and were to represent it in the future.

Others went to the war; in 1914 the Club recorded their sincere appreciation of the patriotic action of their House Committee Chairman, Mr CH McDiarmid, in "enrolling himself as a private in His Majesty's army". McDiarmid was one who returned from war in 1919 to take up his previous position on the committee.

The Club minutes record: "As the war continued the Club was making preparations for hard times. Supplies of coal were laid in, at 20 shillings a ton, to be stored in the bicycle sheds. For the members' convenience thousands of the finest cigars were purchased, including 2,000 Punch cigars, 1,000 Cabanas and 220 Bolivian, together with large quantities of whisky and gin, ordered to circumvent the probable increase in duty to fund the war effort, although a 'war tax' of 2d (1p) was placed on all food and drinks supplied to members. The Club also ensured that there were enough supplies of beer and stout to hold prices steady for six months.

As a further saving towards the war effort it was decided that potatoes would not be served on Saturdays.

"In 1916, the war only halfway through, the green-keeping staff asked for a wage increase. However, as all were in the process of being conscripted, it was decided that a decision be left until hostilities ended, when and if the staff returned, with an exception for those rejected on medical grounds. Men who had been discharged and asked for re-employment, asked for £2 a week. They were offered 35 shillings (£1.75).

"In the meantime, women had been employed to weed the greens and fill in for the shortage of green staff."

In 1919 and the years immediately following the war, alterations to the course continued in the search for that nebulous quality, perfection. It was the time when, at the suggestion of Jack Morris, the incumbent professional, the first motor mower was purchased and one of the greens staff instructed how to use it.

The boundaries of the course were strengthened, wattle and thorn fences erected along the westerly boundaries to prevent the tide washing away the fledgling dunes, the construction of a sea wall, the ultimate barrier to the sea, being dismissed on the grounds of cost. To help fill in the gaps and holes between the dunes and to prevent sand blowing on the course the district council supplied lorry loads of rubbish and members were asked to supply garden refuse.

In 1921 the employment of women on the course was deemed so successful that it was decided to keep them on a permanent basis, their duties to include weeding of the fairways, at the same wage rates as caddies. In the same year a request by Major MacMinnies that a landing ground for an aeroplane be arranged within the course was refused, among the reasons the fact that there were 50 ewes grazing the links.

Preceding page: A close-in focus of the World War I Memorial in the clubhouse, which commemorates members who lost their lives between 1914-18

Opposite: Jack Graham, from a painting by RE Morrison

In 1921, 19 years after the first international match between England and Scotland was played on the course, Hoylake hosted the first international match between Great Britain and the USA. A number of players from that first game were present. Not one of them played; age had given way to youth.

For some years Hoylake's domination of amateur golf had been under threat from the American challenge and they were at Hoylake in force. The great American amateur, Francis Ouimet, spearheaded the team of American amateurs into battle against a team of British amateurs, the sides containing some of the greatest names in the history of amateur golf. The British side, captained by Roger Wethered, included Cyril Tolley and the young 'silver Scot', Tommy Armour. For the Americans, in addition to Oiumet, the team included WC Fownes, Jesse Guilford, Chick Evans and one Robert Tyre Jones. The match was to be the forerunner of the Walker Cup, the first international match between Great Britain and Ireland and the United States which continued the following year at the National Golf Links of America in Southampton, New York.

Open Golf Championship at Hoylake, June 16th to 20th, 1930.

FIRST, SECOND, THIRD AND FOURTH ROUNDS.

No.	Times	PLAYERS' NAMES	Scores 1st Rnd	2nd Rnd	3rd Rnd	4th Rnd	Total
1	8.0	A. PERRY, Leatherhead	78	74	75	82	309
	12.30	H. KIDD, Wilpshire	79	75	85	80	319
2	8.6	E. W. H. KENYON, West Lancs.	79	76	79	80	314
	12.36	HORTON SMITH, Cragston, U.S.A.	72	73	78	73	296
3	8.12	STEWART BURNS, Hendon	77	75	80	75	307
	12.42	ABE MITCHELL, Unattached	75	78	77	72	302
4	8.18	A. R. BRADBEER, Burnham and Berrow	81	74	80	81	316
	12.48	J. J. TAYLOR, Potters Bar	76	78	82	76	312
5	8.24	OWEN SANDERSON, Bradford	83	74	77	78	312
	12.54	BERT HODSON, Chigwell	74	77	76	74	301
6	8.30	H. LARGE, Grange Park	79	74	78	75	306
	1.0	C. W. THOMSON, Royal Eastbourne	81	74	81	83	319
7	8.36	E. RAY, Oxhey	78	75	76	78	307
	1.6	DUNCAN McCULLOCH, Troon	78	78	79	74	309
8	8.42	Mr. DONALD K. MOE, Alderwood, U.S.A.	74	73	76	80	303
	1.12	W. T. TWINE, Bromley and Bickley	78	78	78	79	313
9	8.48	PERCY ALLISS, Berlin Wannsee	75	74	77	79	305
	1.18	D. C. JONES, North Manchester	75	77	82	79	313
10	8.54	TOM GREEN, Copt Heath	73	79	78	78	308
	1.24	F. ROBSON, Cooden Beach	71	72	78	75	296
11	9.0	W. J. BRANCH, Henbury	81	77	78	76	312
	1.30	JAMES BRADBEER, Porters Park	77	77	76	82	312
12	9.6	HENRY COTTON, Langley Park	70	79	77	73	299
	1.36	WILLIAM A. McMINN, Ravensworth Park	82	75	77	80	314
13	9.12	Mr. F. C. STEVENS, Junr., Lakeside, U.S.A.	80	78	No Return		
	1.42	H. RIMMER, Bidston	79	79	79	80	317
14	9.18	ALBERT J. ISHERWOOD, Warrington	75	77	78	80	310
	1.48	Mr. LISTER HARTLEY, Chislehurst	79	78	79	75	311
15	9.24	Mr. ROBERT T. JONES, Junr., Atlanta, U.S.A.	70	72	74	75	291
	1.54	PIERRE HIRIGOYEN, Chantilly, France	75	79	76	76	306
16	9.30	W. LARGE, Huyton	78	74	77	76	305
	2.0	A. J. YOUNG, Sonning	75	78	77	74	304
17	9.36	TOM BARBER, Derbyshire	75	76	72	77	300
	2.6	P. F. WESTON, Birstall	81	77	76	76	310
18	9.42	JIM BARNES, Pelham Manor, U.S.A.	71	77	72	77	297
	2.12	Mr. WILLIAM SUTTON, West Cheshire Artisans.	78	76	81	82	317
19	9.48	AUGUSTE BOYER, Nice	73	77	70	80	300
	2.18	N. SUTTON Wentworth	72	80	76	79	307
20	9.54	Mr. C. J. H. TOLLEY, Royal and Ancient	84	71	80	82	317
	2.24	MARCEL DALLEMAGNE, Saint Germain	79	72	79	80	310
21	10.0	ARCHIE COMPSTON, Coombe Hill	74	73	68	82	297
	2.30	W. NOLAN, Portmarnock	78	79	74	80	311
22	10.6	A. J. LACEY, Selsdon Park	78	79	74	76	307
	2.36	GEORGE GADD, Roehampton	78	78	73	84	313
23	10.12	LEO DIEGEL, Agua Caliente, Mexico	74	73	71	75	293
	2.42	W. G. GIMBER, Seaham Harbour	76	78	81	85	320
24	10.18	Mr. H. G. BENTLEY, Hesketh	76	78	86	78	318
	2.48	Mr. R. H. OPPENHEIMER, Royal and Ancient	79	78	82	82	321
25	10.24	R. A. WHITCOMBE, Parkstone	78	72	73	79	302
	2.54	E. R. WHITCOMBE, Meyrick Park	80	72	76	77	305
26	10.30	SID FAIRWEATHER, Malone	77	78	79	82	316
	3.0	C. A. WHITCOMBE, Crews Hill	74	75	72	79	300
27	10.36	A. H. PADGHAM, Royal Ashdown Forest	78	80	74	80	312
	3.6	CHARLES McILVENNY, Port Elizabeth	76	75	79	83	313
28	10.42	H. CRAPPER, Harrogate	78	73	80	75	306
	3.12	LEN HOLLAND, Gerrards Cross	75	78	80	77	310
29	10.48	MACDONALD SMITH, U.S.A.	70	77	75	71	293
	3.18	PHILIP H. RODGERS, St. Annes Old Links	74	73	76	80	303
30	10.54	E. W. JARMAN, Prenton	76	76	79	80	311
	3.24	W. H. DAVIES, Wallasey	78	77	73	79	307
31	11.0	Mr. DONALD E. B. SOULBY, Fortwilliam, Belfast.	75	82	83	83	323
	3.30						

June 20, 1930.

W. R. Eccles, Printer, Hoylake.

Final score card dated 1930 and signed by Robert (Bobby) Jones

Good weather accompanied the match: a bright sky, the Welsh hills and the mountains of Snowdonia in the background showing clearly, the wind whistling around the clubhouse; not a gale, merely a fine Hoylake breeze.

Darwin writing for *The Times* reported on the match: "Mr Claude Montmorency was the nestor of the British side, very fit and strong. Mr Jenkins and Mr Gordon Simpson, the two Scotsmen who were perhaps the best pair for Britain, were hardened veterans in experience, and Mr Tolley, Mr Wethered and Mr Armour had crowded much golf into a few years.

"But the best that can be said about the British team on that day is that Tolley was magnificent and Montmorency and Aylmer sound. The rest, unfortunately, were disappointing and the American golfers gained an overwhelming victory; from the beginning of the match to the end they played well and gave an object lesson in golf. Their putting was collectively and individually excellent, machine-like in its accuracy.

"The Great Britain players' form was unrecognisable, almost too bad to be true, most failing to play as they could, unable to rise to the big occasion. One member of the team was heard to say 'we've had a jolly good lesson and it jolly well serves us right'."

The Americans won all foursomes matches. For almost the first eight holes the golf of the first American pair, Bobby Jones and Mr Charles Evans, was exceptional. Robert Tyre Jones was the first to tee-off, suffering from the weather and wearing a thick sweater with a big collar and blowing on his hands in the keen Hoylake wind. Theirs was golf that would have beaten anybody. Jones's driving was long and both players straight with wood and iron. They eventually won by five and three having completed 15 holes in two under fours and carding a 34 on the outward nine.

There was at least one bright spot for the Great Britain side in the singles, of which the Americans won five out of the eight. This was Tolley's golf against Evans. Darwin described it lyrically: "one would never have recognised the bored and erratic player of the morning. Now his carriage was superb. Menacing and Napoleonic, he looked every inch a champion.

"To see him filling his pipe while studying his putt and then tap the ball in, walking away to the next before the ball had dropped, was a truly inspiring spectacle. He began with a lovely three and fairly overwhelmed his American opponent with his masterly and powerful golf. He was out in 34, lost the 10th, won the 12th and 13th, finishing off his opponent at the lake with a perfect calm and confidence.

"Mr Montmorency, however, played as well as I knew he would, thoroughly courageous, sound, reliable, against Mr Jones. He was beaten by a longer and stronger player, but I only wish we had more like him. Mr Jones played very finely again. Some people said

8

he would not play well if held for a long time, but he never let it get to him. He is a very great golfer." Darwin himself was one of the three singles winners for Britain.

Following the match, which the United States won by nine points to three, The Royal Liverpool Club presented inscribed silver cigarette cases to each member of the American team as a memento of the occasion. The American team responded with magnanimous letters of appreciation.

One week after this defeat of Great Britain by the United States, the first post-war Amateur Championship was held, again at Hoylake, the growing popularity of golf reflected in a request from a London film company to film the event. Unfortunately the request was denied; a disappointing decision as it would have allowed future generations to see the appearance of Robert Tyre Jones Jnr, only 19 years old, in the Championship, where he would make it to the fourth round before being beaten by Allan Graham, a Royal Liverpool player.

In preparation for the Championship, caddie tariffs of five shillings and sixpence (27p) a day, plus lunch money were agreed. A rabbit catcher was appointed to "eradicate, as much as possible" the rabbits which were creating holes all over the course. This raised the ire of local residents with critical letters published in the Liverpool newspapers. However, a compromise meeting with the RSPCA decided that there seemed to be no alternative to trapping the rabbits; the problem they caused appearing solved when 510 were trapped over the next few months, with a marked reduction in the price of rabbit in local butchers' shops.

The new rules of the Royal & Ancient Golf Club before the Championship stated that "any competitor in the Amateur and Open Championships playing with balls or clubs not in conformity with the new rules regarding the size and weight of balls and that relating to the form and make of golf clubs shall be disqualified."

The emphatic victory of the American golfers in the international match the previous week had made the Americans firm favourites to produce the winner. Among British golfers and supporters the mood was bleak; there was great pessimism about the strength of the American challenge.

The weather during the Championship was blazing hot, the course as hard as brick and the greens had not been watered, making putting a lottery. The American golf commentator, Grantland-Rice, described dramatically the setting before the first blow was struck: "Hoylake the ancient waiting for the day of battle lay stretched out sombrely, a flat-looking plain of granite with blistered fairways and parboiled glistening greens as hard as marble and just about as keen, burnt to a brown greyness by the incessant procession of endless suns that has marched by in long progression with no rain in sight. And almost each day thereafter the sun stalked, 'a tyrant with a flaming sword', to further harden both fairway and green. Hoylake, undoubtedly a fine test when fairly soft with a stiff wind blowing, was now an anxious gamble, a nerve-wrecker for the man who lacked complete control of a delicate touch around the pin.

"It was next to impossible to pitch to the green on most of the holes and keep the ball out of trouble, for the flying white missile landing fifteen feet from the cup would take

Allan Graham congratulates WI Hunter after the final of the 1921 Amateur

one prodigious bound and then scuttle away like a scared jack rabbit for the heavy heather or some waiting trap."

There was one player, however, to whom the word impossible did not apply. Bobby Jones played one of those spectacular shots which, once seen, are never forgotten. At the Dowie, the 200-yard 7th, in his second-round match against Robert Harris, a former finalist, Bobby Jones, cut his first shot into the turfed gully at the right of the green. Most players would have attempted to putt through, but Jones elected to play a pitch onto a narrow green with a surface like rock. It appeared humanly impossible to stop the ball but Jones accomplished it, the ball coming to rest within a yard of the pin. He went on to win the match, five and three.

Jones had opened the Championship against GC Rainford, a Scot. Rainford started with a mighty drive through the early-morning mist which went straight down the fairway. He followed with a magnificent three iron three feet from the pin. This gave him confidence, but it was gradually eroded as Jones outplayed him, winning at the 16th, three and two.

Jones then played an unknown named WC Hamlet, a florist who played over a nine-hole course in Wrexham. Hamlet played bravely but collapsed towards the end, allowing Jones to win on the final green.

It was to be, effectively, a final bright spot for the mighty Americans.

By the end of the second day they were despondent. It was described as one of the blackest days in the history of American golf. None could have foreseen such a slump on the part of so many great golfers on the same day. All the best players were well beaten in the first few rounds. Francis Ouimet was outplayed, Bobby Jones was outplayed. Chick Evans was outplayed, Guilford was outplayed. They were all outplayed. It was a complete demolition of their stars.

Tolley, the main British hope, playing better than any other Briton in the field and, putting superbly, despatched Guilford. Allan Graham, a red-haired giant who had played for Oxford, and a Hoylake man, was Jones's opponent in the fourth round. Graham defeated Jones, six and five. Out in 37, Graham was four up at the turn. Graham then went on to beat HSB Tubbs, to give Hoylake a representative in the final. Only two Americans, Paul Hunter and Fred Wright, were left in the last 10 as the American challenge collapsed dramatically. Hunter was beaten by Darwin, Wright surviving to the last eight.

Johnny Ball, now in his 60th year, having beaten JH Douglas of the American contingent at the 19th in the morning, survived until the fifth round, when he was beaten by Wright. Wright, though, was not destined to reach the final. He was beaten by Darwin who was three up at the 9th even though he completely missed his tee shot on the 10th.

After his role in the match, Darwin recalled how, in Hoylake main street, Market Street, a very fat gentleman held his hand out to him and in a solemn voice said: "Sir, I should like to thank you for the way in which you have saved your country."

In the semi-final Darwin met the Englishman, WI Hunter, the son of Harry Hunter, the Deal professional. Hunter was a post office clerk in Deal and took his yearly holiday to play in the Amateur. He later went to America, turned professional and was very successful. He was too strong for Darwin and the giant killer was himself slain, three and two.

Graham then had to battle it out with Hunter. But Graham was not at his best. On the eve of the final his father had died, but he insisted on playing, which must have had some effect on the result. Hunter played brilliant golf and Graham was outclassed, losing 12 and 11.

Darwin had fond memories of the course and the Club at that time. His recollection was of "a great golf course and one where no warmer welcome awaits". He recalled "how lovely it was when practising by oneself near the sand hills when the summer dusk came on and the lights were beginning to twinkle in the surrounding houses". He reminisced about Jack Morris in the clubhouse, smoking a cigar or reading a newspaper in a chair by the starter's box and of Harold Hilton playing spoon shots in the field and Johnny Ball walking across from the Royal Hotel, chipping a ball with an iron on his way.

In 1921 the Club Secretary was Janion. Always dressed in a black and white check suit, Janion, or Jane to his friends, had been Secretary during the war and a man of great organisational ability who had served on the Championship committee for years.

Darwin said Janion was "a standing illustration of the proverb that a man may steal a horse and another may not look over the hedge. Jane could, metaphorically, steal a whole stable-full."

In 1922, Major Forbes-Bell took over from Janion as Secretary and another milestone in the history of the Club was reached. Ladies were, for the first time, permitted into the clubhouse. After long and often contentious discussion, council decided that members were allowed to bring ladies into the Club, on one night only during the week for dinner, between 15 October and 31 March, and only after 7 pm. The move was not as accommodating to the ladies as it may have seemed. It was expected to lead to a financial gain to the Club.

"There are higher, nobler things than love. A woman is only a woman, but a hefty drive is a slosh." PG Wodehouse in 'A woman is only a woman'.

Ladies' acceptance moved a step further when, in August of 1922, a ladies' room was created at a cost of £300. But lady golfers still had to remember their place. A request that the 1922 Ladies' Cheshire Championship be played over the course was rejected.

ROYAL LIVERPOOL GOLF CLUB
FAR
SURE
AND
POST
Last Collection Time
Monday to Friday
5.30pm
Saturday
12 noon

The Open, June 1930: Cyril Tolley signs autographs for a young Kathleen Algeo

Mrs Pip Critten wrote to say that Kathleen Algeo, and the other girls pictured above, sold programmes during the 1930 Open. She reminisced, "I still remember, all those years ago. The excitement of being a very small part of a great Championship, won by a wonderful golfer, the one and only Bobby Jones!"

These ladies together with Mary Lloyd and last years Captain, Johnny Turner's mother-in-law, Mrs Townley, are still alive and going well at over 90 years of age. Obviously Bobby Jones made a huge impression with a greater audience than just golfers.

But, although the Club moved forward in admitting ladies, no matter how slight the privilege other long-maintained rules were still enforced, including the ban on playing cards in the card room on Sundays.

In 1923 the old Hoylake course became a memory of past glories.

At the instigation of JP Brocklebank, the Captain that year, the well-known golf architect, Harry Colt, was appointed to improve the links, recommend on drainage and layout, and redesign the course accordingly.

But change would not go without protest. Many members felt that 'Old Hoylake' was being desecrated and natural features were being removed to be replaced by examples of modern course architecture.

The great Hoylake course was now one of the sternest tests in the world and began to resemble the course as it is today. It was recognised by many commentators as the most interesting and difficult course in the world, with the advantage of having the most immaculate greens. In 1924 it was the perfect choice for The Open.

The old clubroom at the Royal Hotel on Stanley Road was used as accommodation for the professionals, who were not allowed to use the clubhouse.

On 26-27 June, the days of The Open, the weather was typical of Hoylake. It was hot but the winds from the sea, constantly changing direction, kept the course pleasantly cool. Among the entrants was 'Sir Walter Hagen' who, the previous year, had been runner-up to Arthur Havers at Troon, having won the Championship the year before. He was a man who, like Arnold Palmer of a later generation, was to help precipitate the interest in the growth of the game worldwide. Another entrant that year was the equally flamboyant 'Squire' Gene Sarazen.

Hagen was, perhaps, a great player at the wrong time. His career would possibly have been greater had it not overlapped with and been eclipsed by that of Bobby Jones.

But he undoubtedly gave professional golf a status it had not previously had, by stamping his personality on it in many ways. He was an extrovert showman, delighting in playing poker and drinking until the early hours. He was the first golfer to discard the tweed jacket of previous generations for the casual sweater, which soon became the norm: "I don't want to be a millionaire, I just want to live like one," he said.

Hagen was fortunate to be allowed to compete. His train had arrived 10 minutes late for his tee-off time in the qualifying round at Formby. After some discussion, and argument, The Open Committee allowed him to play. It was a remarkable decision as, at the same time, it refused the plea of another latecomer, Jim Barnes, who had travelled to Formby on the same train as Hagen.

Even then Hagen looked unlikely to qualify, starting his rounds at Formby with a five and seven, his second at the 2nd hitting a spectator which stopped his score being even higher. But, with a brilliant 73 for his second round, he qualified by three strokes.

In The Open itself Hagen was delighted when Johnny Ball, who was playing in his last Open, invited Hagen to play with him. Ball was then 63 and had played his first Open in 1876, some 48 years earlier. But he did not survive the first round. Hagen started with a 77, a 73 in the second round putting him three back from the leaders. In the third round he picked these up with a 73 and set out on the final round on level terms and paired with the Englishman, ER Whitcombe. Whitcombe was Britain's main hope and there was great excitement among the British supporters as Hagen started badly with sixes at the 1st and 3rd. Recovering well, he was 41 at the turn. Whitcombe took 43.

More than 3,600 yards of turf, gorse and sand traps remained. The wind had by now reached almost gale-force and, with five holes of more than 400 yards and two over 500, there could be no relaxing of concentration. Hagen had that concentration.

Whitcombe started back four, three, four, three, and was well-placed. Hagen's description of his own approach shots on the back nine was very familiar to all Hoylake members of the day: "The 14th was a full spoon shot, the 15th a driver, the 16th a brassie and the 17th a straight iron. So I had what practically amounted to five par-five holes staring me in the face." At the 14th, measuring 510 yards, he delivered the shot of his round. A good drive was followed by a low-flying brassie shot into the wind, which came to rest within yards of the cup, allowing him to hole out for a four.

The 17th had been reconstructed for the Championship, almost all the players complaining. The green had been moved back, it was severely trapped in front and at the right and behind it was the out-of-bounds fence. Hagen described his play at that hole:

"I studied the shot for a long time, debating whether to play it safe for a five, which would leave me with the alternative of getting a four at the home hole in order to tie, or go

boldly for it. By this time my firmness had come back, bringing with it my confidence. I had cut my drive a bit and my ball lay in the rough, a position that, while it opened the green for me, made my next shot all the more difficult. With the ball laying the way it was, I was determined to use my straight mashie iron, a heavy club with about the same loft as a midiron but a deeper blade. The moment I hit the shot I knew in my bones it was a good one. It covered the pin all the way and judging by the shout that went up at the green I knew I was somewhere close. Just how close I didn't know until I walked up and found that I was three or so yards away. 'If you can get that putt down, Walter, you're in,' I said to myself. But the ball just slipped past the pin. I now wanted a four to win and five to tie."

At the 18th, Hagen needed a par to win the Championship. His description of the finish needs no embellishment: "I was confident I had victory in the palm of my hand, for here was a short par-four hole with the wind at my back. I got a long tee shot, some 300 yards, leaving me with a short seven-iron shot for my second. Again a series of traps crossed the front of the green. However, they didn't seem to be too troublesome considering the shortness of the shot I had to make.

"I played my second shot too boldly and went past the flag to the back edge of the green. Here I was on this fast green ... on the back edge at that ... and I needed to get down

Preceding page: A view from the course as evening settles in over Stanley Road which leads to Red Rocks

Right: James Pegram, Captain, presenting a medal to TA Bourn, the runner-up of the 1933 Amateur Championship, with winner The Hon Michael Scott, behind. On the right Secretary HC Forbes-Bell, and future Secretary Guy Farrar

in two. I putted down, sloping away, and left myself five feet short. Had I hit a tiny bit harder I would have rolled almost to the hole. But a semicircular ridge held my ball and left me with a most delicate putt.

"With such a fast green I knew my stroke must be delicate. I looked over both sides of the hole. There was a slim chance of a slight roll as it went down a little incline towards the hole. I studied it carefully once more. I decided there was a double roll down the first two feet of the putt to the right, a slight roll to the left in the last two feet. I stood and set myself with one thing uppermost in my mind. I must hit the ball delicately. And in a situation like this delicacy is difficult due to the extreme nervous tension one is under. But then I had a second thought, which helped greatly in executing the shot correctly and in not being over-anxious to see where the ball was going. Should I miss, I'd have to stay over another day to beat Whitcombe in the play-off of the British Championship. If I holed I became the British Open Champion.

"While 10,000 people held their breath, I stroked the ball ... gently but firmly; it righted the last turn, straightened and headed for home! I threw my putter into the air and never saw the ball or putter again. But I sure saw that British Open trophy."

He had finished with a winning score of 301.

No one protested as Hagen's wife, wearing her high pointed heels, ran onto the green to embrace him. He was then carried from the green to the clubhouse on the shoulders of the spectators as if he was one of their own. It was the first American success at Hoylake, the first occasion an American or British player had won the Championship in the other country twice and Hagen recollected that it was one of the best experiences of his golfing life.

After he had signed his card, Hagen and his wife were invited into the clubhouse for a champagne reception. It was the first occasion a woman was to cross the threshold of the clubhouse proper.

Also competing at Hoylake that year was Arthur Gladstone Havers who the previous year had beaten Walter Hagen to win the Championship at Troon. Among Havers's friends was the wealthy seed merchant, Samuel Ryder, and, over dinner during the Championship, a conversation between the two resulted in the idea and format of the Ryder Cup, the first-ever match being played the following year at the Worcester Country Club in Massachusetts.

In 1925 the first English Close Championship was played in April. The first Champion was T Froes Ellison, a member of Royal Liverpool and a founder member of the Hittite Golfing Society, which was formed the following year by a group which included Guy Farrar.

Suggestions Book, April 1923

It is suggested that bridge be played in the Club on Sundays.

This was granted.

Suggestions Book, July 1923

That the council consider the question of playing on Sunday.

This was signed by 95 members.

Suggestions Book, April 1934

About 12 months ago an old member of the Club, presented a case containing old golf clubs and balls, etc. For a time this case was on view in the Secretary's room. It has now disappeared. I should be glad to know what has become of it.

(Author of this book, "so would I".)

The new society consisted mainly of the best golfers from The Royal Liverpool and Formby Golf Clubs, among them Dr W Tweddell, who was to become the Amateur Champion in 1927. The aim of the new society was to promote foursomes golf and to play scratch foursomes against other golf clubs and like-minded societies. Membership was by invitation.

In 1927 the only single competition that the society plays was initiated at Hoylake. This was the John Ball Putter Competition, the prize being a putter presented to the society by Ball. It is still in the clubhouse. In 1927 Hoylake again hosted the international, England v Scotland, one of the most exciting to have taken place and ending in a draw.

Of the 17 Hoylake members who entered the 1927 Amateur Championship, the greatest interest was focused on Ball and Hilton, both trying to win their 100th Championship round. Although both failed, for a short while the years were rolled back as Ball, dormie five down, obtained fours at the next two holes and, if his opponent had not holed a long putt at the Dun, the match would have been extended further. But age had caught up with the old warrior. This ended his last game in the Amateur Championship which he had first played in 1885 and won eight times.

Tweddell, little known before the event, progressed serenely to the final where he met Eustace Landale a fellow member of Royal Liverpool who won the 1st, halved the 2nd and then quietly faded away. When dormie nine, Tweddell became so nervous at the thought of becoming Amateur Champion that he took three putts on both the 10th and 11th greens; but at the next he obtained the required half, winning seven and six. In 1928, Tweddell was appointed Captain of Hoylake and, subsequently, Captain of the Royal & Ancient Golf Club and made an honorary life member at Hoylake.

In the same year, Dr Frank Stableford, another RLGC member, invented the Stableford scoring method. This was slow to catch on but, at Wallasey Golf Club, where he was also a member, in 1932 it was given a trial and from the beginning was a complete success. It was, however, to be many years before the R & A gave the method their official sanction.

1930 was one of the most momentous years in golf and the most memorable in the history of The Royal Liverpool Golf Club. Hoylake again hosted The Open, one which will always link Hoylake with America. It was held on 18-20 June, with qualifying rounds at Hoylake and Wallasey on 16 and 17 June.

It was the year of 'Impregnable Quadrilateral' or Grand Slam, when Bobby Jones eclipsed everything that had gone before. It was the year when Jones, who had already won two Open Championships, was to win both Open and Amateur Championships on both sides of the Atlantic.

Like Ball and Hilton before him, he was already a legend in his own lifetime, a member of the USGA Executive Committee and a charismatic character, loved by the galleries not only for his golfing prowess but also for his easy-going manner and sportsmanship. It was a time of big changes in golf equipment and the advent of

1921 Amateur Championship. Picture taken from present 8th green. The green was moved in 1924, one of Harry Colt's changes

steel-shafted clubs, although Bobby Jones resisted this innovation, winning his grand slam with hickory-shafted clubs.

Playing with these clubs, he always appeared to drive the ball well within his power, but, when occasion demanded, was capable of producing shots of remarkable length, his swing repeating like a machine. He appeared to have the ideal temperament, outwardly calmly in control and immensely confident. But his appearance hid the nervous tension he suffered in competition golf. It affected his digestion so much that he scarcely ate anything but buttered toast during a tournament, drinking innumerable cups of tea. He did though celebrate the end of a round with a large Scotch.

Before The Open, Jones had already triumphed in the Amateur at St Andrews. Afterwards he said: "Honestly, I don't care what happens now, I'd rather have won this tournament than anything else in golf. I'm satisfied." Perhaps because of this he approached The Open in a relaxed frame of mind. But when he embarked on the qualifying rounds at Wallasey and Hoylake his competitive spirit took over. Whilst he qualified with something to spare, his play had been only moderate. One golf writer was prompted to say that he "took a turn amongst the ordinary mortals by compiling a round of 77".

Jones complained about his game at the time: "I simply don't know where the darned ball is going when I hit it. I guess I'm trying to steer it and, of course, that's the worst thing in the world to do. But what can I do? This [Hoylake] is a tight course. You can't get up there and slam away and trust to freedom of action to take care of the shot. You simply have to exercise some control of the ball. And it's the most hopeless job I've ever tackled. I never have worked so hard before." He continued to describe the course as a "long-hitters' paradise" but the last five holes as "the most difficult finishing stretch in the world".

Above: The Hon Michael Scott from Westward Ho! (The Royal North Devon Golf Club), winner of the 1933 Amateur Championship

1936 Open Champion, Alfred Padgham

Despite these concerns he played the first three rounds of The Open itself on par.

The thing that impressed Guy Farrar was Jones's putting: "a symphony in rhythmic movement. With his head locked one side, he gently pushes the ball towards the hole. Heavens, you think, he must be short, but the ball rolls on and on and on until it reaches the hole, gives a last lingering look and finally disappears."

When the meeting proper started, the weather was perfect – the course in excellent condition with a thunderstorm on the day before the competition having slowed the fairways.

At the halfway stage Jones had a total of 152 and in the third round finished poorly with a 74. The tall, blonde Archie Compston, a huge man, friend and golfing tutor to the Prince of Wales, returned the course record of 68. It was the first round under 70 recorded in an Open at Hoylake. He gave the British crowd great cause for optimism as he held the lead, with Jones a shot behind.

In the final round Compston fell away with an 82. Having started full of confidence, he missed a 30-inch putt for a par at the 1st hole. If it had gone in it may have settled him down and led to a winning score. However, he went to the 2nd knowing Jones, playing ahead of him, had picked up a birdie three. This was the point, perhaps, at which Jones won the Championship. His towering drive at the 2nd was seriously off-line and rebounded from the head of a steward, carrying some 50 yards onto the adjoining fairway and into a bunker at the right of the 14th. Jones had a clean lie and from the sand he played an astounding shot 140 yards to the green, before holing a 20-foot putt for a birdie three when he was looking at a five. This score was nullified when he took three putts on the next two greens, but he continued on par until he reached the 8th, where disaster called.

After two wooden shots, he was left with a chip to reach the plateau green. He elected to run the shot, which finished halfway up the slope, and then, in an attempt to hole his next, he raced it past and took three putts, dumbfounding the crowd as he returned a seven. Jones was later to remark: "It was the most inexcusable hole I have ever played. An old man with a croquet mallet would have got down in two. I will play that hole a thousand times in my dreams." But Jones, focused and determined, played composed golf to finish in 75.

One stroke may have secured the Championship. At the 16th hole, the Dun, a 532-yard par five, his second shot finished in the left greenside bunker very close to the left-hand wall. The ball could only be struck with a sharply descending blow, with his right foot placed on the bank behind him. Knowing this was a dangerous shot, but needing a four, he used a recently acquired 25-oz niblick sand wedge with a concave face and lifted the ball out of the bunker. It rolled across the green, trickling past the edge of the hole just beyond. Jones claimed this as one of the greatest shots of his life and it was this birdie four which clinched victory. By now Compston had wasted too many shots and was definitely out of it. Jones had played the second nine on par and won by two strokes to clinch the second part of the Grand Slam. His winning score of 291 was the lowest recorded in an Open at Hoylake.

Royal participation: the Prince of Wales, the future Edward VIII, in 1929. He had visited the Scout Jamboree at nearby Arrowe Park. The Prince is playing in his scout uniform, the first time anybody had played Hoylake in shorts

To mark his triumph, Bobby Jones was elected a life member of The Royal Liverpool Golf Club.

"On the golf course, a man may be the dogged victim of inexorable fate, be struck down by an appalling stroke of tragedy, become the hero of an unbelievable melodrama, or the clown in a side-splitting comedy – any of these within a few hours, and all without having to bury a corpse or repair a tangled personality." Robert Tyre Jones

In the year of the Grand Slam, other events within the Club maintained the image and growth of amateur golf. The Captain, JGB Beazley, presented a cup for annual competition for members under the age of 25. JB Bond was the first winner, JD Rennison the runner-up.

In 1932, Bruce Thompson, a member of The Royal Liverpool Golf Club, won the Belgium Amateur Championship. The Amateur final of that year was between Dale Bourn and the Hon Michael Scott. In the semi-final was the famous 'macintosh incident', where Cyril Tolley played a shot out of a spectator's macintosh. Scott, driving and putting well, at 53 became the oldest winner.

In 1933, John Graham (Jnr) at the age of 16 recorded a score of 77 to win the Boys' Medal. He was the first boy to record a score under 80.

1936 Open. Henry Cotton and wife, Tootsie, centre, with Guy Farrar on left, holding stick

Also in 1933, the first official Colts' match was played at the West Lancashire Golf Club, The Royal Liverpool team winning seven matches to one. The following year, apart from The Royal Liverpool, seven local clubs took part in the competition, Formby, Fulwood Park, Leasowe, Wallasey, West Derby, West Lancashire and Woolton. Four of the original Royal Liverpool team would go on to serve as Captains of the Club.

In 1936 The Open was again played at Hoylake. The course had been extended to 7,078 yards. In those days it was the host club that set out the course for the event, unlike the present day when the R & A takes control.

The object of these changes, according to Club Secretary, Major HC Forbes-Bell, is as apt today as it was then: "Our object all along has been to produce the best golfer of the year – that is all. We are not in the least concerned with what score he will do it. First-class golf should be a matter of accuracy as well as length. Under modern conditions, unless you stretch your course length is bound to predominate. These men hit the ball so far that the original bunkers no longer come in to play and they can get the greens with their second shots wherever their drives finish. They can play one bad shot and still get their four and that is what we have tried to stop. We want them to play four good shots out of four. We regard ourselves as being on trial to produce the best golfer in the world. We are not the least concerned what the score shall be."

The first round left Alfred Padgham, Henry Cotton and Gene Sarazen level at 73. At the end of the next round Padgham was one stroke behind the leaders, Cotton among them. On arriving at the Club for the final round, Padgham found the professionals' shop was locked and a window had to be broken for him to get his clubs, after which he went round in 71 to beat Jimmy Adams into second place. Padgham had bettered Jones's 1930 winning total by four shots, with 287. *The Times* reported that he

Henry Cotton in full swing

had won it over the greatest, longest and sternest course that had ever been set.

Adams, a man with an easy, lazy swing, who was an inspired putter, soon after became the professional at Hoylake. Another entrant that year was the slight figure of AD Bobby Locke, who, on a business trip to London, took the opportunity to play. Still only 19 years old, he won the Amateur Medal, finishing only seven behind Padgham.

After the Championship, in reply to the adverse comments concerning the length and difficulty of the course, the response of Henry Longhurst, the golf journalist, is worth repeating:

"The people who were responsible for the new course were assailed with much criticism, written and spoken, long before the Championship began. The course, it was said, was too long, the players would never get round it, golf was becoming a matter of endurance and so forth. To all of which the reply was 'wait and see'. We waited, we saw and we were conquered. Hoylake, as it played during the Championship week, turned out to be the finest test of golf in the world. So many persons whose opinions are entitled to respect were agreed on the point that such a statement ceases to be dogmatic. Gene Sarazen, who has travelled all over the world in pursuit of golf, remarked time and time again, 'it is the greatest course I have ever seen'."

In 1939, the Amateur Championship was the last of any kind to be played before the onset of World War II. Jimmy Bruen, an Irishman, was a strong favourite to win and on the way to the quarter-final had beaten Hoylake's John Graham (Jnr). His next opponent was the Scot, Alex Kyle. Kyle was one up on the 18th but put his approach shot in the cross bunker at the front of the green. Bruen was on in two and a play-off seemed likely. Kyle, however, laid his bunker shot dead and the match was over, Kyle going on to beat Tony Dunne of Wales at the 35th hole to win the final.

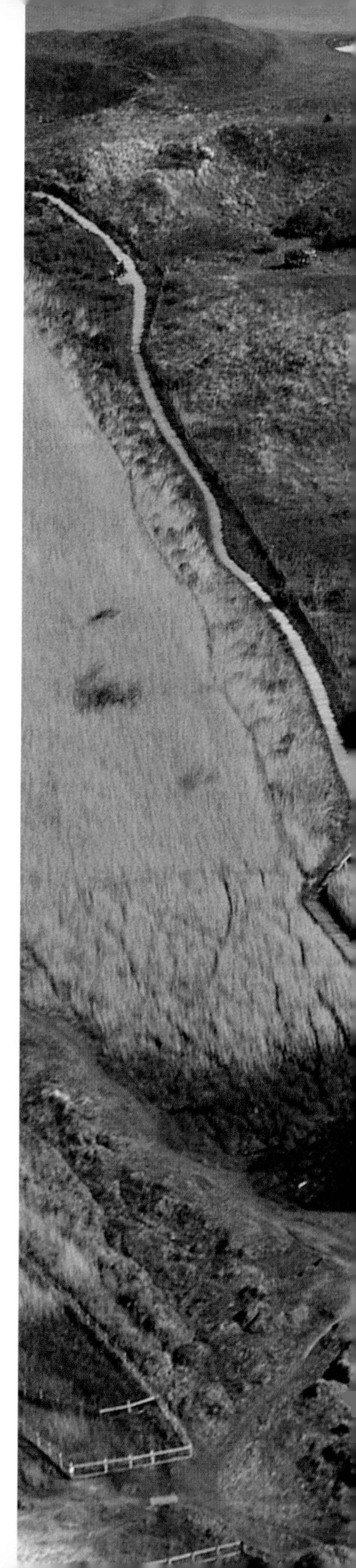

Chapter Nine

9th hole

Bobby Jones: Essay to a Champion

Everybody knows that Bobby Jones achieved immortality by winning golf's Grand Slam in 1930 – the supposed 'Impregnable Quadrilateral' of US and British Opens and US and British Amateur Championships.

Everybody knows the 1930 British Open was at Hoylake, when despite being beneath his best, Jones held off first Archie Compston then Leo Diegel and Macdonald Smith to win by two shots.

But behind the legend lies a thread of complexities that made up the character and achievements of perhaps golf's greatest ever exponent. And one of those threads leads to the conclusion that Hoylake made Jones the golfer he became.

Pick up another and you learn that Hoylake also shaped the other triumph of Robert Tyre Jones's life – the creation of the Augusta National Course.

Jones, already a consummate golfer, played his first golf overseas at Royal Liverpool in 1921 as one of a group of Americans in a vanguard that later became the Walker Cup. Hoylake proved a new and a chastening experience, as did the Old Course. "I shall never forget how I cursed Hoylake and St Andrews," said Jones years later.

"At the time I regarded as an unpardonable crime, failure to keep the greens sodden, and considered a blind hole an outrage. I wanted everything just right to pitch my iron shots to the hole. It was the only game I knew, so I blamed the course because I could not play it."

His confidante and biographer OB Keeler agreed: "Old Hoylake taught him in 1921 that he really knew very little about playing golf in a wind; or getting the ball on greens baked hard and glassy; or putting on such greens when he did get there."

This first foray into British seaside golf had left him with what Bernard Darwin called a "puzzled hatred for the links", an emotion that was to turn into fascination and later adoration as he determined to teach himself how to play links golf.

In 1930, wins at Hoylake and at St Andrews gave him half of his quadruple and the satisfaction of knowing he had succeeded.

1930

After Bobby Jones's seven on the 8th hole he played the final holes to perfection until approaching the 16th green.
His ball gently rolled into the back of the bunker. At this moment he decided to try his new-fangled sand-wedge, a club he had just acquired, but had hardly swung in anger. If he could chip up the ball almost vertically it may just make the green and roll in the direction of the pin. He played the shot to perfection and finished within two inches.

The Grand Slam was always in Jones's sights. He had told Keeler that he intended to try to pull it off and set a record that could never be bettered. He was not a man who would founder on lack of mental strength. The great golfer Francis Ouimet said that playing Jones was like being caught in a buzz saw.

The first leg of the Slam was at the Old Course and Jones escaped some close calls in the early rounds before defeating Roger Wethered seven and six in a 36-hole final.

He then spent some time with his wife in Paris before returning to Britain and to Hoylake for The Open. After rounds of 70 and 72 Jones had the lead by one shot. But Archie Compson fired a 68 to take a one-shot advantage into the final round. The Jones' buzz saw, though, was not to be denied. He won by two, becoming the first man to pull off the British double in 40 years. He was halfway to his goal.

Preceding page: Robert Tyre Jones, from an original painting by John AA Berrie

Right: 1930. The Captain, Jeffrey Beazley, presenting Bobby Jones with The Open trophy. This was regarded by his grandson David as the height of the Beazley family's sporting traditions

Next was the Interlachen Country Club in Minnesota for the US Open. Jones managed to stay in touch with the pacesetters for the first two rounds then spread the field with a scintillating 68. Even a closing 75 was not enough to deny him the third leg of his quest.

And so to Merion Cricket Club, just outside Philadelphia. Jones, as befits a true sporting giant, saved his finest form for when he needed it most. He won the qualifying medal with rounds of 69 and 73. He was not challenged in the early rounds and won his quarter-final six and five. In the semis, Jess Sweetser was blitzed nine and eight, setting up a final against Eugene Homans.

It was no contest, Jones ran out an eight and seven winner. The 'Impregnable Quadrilateral' had been breached. The Grand Slam was complete.

Two months afterwards, Jones, a nation's hero, wrote to the US Golf Association announcing his retirement. On the course at least, there remained nothing left to accomplish.

Bobby Jones though, needed a challenge. And again, Hoylake helped to shape his destiny. He had become an avid student of golf design and felt that American courses were generally penal in nature, for they did not allow for options. There was one safe choice and the ball must be placed there.

The result was an unthinking player who had the ability to play only one way. The British seaside links required strategy, the fairways were wide and the greens were firm and naturally undulating. As Jones himself put it, a seaside course like Hoylake could "not be played without thinking. There is always some little favour of wind or terrain waiting for the man who has judgment enough to use it and there is a little feeling of triumph, a thrill that comes with the knowledge of having done a thing well, when a puzzling hole has been conquered by something more than a mechanical skill."

Bobby Jones Takes The Hoylake Gallery.

Snaps at Hoylake to-day showing Bobby Jones on the twelfth green, and inset, on the right, driving from the eleventh tee. His partner Mr. Norman Newton, is on the left of the inset.

Top: A rare postcard of Bobby Jones in action at Hoylake circa 1930

Below: Bobby Jones and Francis Ouimet practise before the 1921 Amateur Championship and the first international match between Great Britain & Ireland versus the USA, the precursor to the Walker Cup

Overleaf: Snow on the Hoylake links, March 2006

Royal Liverpool Golf Club,

HOYLAKE,

Wirral,

Cheshire. L47 4AL.

8th January 1969.

Robert T. Jones Jr., Esq.,
6th Floor,
Haas-Howell Building,
Atlanta, Georgia 30303.

My dear Mr. Jones,

As you may know, 1969 is the Centenary Year of the Royal Liverpool Golf Club. I am writing you a personal letter at the request of my Council and Members, to ask you to accept from us a small token of our regard. This letter I feel very honoured to write. The token is inscribed : "With affectionate esteem" and I can assure you that this is most sincerely felt by all of us here, and indeed I am sure it expresses the feelings not only of the members of this Club, but in fact of all British golfers.

Your portrait hangs on the top of the stairway in the Clubhouse, just outside the Club Room and gives great pleasure to us all and, I know, will give great pleasure to the many visitors we are expecting to receive during our Centenary Year.

With my kindest regards and best wishes.

Yours sincerely,

John La...

Captain.
(J.C. Lawrie

ROBERT TYRE JONES, JR.
75 POPLAR STREET, N. W.
ATLANTA, GEORGIA
30303

January 29, 1969

John Lawrie, Esq., Captain
The Royal Liverpool Golf Club
Hoylake, Wirral, Cheshire
England

Dear Mr. Lawrie:

I am deeply touched by your letter of January 20th. I have a great affection for Hoylake, the Royal Liverpool Golf Club, and its members. That they should choose to honor me is pleasing indeed.

You may be interested to know that it was at Hoylake that I first played in England, and there that I last appeared in a British championship. Naturally, all these things are happy memories.

With warmest regards to all,

Most sincerely,

Bob Jones

...rt T. Jones, Jr.

ROBERT TYRE JONES, JR.
75 POPLAR STREET, N. W.
ATLANTA, GEORGIA
30303

March 24, 1969

John Lawrie, Esq., Captain
The Royal Liverpool Golf Club
Hoylake, Wirral, Cheshire
England

Dear Mr. Lawrie:

The lovely silver ash tray arrived over the weekend, and was a most welcome greeting when I arrived at my office this morning. Please accept my sincere thanks and express my gratitude and appreciation to your Council and Members. I shall treasure it as an evidence of many happy memories. I am most pleased by the inscription, which I assure you is warmly reciprocated.

I have no doubt that the Centenary Year of the Royal Liverpool Golf Club will be memorable. Certainly, my good wishes will be with you throughout.

With kindest personal regards,

Most sincerely,

Bob Jones

Robert T. Jones, Jr.

RTJ:jsm

The Club, through the good offices of John Lawrie, invited Bobby Jones to the Centenary Dinner in 1969. Jones was unable to attend so the Club sent him a silver ashtray

Jones had discovered a new goal: to produce a course that would attempt to recreate the thinking dimension of the great British links courses. "The main idea was to bring to inland Georgia the closest possible approximation to British seaside golf," he explained. "It was intended to be an expression of my ideals in golf course design."

The Jones' ideals were:

1. Give pleasure to the greatest possible number of players
2. Require strategic thought as well as skill
3. It must give the average player a chance, while requiring the utmost of the expert
4. All natural features must be preserved.

The result? The Augusta National, and the Masters tournament held annually since 1937. It was Jones's lasting and monumental legacy to the game he played so wonderfully.

Robert Tyre Jones died of syringomyelia, a rare and degenerative disease of the nervous system, in 1971. He was 69 years old.

There was something of Johnny Ball about his stoicism as the disease crippled and pained him more by the year. "Just remember son, you always play the ball where it lies," he would say when people sympathised with him about his illness.

And like Ball, the occasional, witheringly brilliant shaft of humour. Informed at a tournament that it was "100 degrees in the shade" he replied: "It's a good job we don't have to play in the shade!"

Shades of Ball too, when asked why membership of the Augusta National was kept so small and select. "I like the human race as a tribe," he explained, "but only in small doses."

Hoylake shaped the legend that is Bobby Jones, and Jones shaped the institution that is Hoylake. With Ball, with Hilton, he sits at the Club's highest table.

ROYAL LIVERPOOL GOLF CLUB.

OPEN CHAMPIONSHIP, 1930.

Player R. T. Jones

Friday, June 20. Fourth Round.

Holes		Total	Holes		Total
1	////	4	10	////	4
2	///	3	11	////	4
3	/////	5	12	////	4
4	////	4	13	////	4
5	////	4	14	////	4
6	////	4	15	/////	5
7	///	3	16	////	4
8	///////	7	17	////	4
9	////	4	18	////	4

Total Out 38 Total Home 37

Player's Initials: R. T. J. Jr. Total Out 38

TOTAL ROUND 75

Marker [illegible]

Above: Bobby Jones's last score card in The Open, 1930

Overleaf: 2006 Treasurer Nigel Lanceley attacks the 4th green

When Bobby Met Johnny by Harold Hilton

I suppose you could call it flattery but why Mr Jones even suggested that my well-forgotten book published in '07 was other than an irrelevance I will never know.

"Yes," explained the great American golfer, "I have read your book many times but why do you not mention in more detail your strong rivalry with Mr Ball?"

"Why? 'Cause there was not any strong rivalry," I proclaimed.

"No strong rivalry! You cannot be serious, (these Americans!). I thought you would almost have been at blows every now and then?" These Americans are certainly different, though I must make it clear I really do love their attitude to golf and life in general. A bit frightening, but refreshing.

I tried to talk to him about his own game. Just a few hours earlier the man had won The Open at my home green of Hoylake, but much like Johnny he didn't care a jot for chat about personal triumphs.

Instead he marched around the Hoylake clubhouse like a child in a toyshop.

"You must have had a hell of a time playing against those Scottish gentlemen? And in those clothes," he said, pointing to a portrait of the two of us on the staircase at the Club.

I pointed out that I was wearing the same clothes today. He looked a little embarrassed. Well, if not embarrassed, certainly aware that he may have offended me. I assured him that was the way it was then. I might look a little gauche in 1930 but I cut a dash in those days.

For such a great champion, Mr Jones had a bewildering fascination with the achievements of others. Johnny's deeds, in particular, caused him to fire question upon question in my direction.

I ventured: "You should ask Johnny himself. I'm surprised you haven't done so before now." It was then that he took me by surprise.

"But we have never met."

"Never met?" I exclaimed, "I am astonished, I thought you must have."

"No," said Mr Jones, running a bear-like hand through his mop of thick, pale brown hair in a gesture of some frustration. "Every time I make an effort to meet him he sort of, well, disappears."

I chuckled. I was amused but hardly surprised.

"Oh that's Johnny certainly, but please do not think he is being rude, far from it, he's just, well, rather reluctant to push himself. Bit shy, old Johnny."

By now the great American golfer was in a state of some excitement. He was all but oblivious to the well-wishers in the Hoylake clubhouse. Only one thing seemed to matter to him and it wasn't his deeds on the links just a short while earlier.

"But I would love to meet Johnny. Do you think there is a chance? I am leaving for Liverpool this evening for some meetings."

"How much time do you have?" I asked. "Not a great deal," he said sadly. "I'm not sailing until later in the week but I do have a few engagements before I return home."

I called the steward and asked if Mr Ball was still in the clubhouse and was informed he was with Jack Youds, the Club professional, in his shop.

"Can I see him? Can I see him?" He was now hopping on the spot.

"I will ask for him to come up," I said, but he was having none of it. "No, not at all, I will go and see him."

"If you wish. I'll show you the way."

So off we went down the main staircase. There were many members still around. All they wanted was a glimpse of this extraordinary golfer. Shouts of "well done" erupted and grown men were cheering like children. How odd, I thought. Many of them were usually such miserable sorts. It was the first time I had ever seen some of them smile. I advanced through the swivel doors round the back of the Club and up the stairs to Youds' shop.

Opposite: Jenny Legg and Mavis Barlow in action at the 11th – known as the Alps – overlooking Hilbre island and the Dee estuary

There, among the shadows of the rusting brassies and half-repaired mashies sat Johnny. It was Jack's shop though and thus he was accorded first greeting. "Hello Jack. My putter ready yet?"

"Mr Hilton!" said the pro, leaping up and thrusting his hand out to shake mine. "I've got it through the back. Just needs a leather patch gluing to the grip. I'll get it now."

"No, no, no Jack," I laughed. That's not really why I'm here. It wasn't you I'm looking for actually. I've come to see Johnny."

"What do you want now Harold," Johnny said in his usual off-hand manner. I have never taken exception to his manner. We had known each other for over 50 years and it has always been his way of coping with what he refers to as my "over-energetic attitude to life".

"I have someone who wants to meet you," I said, cocking my head towards the door, where the new Open Champion stood outside.

"Oh have you? And what if I do not wish to meet him?" Johnny, in his late-60s and somehow smaller than in his great days, still bristled with a mock indignation that would always make those who knew him laugh, and those who didn't wary.

"You will, Johnny. You will."

A splash of colour as spring appears: Alan Booth, 1971 Captain, planted daffodils all over the links

"Mr Jones?" I shouted, and turned round and saw him still stood at the top of the stairs. "Do come in. Mr Ball is here." He gently advanced over the threshold, dipping his tall frame through the door. Johnny shot to his feet. There was a silence I was not expecting, something Johnny would put down to my lack of sensitivity at eschewing some form of advance notice.

They stared at each other. I looked from one to the other and decided an introduction was unnecessary.

Eventually the American held out his hand: "My name is Bobby Jones and I am delighted to meet you Mr Ball, I have heard and read so much about you and am only sorry it has taken so long to make your acquaintance. Let me say what a real honour this is for me."

Johnny liked praise about as much as he liked losing at golf. He was most ill at ease and I realised that I should not have barged in. "I can assure you it is more than an honour to meet you Mr Jones," he said stiffly.

"Please call me Bobby." "Well then, please call me Johnny."

"Do you mind if I do?" Mr Jones seemed somewhat in awe.

"Everyone else does, it's the modern thing don't you know!" They both laughed. Good old Johnny. If the steely core of yore remained, then so did the perfectly chosen and witty remark. It broke the tension nicely.

"Bobby was telling me you have never met, I can't believe that?" I said to get the conversation flowing.

"I have seen you many times, though, Mr Jones. First in '21 when you first played over here."

"Oh? I guess that's maybe the reason you did not wish to meet me?" said Jones, wrinkling up his face into a mask of discomfort.

"What do you mean?" asked Johnny. "Well, I realise that my behaviour was not what it should have been, but I was a young man and I can assure you I have learnt from my errors."

I nodded inwardly. Back in '21 Jones was a lovely player no doubt. But the windswept Hoylake links was new meat to him, and at times he looked like a 10 handicapper with a hangover. He played badly and his irritation was a little too close to the surface at times.

"Please don't give it a thought," said Johnny hurriedly. "It was no more than youthful exuberance."

"You never said that about me, Johnny," I exclaimed in recollection of the dressings down I'd received from Johnny when my own passions got the better of me.

"To get back to you, Mr Jones," said Johnny, silencing me with a glare. Your odd misdemeanour did not bother me as I was so intrigued with the way you played the game, I had never seen anything like it.

"But hold on, you guys could play," said Jones with that last-word emphasis American insist on using to stress a point.

Johnny though was having none of it.

"Nothing like the game you play, Mr Jones. You play a game with which we are not familiar."

At this Bobby looked embarrassed and insisted Johnny and I did not have the equipment they have these days.

"The courses were not as well maintained," he went on. "You didn't even have rakes in traps and those jackets you played in ... well, I think you are being most harsh on yourselves."

He made some points I suppose but I was with Johnny on this one.

"Johnny's right, Bobby. The game has changed more in the last 20 years than at any other time in its history. You are playing at a wholly different level."

Just then, Jack joined in. In the reverent way of pros he was not about to offer an unsolicited opinion. What he did have to offer was just as welcome.

"Excuse me butting in," he said, "but if you three cannot agree about anything else perhaps you'd agree to join me in a dram?"

"I beg your pardon," inquired Bobby.

"Whisky. Can I help you to one?"

Bobby smiled. "As this is a special occasion, yes please."

"Not every day you win The Open," agreed Johnny.

"Not that," Bobby shook his head. "For me, meeting you is the occasion."

Jack retired to his back room and emerged with whisky in four glasses. Soda was dispensed and the atmosphere became warmer.

We talked of nothing but the game and were amazed when Bobby told us that this was the last time he would be playing golf in Britain.

"Why?" all three of us exclaimed. "Don't you like this country?"

He was almost apologetic and informed us that he loved Britain dearly but the pressure of these big tournaments was having an effect on his health.

"I hope I do not sound pathetic," he said, "but I can hardly eat during a major competition."

We were astonished at this revelation.

"But will you play when you return home?" I asked.

"Just two more tournaments and that will be that. I am a lawyer in Atlanta, my home city, and it really is time to do what my father terms some 'head-down, real work'."

I felt a little awkward at this point.

My father had the same hopes for me and, though he died 30 years ago, I have yet to meet his expectations as far as careers go.

"What tournaments will you play if there are to be only two more?" asked Johnny.

"It has been my ambition for some time to win the United States Open and Amateur in the same year as I won their British equivalents. Now that I have managed the first two it appears appropriate that I should really go for the Grand Slam."

"Grand Slam! What on earth is that?" I asked.

"All four major titles in the same year."

For a few seconds, nobody spoke.

"That is an almost-impossible task," said Johnny.

Bobby looked squarely at him and after a slight pause said: "You did the Slam in 1890."

"How did you know that?" Johnny was genuinely mystified. "And anyway, that hardly counts because it was only two tournaments," said Johnny, brushing away the plaudit.

Jones wasn't finished: "And Harold. In 1911 you won both the British Amateur and the US Amateur at Apawamis."

He was kind. But we were never about to let our deeds stand comparison with his great quest. We insisted that two events in a year would never measure up should he reach this extraordinary goal of four.

"Whatever the reckoning, Harold, you cannot deny that you had a major influence on golf in America," said Jones, Jack's rough spirit clearly working on his inhibitions.

"Me? Come off it," I squirmed.

Proceeding the 1930 Open Championship the Club held a dinner in the clubroom and invited many of the top amateur players. These included Bobby Jones who was seated next to the Captain of the previous year Kenneth Stoker, a man of substance and a fine golfer himself.

Jones was so taken by the red coat that Stokers was wearing that he made numerous enquiries. Why do you have a red coat? To be informed that in the early days golfers played in red coats to identify them amongst the general public who were allowed to walk the links as it was still common ground. Today Jones was informed that the Captains wore the coat on official occasions.

And why do you have a green collar?
And why brass buttons?
Jones was intrigued by the coat.

Kenneth Stoker, realising the great man's interest, said that if he won The British Open this week he would present him with the coat. History tells us that Jones did win and Stoker presented his coat. Stoker, who only died in 1982, always said that was the reason Bobby Jones presented a jacket to the winner of his own championship, The Masters.

Kenneth Stoker's coat is on display at the Atlanta Athletic Club.

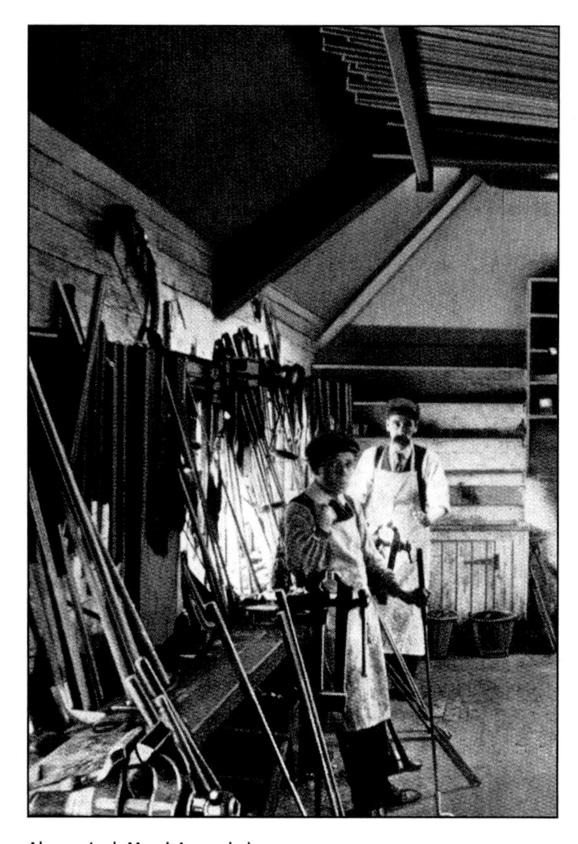

Above: Jack Morris's workshop

Overleaf: The famous Red Arrows demonstrate their flying skills over the links, August 2005

"No. It's true. You made those New York guys stop talking for once and made them realise that we were a long way behind in the world of golf."

Johnny seemed lost in thought. Then, as if a great thought had struck this quiet man of Hoylake, he sat bolt upright and announced: "I believe you will win it. The whatdoyoucallit, the Grand Slam." You have the game for it and, more importantly, you have the desire."

"Kind of you," said Jones.

"But see, it's not the actual playing that concerns me, it's the days before that worry me. The sleepless nights, the churning in my stomach. Last week at St Andrews I was in a terrible mess and this week at Hoylake even worse."

"That," said Johnny sagely "is why you will do it. That's the desire."

"What will you do if you don't win?" I asked.

"Harold," barked Johnny, "you really do come out with some brainless remarks. Of course he'll win. I've told him so, haven't I?"

"Another dram," said Jack, and we thrust our hands in the direction of his bottle.

By now, The Open Champion was lost in a fug of whisky and nostalgia.

'It is just marvellous to meet you guys. Hey, you guys go back to the beginning of the game."

"Well, not quite." This time Jack couldn't stay quiet. "My predecessor here was Jack Morris," he said. "Now his cousin, Young Tom, he was a player."

"Mr Youds, I can assure you I know all about Young Tom. I visit his grave every time I'm at St Andrews. What a man he must have been."

The story swapping began again.

How Young Jack won the first professional tournament in England on these very links. How he died tragically at the age of 25.

A rattle at the door interrupted the badinage. A large man with a cap appeared and announced himself as Bobby's chauffeur, and that Mr Jones was due in Liverpool within the hour.

"I do apologise," he said to us, and asked the driver if he could put the appointment off. The driver looked uneasy. "It's the United States Ambassador, Mr Jones."

"You be on your way Mr Jones," demanded Johnny and, reluctantly, the champion golfer stood up and inched towards the door.

We all arose too and shook his hand.

"I do not know when I will be here again," he said, "but I would love to play a few holes and continue our conversation. Hey, you guys! Why not come over to Atlanta and we'll give you a party? We're good at parties in Atlanta."

Johnny laughed. "Bobby, we are old men now, so thank you, but we would be more than honoured if you visited us – and the invitation is open to you at any time. You can stay at my hotel over the way.

"The old clubhouse?"

"Do you know everything about Hoylake?" I queried, again amazed at his knowledge.

"More than you will ever know."

Just then the American stopped. "Johnny," he said, "I thank you, sincerely, for saying you think I'll do the Slam. And I take your point on desire. But however much I want it, I think Merion in the US Amateur will be a step too far. Such a lot of matchplay you see – I mean, physically, I'm so tired these days. One day at least I'll struggle and fatigue will get the best of me."

Johnny nodded and thought. Then he said: "You can do it. The thing with matchplay when one is tired is to start well. Get the other chap on the back foot from the first hole. Hammer out a big lead when you are fresh and you will destroy their spirit. They'll find no way back. Never take your foot from their throat."

With that Bobby Jones said his goodbyes. He was especially sad to say farewell to Johnny but it didn't bother me. I have always been in Johnny's shadow and I've grown used to it.

We've talked of Bobby Jones many times since. Johnny always ended with the remark: "a lovely man, a gentleman". For a man of few words it was the ultimate compliment.

And the Grand Slam? Bobby did it. He won at Merion and was never behind in a single match. Even in the final he walloped Gene Homans eight and seven. I read a report in the *Liverpool Daily Post*. They say he never took his foot off Homan's throat.

Chapter Eleven

11th hole

The Powers That Be ...

Thomas Owen Potter

The first great Secretary of Hoylake was Thomas Owen Potter (Tosper). A county cricketer who, after finishing with his flannels, devoted his life to golf and, in particular, The Royal Liverpool Golf Club.

His greatest accomplishment must be that by force of personality he instigated the first Amateur Championship in 1885. There was opposition but there always is from those strange and negative sections of golf; these he calmly overcame. What a great monument that is to "a man who commanded affection from many and respect from all".

He made his home at the Royal Hotel and played regularly with John Ball Snr, the proprietor of the hotel. On many occasions a hamper was arranged and sent to the furthest part of the course. On their arrival they tucked in and "started for home like giants refreshed".

Tosper was a great character and led the members in singsongs after the dinners. The wand he used for these extravaganzas is now 'the Captain's wand of office' that can be seen in the display cabinets today, a fine ivory baton.

Tosper is also responsible for the comprehensive books of newspaper and magazine cuttings that are in the Club today. They date from 1869 to 1909, the year of his death.

When he stepped down as Honorary Secretary in 1894, the year before the clubhouse moved across the course, there had been a number of disputes between the Club and John Ball Snr over rents, rights for

Above: Harold Janion, the Secretary, at leisure. Fine golf shoes, even finer suit!

Preceding page, 194: The Captain's wand of office, presented by Thomas Owen Potter

Preceding page, 195: Thomas Owen Potter conducting the members in a singsong. Pendulum Brown plays the piano

farming and rights for shooting rabbits. So, when the move was made Tosper, as he was still living at the hotel, decided to resign.

Harold Janion

The workload for a person in an honorary position had become impossible for any other man and the first paid Secretary was W Ryder Richardson, but he soon moved on and, in 1900, the second great Secretary, Harold Janion, took control and presided over the Club until his death in 1922.

He was a man of action. His remarks, if repeated, would sound rude but few took offence. It is difficult to understand how he could be called 'Jane'! Today this would be taken in an offensive way, perhaps those late Victorian men were less sensitive than today's man? Or just very thick skinned.

He did, however, make enemies, which was inevitable, "but to his hosts of friends he was always 'Jane', the beloved Secretary of The Royal Liverpool Golf Club". Bernard Darwin wrote of him, "He was a standing illustration of the proverb 'that one man may steal a horse and another may not look over the fence'. Jane could, metaphorically, steal a whole stableful." Regrettably, I do not have a clue what that means.

He was responsible for staging the first International match. It was between England and Scotland in April 1902. Having grown irritated with trying to persuade the R & A at the time to do anything about it, he just got on with it. His position at Hoylake was unique as he was The Royal Liverpool Golf Club.

Once, at a Green Committee meeting when members became too loquacious he terminated the proceedings, closed his book, stood up and declared: "Well, I am off home. You can stay all night talking if you like." He believed that there were only two golf clubs in the world – one at Hoylake and the other at St Andrews – and it was believed that he secretly regretted the decision allowing the Amateur Championship to be decided on any other course.

The Club's first 50 years were an outstanding period in many ways due to the administrative excellence of 'Tosper and Jane'.

Major HC Forbes-Bell

For the next 20 years Major HC Forbes-Bell oversaw three Opens, including Bobby Jones's in 1930.

By 1936, The Open was played over 7,000-plus yards. The clubs in those days virtually ran the event and when asked why the course was so long he remarked that, "The idea was to find the champion golfer. Wait and see, we will be judged by the result."

And indeed they were. Henry Longhurst said: "it was a triumph for Hoylake" and Gene Sarazen, who did not win, thought it was "the greatest course he had ever played".

Guy Farrar

Forbes-Bell died in 1942 and with great persuasion Guy Farrar took office. Farrar was one of 'the great men of Hoylake'. He ran the Club as if nothing had changed since before the war.

As with a fair number of fellow members he was a man of independent means. His life had always been the Club.

He had, however, considerable knowledge of agronomy and wrote articles on the subject. He was also the chairman of the local ornithology society and a fine photographer.

It was told that he developed all his own photographs and, whilst performing the process, used to remark that the secret to good results was cleanliness, at

Major Forbes-Bell, Secretary 1924-42. He oversaw three Opens

the same time as having a cigarette with a tail of ash hanging from his mouth. He was in that respect similar to Harold Hilton, a chain smoker.

He did a great deal to move the Club forward after the war and had the course in such good condition that The Open was played but two years after the conflict in 1947.

In a fascinating conversation with perhaps the best golfer Hoylake has produced in the last 60 years, Michael Pearson, he told me that it was Guy Farrar who asked him to become a member. Now this may sound strange to some, but in the '40s this was still a stuffy country; in fact so was the Club. Pearson was in the meat trade and men in trade were not the sort who frequented the Club. Perhaps this was the beginning of a change? And in all probability a change that was urgently required.

The Club was full of wealthy men, some of whom had never worked from families who had made their fortunes in cotton, shipping or insurance. In those days it was almost looked down on to do a day's work.

Pearson tells me that Farrar was not one to suffer fools gladly, which really means that he was not a tolerant man. If he liked you, fine, but if not one of his most used phrases was, "God bless me soul, the man's an idiot". He was, in fact, a shy man whose abruptness is often associated with such men.

The Oscar-winning actress Glenda Jackson, now an MP, presents prizes at the Hoylake Village Play's Annual Dinner. Behind the cup Vernon Sangster looks on with great interest. Glenda Jackson's father was a member of the 'Village Play'

The only criticism was that he ran the Club as if the war had not taken place, blissfully unaware that the world was moving towards a technological future.

He carried on in the accepted fashion, but the time had come when the future had to be faced. Farrar was now over 65 years old but had little inclination to resign. The nettle had to be grasped and he was eventually advised that that was the Club's wish. When news reached the members there was an outcry, but as is the way when the emotions had died down the events were seen in perspective.

Herbert McPherson

Herbert McPherson was then appointed, having previously been Secretary at Westward Ho! An efficient man, who won many plaudits for his handling of the last Hoylake Open in 1967.

John Davidson

John Davidson became Secretary in the mid-70s and started to see in a number of changes, slow but sure, far-sighted ideas that eventually took hold. He was a sound, capable man who worked tirelessly for the Club during those difficult times. It was very sad that he died in office but he did live long enough to see the upturn in the Club's fortunes.

Group Captain Christopher Moore

We were now moving into an exciting period, with the course now more than acceptable and the clubhouse recently refurbished. Group Captain Christopher Moore succeeded to the position in 1993; an energetic and enthusiastic RAF officer he soon made his mark with straightforward simple efficiency. He has carried the administrative torch of The Open with great skill, as he did when overseeing the two Amateur Championships and numerous other events in the last 13 years.

When Thomas Owen Potter (Tosper) was resident at the Royal Hotel there was a friendly parrot that greeted him every morning with a "Hello Tosper".

One morning the bird flew to the window ledge and squawked "Goodbye Tosper", and disappeared out of the window, never to return.

During a visit in the 1950s Leonard Crawley, the great golf correspondent of the *Daily Telegraph* was staying with the Stern family during a major event and at breakfast was adjusting his moustache with the help of the sugar tongs.

On approaching the dinning room the elderly Mrs Stern witnessed the event and demanded that Crawley left forthwith. The *Daily Telegraph* golf correspondent never returned to the Stern abode.

Societies

The Hoylake Village Play was formed in 1895 following the great tempest that brought great suffering to the fishing families of Hoylake, who lost 38 men. The Club had meetings with the local tradesmen and agreed that a club would be formed. They would join the Artisans golfing society but, thankfully, the name of the Hoylake Village Play has continued.

The members give their time to help with the upkeep of the course, and a marvellous job they do. Two matches are played against the Club: the Glover Cup and the Dan Tobey, always in the most competitive spirit, nothing given, and a good day out is had by all.

The Village Play have always had a first class set of officers, none more so now than with Jim McVey as Chairman and Peter Williams as Secretary. There are so many I should mention, but suffice to say that we have the most marvellous relationship and long may that last.

Hoylake is also the spiritual home of many other groups from the British Golf Collectors' Society, who play their annual competition on the links. Their first President was John Behrend, after his untimely death was succeeded by that great amateur golfer, John Beharrell, who presides over his duties in his delightfully, dignified way. The dinner followed by the

A change from golf: Dermot Staunton of the Hoylake Village Play bowling to Secretary Chris Erickson, with keeper Roger Greenway and slip Tony Jorden. July 1993

auction is one of the golf highlights of the year.

Youth golf has become a major element of Hoylake golf. Every Sunday scores of members and local children can be seen whirling away under the scrutiny of John Heggarty and his assistants. Further up the age scale Liverpool University has used the links as home for many years.

Many others have their dinners at the Club: the Spasmodics Cricket Club to the Liverpool Crystal Ballgazers' Society.

In 1992 John Behrend approached me and pronounced that the last cricket game to be played on the Hoylake practice ground was in 1886, knowing that I was President of the Spasmodics CC he suggested that we play another game. This required little encouragement and we played the following summer.

The Spasmodics are not the greatest cricket team in the world and even the better players are too old to perform as they wish. Their major objective is to enjoy the game and what better opposition than the Golf Clubs Winter League team? Everybody made a great effort. I think the Spasmodics won but the greatest outcome was seeing these fine golfers hardly able to hold a club for weeks after due to using muscles they rarely used or even knew they had. The fixture is played around the third Friday in July so let us hope that this tradition will carry on. I see little reason why it should not; I mean what else takes place at this time of the year at Hoylake?

The Hittites

The playing of four ball golf was the main reason for the founding of The Hittites, formed in 1926 with the specific intention of playing and encouraging foursomes golf.

After Oxford and Cambridge, the Hittites are the most prominent society in the country. Early members included Guy Farrar as Secretary and Froes Ellison, who had retained his English Amateur Championship earlier in the year. The Hittites name has many variations. I can only confirm that Guy Farrar said it was a combination of hitting the ball and then getting slightly tight! Hittites were selected, as is still the case today. Initially the best players came from Hoylake and Formby, but as the society grew selection was widened to cover all of north west England. The list of notable golfers includes Walker Cup and international players and administrators of the highest order, including Colin Maclaine of Royal Lytham, David Marsh of Southport & Ainsdale, Gordon Jeffery of Royal Birkdale and John Behrend of The Royal Liverpool, who have all been Captains of the Royal & Ancient Golf Club of St Andrews.

There are a number of annual events, including the John Ball Putter. This was presented by the great man and is played at Hoylake, their spiritual home, after the AGM and dinner at the end of each October.

They have travelled the world playing against like-minded golfers, a society at the pinnacle of quality club golfers.

Chapter Twelve

12th hole

1939-1967

During the six dark, desperate years of war the course was used as a fortification against impending attacks. A short strip of land by the shoreline from the 9th to the 12th was heavily fortified with land mines.

I am indebted to Tony Colvin, Captain of the Club in 1987, who recalled the Club during these times: "The golf club found itself at the centre of much local activity. Search lights were erected in the practice field and ack-ack battalion personnel were allowed limited use of the clubhouse. In July, an air raid warden's post was built in the corner of the course by St Hildeburgh's church, where the Village Play clubhouse stands today. After the outbreak of war the Council met and made a number of decisions:

1. During the conflict the course would remain open, as would the clubhouse, but with restrictions.
2. One hundred sheep would be allowed to graze on the course.
3. There would be no subscription charged to members in the forces and non-member officers in the services would be freely welcome in the clubhouse and on the links.
4. E Otto Glover was appointed Captain for the duration of the conflict.

"In August 1940, with the possibility of an enemy invasion, sleepers and posts were installed on most fairways to prevent aircraft landing, they also created additional hazards to the playing members.

"Of the distinguished service officers who visited the Club, I remember in particular Admiral Max Horton, who had been a distinguished submarine commander and hero of WWI, but was in WWII as the officer commanding the combined HQ of the Western Approaches.

"Derby House in Liverpool was a hive of naval activity, including numerous WRNs who did daily PT on the flat roof beneath my family firm's offices. This was Martin's Bank building, which housed gold bullion for the Bank of England.

"Admiral Horton's office was also in Derby House and he lived in the Adelphi hotel. He was given a starting time on a Sunday morning and senior members made up a four. He would arrive in a Humber staff car driven by a charming WRN officer and two naval ratings who for security purposes accompanied him throughout his round.

"These notes would not be complete without mention of the Home Guard commanded by senior members of the Club, often referred to as 'The Hoylake Horse'. They met in the clubhouse or the Green Lodge pub and were responsible for nightly patrols along the coast from the 9th tee to the 12th green. We schoolboys attached ourselves during the school holidays to the Home Guard as runners, taking messages to and from the patrols. Considering that between July 1940 and January 1942 German bombers made 68 raids on Liverpool in which 4,000 died, it was a scary operation for youngsters to cross the links in the black of night. "The sounds of enemy aircraft and the sight of the searchlights from the battery on the practice field created boyhood memories still alive today.

"Undoubtedly, enemy planes were often overhead, confused by the flares in the river Dee which were used to distract hostile aircraft away from Liverpool.

"The congregational church, a quarter of a mile from the clubhouse, was set alight by incendiaries and I was one of many who carried buckets of water along Meols Drive to assist the fire brigade.

"The Leas School (on the left of the 6th) was evacuated to the Lake District and the RAF requisitioned the buildings for a hospital. The RAF also attempted to requisition the clubhouse. This was resisted and eventually rejected, but RAF personnel and also USA nurses who were stationed in the then Stanley Hotel were given extensive facilities in the Club.

"In early 1942 the sea-boarding area of the links along the shore was requisitioned by the army for the creation of a minefield. The Club was paid an annual rent of £130.

"The 12th green was lost and recreated inland from the 13th tee, which was also moved forward. (The 12th green was the only one out of use and even then it was arranged to have a path through the minefield to push the mower so that the green would not be neglected.) Local rules pertaining to the minefield were subject to many arguments but how lucky we were to be playing at all with the war at its height.

In February 1942 our Patron, the Duke of Connaught, died and Royal patronage was suspended for the duration. This remained the case until March 1946 when His Majesty King George VI became Patron of the Club.

In August 1945 Western Approaches ceased to exist and a grateful letter was received from Admiral Sir Max Horton thanking the Club for all the hospitality received by him and all members of the services during the war."

Preceding page: John Heggarty, the Club professional since 1982

Bobby Locke, 1956

Tony Colvin was called up in 1943 and demobilised in September 1947 to find that he had been elected a full member in 1944, the year in which membership of the Club recommenced.

The only damage sustained to the course was three ack-ack shells that landed on the 15th. A knowledgeable member examined the damaged and proclaimed that they would eventually sink and be quite safe. There is no record of them ever having been removed to this day.

At the end of this dreadful conflict the full implications of the horror would take decades to unfold. It was time though to reflect and then look forward. The Duke of Connaught had died after 70 years of Patronage and the two great heroes of the Golden Days of Hoylake golf had passed away. Johnny Ball, who is buried in the graveyard in Trinity Road off Market Street in Hoylake, and Harold Hilton who had died in Gloucestershire. What a shame they could not have been "sent-off" with the full gratitude of all their friends and admirers.

Further, the Secretary Major Forbes-Bell had died and after great persuasion Guy Farrar accepted the position, a decision that was to bear fruit as soon as normal life recommenced in 1945.

That summer, an inspection of the links concluded that it was in amazingly fine condition. Secretary Farrar was soon in touch with the R & A to inform them of the state of play. He told them we could stage The Open, but St Andrews, having resisted the Nazi menace with similar results to Hoylake was also in great shape and ready for action, and so the 1946 Open was played there.

From 25-28 September 1946 Hoylake staged the Professional Golfers' Association Matchplay Championship, the first time this event had ever been played on a links course.

The winner and still at the vanguard of British golf was the maestro himself T Henry Cotton, beating former

Hoylake professional Jimmy Adams eight and seven in the final. Cotton had beaten Bobby Locke in the semi-final.

But Guy Farrar was not to be thwarted and The Open of 1947 was played at Hoylake. The holder Sam Snead did not enter, explaining: "The journey would cost more than the prize money." For all his flippancy, Snead surely never resented the expense that earned him the winner's trophy a year earlier.

It had been 11 years since The Open had been played at Hoylake, the longest fallow period since the first Championship in 1897. Considering six years of war this was understandable. The course was "a miracle of velvety smoothness" reported *The Times* correspondent who described the greens as "lovely, of a comfortable pace".

The Championship was as exciting as could be with four players, including Henry Cotton and the Irishman Fred Daly, tying for the lead going into the last round with a further five in contention.

Again the golfers went out in a willy-nilly order, not as it is today with the leaders out last. Fred had a fine round. He also had a "fine waggle and a lovely whistle". When asked why he spent so much time waggling before his shot he explained: "I waggle until I'm good and ready."

England Boys' Team 1946. Seated extreme left Peter Alliss, seated extreme right Michael Pearson, standing second right Guy Wolstenholme

He ended his round with a fine pitch to the last green and sank a 35-foot putt. This was too much for the Irish supporters. They tried to lift him shoulder-high and chair him to the clubhouse, but Fred would have none of it as there were still two hours to go before the rest were in.

It was not Cotton who threatened but the American amateur Mr Frank Stranahan. On the 16th tee he needed two fours and a three to tie. He secured his four on the 16th but three putts from short distance on 17 looked to have scuppered his chances. Even then, a two on the last would have forced a play-off. A mighty drive down the middle of the fairway placed him in a fine position and he actually walked the 100 yards to the green to examine the pin placement. Returning to play his shot he executed the most marvellous pitch but it missed by a fraction. And so the great Fred Daly became, and in fact still is, the only Irish winner of The Open.

In 1987 when Tony Colvin was Captain he held a dinner in Fred's honour at which the Irish legend recounted the events of '47:

"On arriving at the clubhouse with Harry Bradshaw we were approached by the commissionaire. 'Sorry we've no tickets, so please be off – both of you.' We were humiliated and were given the impression he thought we were a couple of Irish navvies looking for

Right: Fred Daly, champion 1947, still the only Irish winner of The Open

work. Old Cyril Hughes, the professional, then played a round with us and shortly after finishing Commander Roe, the Secretary of the PGA and a lovely man sorted out the confusion. I laugh now, but before such an important event it was a wee bit upsetting.

"The event was sensational, with a large international field, but I loved every minute and always thought I could beat Henry (Cotton). I do have this recurring nightmare, in which a voice at the other end of the phone exclaims: 'Fred, you are never going to believe this, but Stranahan really did hole that pitch. Could you dig out the clubs again and get over here for the play-off.'"

Fred was just about the most popular visitor to Hoylake. We loved him and I really do believe he loved us.

The running of the Club was now firmly in the hands of Guy Farrar and the various committees. The biggest problem the Club faced was money, or lack of it. It is hard for some of us today to realise that the Britain of the 40s, although pleasantly bumbling along, was fiscally poor.

In 1964 the Club asked Edward Birchall and Roy Smith, both former Captains, to write the second history of the Club in time for the centenary. They were asked if five years was sufficient time for the project and agreed that the book would be ready for publication in time for the centenary in 1969. Birchall took responsibility for the project and started from where Guy Farrar left off in 1932. They were going to use an "updated version" of Bernard Darwin's original foreword.

The structure of the book was agreed and work was underway, the first chapter dealing with the state of the course. But misfortune befell the project, Birchall dying soon after beginning work. Nobody picked up the task and all we are left with are some early outlines of the chapters and the beginnings of the book.

Reading his early transcripts it was apparent that it was a never-ending job maintaining the Club's solvency.

1947 Open runner-up, amateur Frank Stranahan of the USA

Wealthy members such as Vernon Sangster of football pools fame paid for all sorts of necessary work in the clubhouse and Sir Douglas Crawford of biscuits fame paid for the complete refurbishment of the clubroom. Howard Shone provided benches on all the tees.

During the time of Sir Douglas's incredibly generous refurbishments, he told the Captain of the day, Jock Warnock, that he wished the gesture to remain anonymous. It was a request that Jock respected but the truth leaked out.

Neil Jacobs (of cream cracker fame) approached Jock and moaned: "I don't like these alterations. Now I know Douglas paid for them, I'll pay for them to be put back the way they were."

"But what is wrong with them?" enquired Captain Warnock. Jacobs didn't hold back: "Well, for a start they remind me of a cross between an Armenian brothel and a Torquay hotel." Poor old Jock struggled for comprehension, arguing that he'd never visited either one of those establishments. Needless to say, within a few weeks the refurbishments were hardly mentioned and we have lived happily with them for the past 40 years.

Running the golf club through the 50s and 60s required a financial balancing act of great skill. It was accepted that nothing was bought in the last few months of the financial year, as we had no money. Any purchase had to wait until December when the subscriptions for the following year started to roll in and spending on a small scale began again.

A major problem was the reluctance of the 'powers that be' to increase the subscription level, a failing which continued well into the 70s. When I joined the Club in March 1970, aged 24, I was asked for 26 pounds 3 shillings and 9 pence (£26.19) to comprise both my subscription and the entrance fee. I was amazed the amount was so low. Realising a bargain, my money was in the post by return.

I've never paid a bill so promptly – before or since. The point is it was ludicrously cheap and the Club suffered from its inability to grasp nettles.

The gentlemen running the Club were fine men, incredible characters who were held in the highest esteem. Nearly all of them had not only served in the war but had seen action at the Front; many had been decorated. Some had even been captured and became prisoners of war. Some who should have been enjoying the fortunes of peace had given their lives for their country. I am sure nearly every club in the country had been affected in this way.

Royal Liverpool though fell a long way in a short time. The men in charge were trying to deal with matters for which they were ill-equipped. Together with many of their generation they had witnessed atrocities too brutal to recount; they had given, in many cases, the best years of their lives. Business careers were put on hold in some cases for up to eight years. They had lost some of their dearest friends at home and on duty in foreign fields.

An indelible impression had been made on them mentally, and it was a difficult position from which to restart lives. On top of this, many were renewing relationships with young families they had hardly seen.

They arrived home to a "land fit for heroes" only to find misgovernment on a high scale. Rather than encouragement for the entrepreneurs, all they found was nationalisation and the creation of mediocrity. The country was crying out for enterprise and all we had was rationing, a situation that lasted for seven years after the war. Europe was only saved by America's "Marshall Aid", in the 40s when the Russian threat was at its height. It took Britain many years to recover. One wonders now how the Club kept going.

There were though opportunities. There was a stream of major competitions both amateur and professional that came to the links, notably the Dunlop Masters in 1950, won by the dynamic little Welshman Dai Rees.

The first Amateur we hosted after the war was in 1953 when the imperial Joe Carr won, so keeping the Irish connections at the high table of Hoylake champions. Carr beat a splendid amateur golfer Harvie Ward of the United States in the final.

A few years later came The Open of 1956 when the majestic Peter Thomson won his third Open in a row. The superb Australian had a comfortable victory as he became the

Former Secretary Herbert Macpherson and head greenkeeper Mr Smith look towards the 5th dog-legged hole at Hoylake in 1965. Picture courtesy *Daily Post*

first three-in-a-row winner since The Open became a 72-hole event. When you consider all the great players who had not accomplished such a feat, from Vardon to Jones, Hagen to Cotton, Nicklaus to Woods, it shows the magnitude of the Australian's win.

The British were keen to make the most of this achievement and, while accepting the deeds of Ben Hogan and other Americans, they decreed that nothing came close to Thomson's victory. If one considers his many other wins and that he came so near to winning the US Open, Thomson can lay claim to being the finest golfer of the 50s.

Perhaps this was not his greatest victory, as many believed from the outset that it was a one-horse-race. There were fine performances from Van Donck and Roberto de Vicenzo, but I feel it was always Thomson's to lose. Expectations tend to belittle an outstanding achievement.

Thomson was a modest and unassuming man. On the final green after he had holed his winning putt he asked for silence when his partner was putting out. That sportsmanship was not lost on the crowd.

There was very little doubt then that Thomson was a great champion and he was expected to win many more tournaments. He did not disappoint, winning The Open on two more occasions when confronted by the might of American golf.

Right: 1948, driving off at the old 5th, which is the site of the current 3rd green

John Graham (Jnr) was Captain that year and tells the tale that he was known in Hoylake as "the man who plays golf" and many did not know his real name:

"After the prize-giving, I had to pose with the winner and the jug. The next day our pictures appeared in the press both holding the jug. A fortnight later I was walking along Market Street in Hoylake, when I was stopped by a middle-aged lady who congratulated me on winning The Open Championship. 'I saw a picture of you, in the papers, being presented with the winner's cup. Well done!' With that she went on her way. I am afraid that I have never told her the truth! But it was a nice way to close my file on the 1956 Open."

Major tournaments continued to be played at Hoylake. The following year came the English Amateur and a young South African, Arthur Walker, who qualified as his mother was English. He won comfortably but apart from an appearance in the semi-final of the British Amateur we did not see much of him again. He did though win many events in his home country.

The Brabazon returned in 1961, with that outstanding amateur of the day RDBM Shade winning. The RDBM many thought stood for "Right Down the Bloody Middle" but he always answered to Ronnie. He had a fine amateur record and also a number of wins when he turned professional.

The Martini came to Hoylake in 1963 and was a tie between Neil Coles and Christy O'Connor.

Changes to the course were still being considered and one concern was that the sand hills did not come into play until the 8th hole. The Club brought in the well-known course architect Fred Hawtree, with the instructions to encompass the hills earlier in the round. However, he had to deal with one of the oldest holes on the links, the old 3rd. I only played Old Third once and that was in August 1963. I shall never forget at the end of the round walking back home with lots of thoughts about the course and rehearsing with great excitement what I was to tell my father. How will I describe my approach to the 18th green with a hickory-shafted mashie to 18 inches. When I burst in, the whole family were watching the news, "Quiet" they insisted. I thought another war had broken out, but no, there had been a sensational robbery from a train and a great deal of money had been stolen. This turned out to be the Great Train Robbery when over £2 million was stolen from the night train from Scotland to London. I was a little disappointed not to recall my mashie niblick approach, but at least I remember whenever that robbery is mentioned where I was that day. It was the day I played my first round at Hoylake.

Though the main concern to those running the Club was one of money there were still major events taking place at regular intervals. So with the future in mind the Green Committee put forward the idea of changing the 3rd, 4th and 5th holes. This was really quite revolutionary considering the climate of conservatism that pervaded the Club. Thankfully the 'powers that be' went ahead with this inspired idea of golfing architecture. There was still opposition from some, but, thankfully, the whole project was pushed through

The old 3rd was one of the oldest holes on the course. The teeing area was the same as today but instead of the dog-leg left you played straight into the prevailing wind for 469 yards. There was internal out-of-bounds down the left, innumerable bunkers and some filthy rough on the right. To use a technical term – an absolute stinker of a hole.

Creating the dog-leg to the left necessitated playing onto the old 4th green. Very few alterations were made to the angle of the green or the bunkers surrounding it. I believe not terribly much was done with the terrain, apart from scything through the rough in the direction of the old 4th green and leaving the rest to nature. Once again nature did the trick.

The new 4th as we play it today was perfect land for the recommended alterations. It also brought into play the dune area. However, one small problem remained. There was no green.

A prominent member at the time, an eminent Liverpool orthopaedic surgeon Nobby Roberts, was against spending further money on the project and told the Green Committee to find a solution. What they came up with was most ingenious.

Before the days of motoring, and consequently car parking, there were two attractive lawns on either side of the drive when you approach the clubhouse from the main road. These were often used as bowling greens. One of the lawns had already been removed for the benefit of the cars there were and it was proposed that the other should also be removed in the near future. Ah ha! Why not the redundant lawn to turf the new 4th hole?

Michael Pearson playing from the 'cross bunker' in front of the 18th, early 1960s

For some reason, around 1960 we produced a good number of University Blues. Roger Robinson lead the way back in 1954: he was a fine iron-player. His great friend John Behrend just missed out on the honour; these were the days when the University Match was regarded as a major event in the British sporting calendar.

After great debate this was agreed and the grass duly rolled up, placed on wagons and transported to the designated location. With a little will and imagination two problems were solved in one glorious movement. Even the great Orthopod was happy with the outcome.

But why, oh why, was the hole not called 'The Bowling Green' rather than the unbelievably unimaginative name of 'NEW'? What a lack of soul. Perhaps some day that will be rectified?

Nobby Roberts was a marvellous character and wonderful with new young members. He lived with his wife Pat, a stalwart of the Club, on the adjacent Stanley Road. Their eldest son Michael was a fine golfer and an eccentric from an early age.

Michael played off scratch and you could never meet a more interesting and different character. One of the great men of my life. What a terrible shock when he contracted an illness that, despite great courage, was to take him at the age of 40. He is greatly missed by his legion of friends.

One of Michael's great feats was to hit a golf ball from the lawn in front of the Green Lodge public house, over St Hildeburgh's church onto my parents' back lawn, which is now flats overlooking the practice ground. He never failed. I tried once and hit the church. No damage, vicar.

Nobby, at one of the Club's annual general meetings finished his Treasurer's report and asked if there were any questions. One seasoned member rose to his feet and posed a rather difficult query that was well beyond Nobby's field of financial knowledge. After a prolonged period of pained silence Nobby, removing his spectacles from his nose, looked sternly at the offending enquirer and proclaimed: "We don't like snipers at this club." Many members, equally confused by the question, chanted "here, here" and the AGM came to a hasty close.

The Open Championship of 1967 was soon upon us and came as manna to a club which had watched with envy as go-ahead Royal Birkdale held the event in 1961 and 1965. As Hoylake's day approached there was no feeling that this could be the end of the road for Royal Liverpool hosting the event.

There were some difficult days ahead but they do not sully the memory of that magnificent win by Roberto de Vicenzo. His win was a tonic for all romantics.

But The Open had gone. The Club required new ideas for the future and new blood to move forward as those dynamic men of 100 years before had done.

There were many cobwebs to dust away.

For instance, soon after The Open, there was a Special General Meeting called by a past Captain, Bill Gates, proposing "that no more professional golf events were acceptable to the members of RLGC". Thankfully, this was rejected. The thinking behind such a motion was that Hoylake was a course for the amateur golfer and was only proud to host amateur events.

I believe the members talked themselves out of the idea of the Big Event having been told by the Secretary of the R & A that the course was no longer suitable and nor was the area and its infrastructure. The R & A had appointed a new Secretary, Keith MacKenzie, who was not impressed with the course nor with the Club. I do not believe the Club was impressed by Keith MacKenzie either.

One can see though that future Open Championships must have seemed out of sight to many of the members. The growth in the size of the Championship made the infrastructure of the course, the Club and the district unsuited to hold such a major sporting event.

We will see later the lengths the Club had to go to, to persuade the R & A to consider Hoylake again.

In those days there was no extra land available on the site of The Leas School. There were no motorways on the Wirral, the local authority were not enthusiastic supporters of the Championship. A story is told of a local councillor when asked whether the Municipal Course would be made available for parking suggested holding The Open on the Municipal and parking the cars on "The Royal".

Car parking was a serious problem – this was before the days of Park & Ride – a suggestion was even canvassed of building a temporary dam to allow parking beside the sea holes between West Kirby and Red Rocks.

It was going to take more than the membership at that time could stomach to return the Championship to Hoylake. Little wonder therefore that members reverted to the line that Hoylake was the custodian of amateur golf in England. Those words served both as a comfort and an excuse.

If you cannot have something – or believe you cannot – best to say you do not want it. And then there is no need to try and get it.

As with many other clubs, it was a case every year of "roll on December" when the subscriptions, meagre though they were, came in and bills could be paid.

What was not envisaged was how quickly the reputation of the Club would suffer. An example of this was when the Fairway Shipping Company, who had a number of their ships named after well-known golf courses, renamed one of their vessels – originally called Hoylake – as *Cypress Point*.

Open championship spectator arrangements

The following arrangements are being made at Hoylake for the benefit of spectators at the Open championship which is set for 12th-15th July :–

SPECTATOR STANDS

Tubular stands are being erected at vantage points on the course to facilitate viewing. They will provide accommodation for over 5,000 spectators and will be located in the following positions :-

Fourth Green–for 300 spectators, Fifth Green–for 300 spectators, Ninth Green–for 600 spectators, 15th Green–for 500 spectators, 16th Green–for 500 spectators, 17th Green–for 500 spectators, 18th Green–for 2,500 spectators.

In addition there will be two bridges at the back of the 12th and 13th greens and a club stand at the back of the 18th green for members of The Royal Liverpool Golf Club with reserved space for members of the press.

There will be no additional charge for admission to the stands.

SCORE BOARDS

In addition to the main score board in the Tented Village, there will be another large hole-by-hole score board at the ninth hole and " leader " boards between the first and second holes, at the 13th hole and 18th hole.

The main " leader " board at the 18th green will give the scores of players after the 17th hole and will also show the position of the ten leaders.

Spectators in the stands at the 18th hole should be able to read the detail on the leader board which will be large and legible.

As has been done in the past, mobile score boards showing the competitors' position in relation to par will be carried with selected matches on the first two days and with all matches on the Friday and Saturday. The leading matches on both these days will have a special board showing the competitors' position in relation to par for the whole championship in addition to the current round.

A daily draw sheet will be on sale at the course.

CROWD CONTROL

The fairways will be roped and fenced. Only the players, their caddies, markers and score board carriers, press and photographers wearing special armbands will be allowed within the ropes.

CAR PARKS

Ample public car parking arrangements are being made near the course.

Top: Press release, 1967 style

Below left: Editorial in *The Times* 17 July 1967

Below right: A Bailey Bridge being erected over the railway line for the 1967 Open. For the 2006 Open the railway was closed for 10 days

THE ROYAL AND MODERN

For years it used to be said that golf was a game to be played and not watched. The difficulties of following a round and the uncertainties of timing made it for years the Cinderella of the major sports on television. But the large amount of equipment used by the television services at the Open championship this year, including some for relaying it live to America, showed how completely that attitude has changed. The American Masters and the American Open have been seen live on television over here this year, and the B.B.C. has made its own series of films of contests between the great players of the world.

Times have changed, too, for the spectators on the spot. Some may have been dismayed by the amount of chestnut paling insulating them from the fairways at Hoylake, but many found consolation in large stands put up at points around the course. They happily waited for the golf to come to them.

A rigid control of spectators is desirable not only for the competitors but for the proper presentation of the Open as a growing spectacle. Much has already been done in recent years, and the championship committee of the Royal and Ancient will no doubt be encouraged now to do more. Permanent stands are a success. Another way in which the watching might be improved is by banking the ground alongside fairways to form natural tiers.

All this requires much preparation and can be achieved only if the Open championship is kept to a fixed number of places. Deciding where the championship is to be played is one of the biggest difficulties the Royal and Ancient has to face. The requirements of an Open in accommodation and parking space limit severely the number of possible sites, but enough must be found to give a breathing space to clubs between one visit and the next. Hoylake was in a sense on trial last week, not as a course but as a venue. It emerged from that trial with success.

Part of the reason for the success was the weather. Another part was due to the remarkable popularity of the winner. The rest came from foresight and hard work, and it encourages the hope that the south of England may stage the championship again.

The biggest tonic golf could have would come not from administration or presentation but from the players themselves. ROBERTO DE VICENZO, holding the Open trophy in his arms at last, said in a speech which no script-writer could have bettered that next year he wanted to hand it on to some young British player. New hope that the end of foreign domination in golf's biggest event is in sight has arisen from the performance of a handful of our younger players. It found expression in the words of the oldest man to win the championship this century.

ARMY TEAM WORKED ROUND CLOCK TO BUILD 'OPEN' BRIDGE

Peter Thomson

Nicko Williams has a day with Peter Thomson

No sportsman will ever forget the summer of 2005, the year that the Ashes returned to England. On the morning of the decisive final test at the Oval I decided to watch the morning's play on the card room TV at the Club and as I sat down another member joined me. I glanced round, and to my astonishment recognised Peter Thomson – five times Open champion, former Australian MP, and keen cricket follower who was at Hoylake on a golfing photo shoot.

What a man to share a morning's cricket with.

Peter was a delightful companion, modest, knowledgeable, kind in his opinions. He had not really recognised Hoylake from his 1956 triumph but was looking forward to the 2006 Championship. Would the course be long enough? Would Hoylake's magnificent greens make life almost too easy for the present generation of master putters? Peter felt that the best defence against the modern player was to let the greens grow: "Make them hit the ball – not stroke it; that would sort the men from the boys."

He was generous to his golfing peers and competitors. Especially to Bobby Locke and Sam Snead, neither particularly popular

Left: Peter Thomson, 1956 Open Champion

Right: Peter Thomson making his victory speech. Right of him John Graham (Jnr), Captain, and Guy Farrar with the golfing public. He had played much exhibition golf with both players in their native lands and learned a golden lesson from Sam Snead, in his view the best golfer from tee to green of his era.

The athletic and magnificently built Snead had out-driven him by 50 yards and more, yet when it came to iron-play Thomson was surprised to see Snead take either the same or sometimes a longer iron. Snead's explanation: "Why press for length to the green when what you need is accuracy?"

Peter, a completely self-taught golfer, immediately recognised the age-old truth of this and as a result became even more accurate with his iron-play to the green. You do not win five Open Championships and a host of other tournaments around the world just by beautiful ball-striking and masterful chipping and putting and Peter's opinion of the proliferation of sports psychologists on the present day circuit was highly entertaining.

One could not help getting the feeling that whatever path Peter had chosen he would have reached the pinnacle of any career.

How fortunate we are that one of the truly great Champions won an Open at Hoylake.

Chapter Thirteen

13th hole

A Hoylake Memoir

by Peter Alliss

My first view of The Royal Liverpool Golf Club was in 1947. The Open Championship was being played there that year and my father, although 50, decided to compete and, would you believe it, take me along for "experience".

At the end of the first couple of days I was a long way from qualifying but what I had seen intrigued me, not least the style of the clubhouse and its grandeur, the condition of the course and its greens, which were absolutely magnificent.

But oh, that diabolically difficult 1st hole (now the Championship third) which, if you negotiated it safely, only set you up for another three or four holes which, if not quite as formidable, certainly had the nerve ends twitching by the time you got to the 18th tee!

My next visit was in 1949. I had been summoned to do my National Service and reported to West Kirby, not a million miles away, where lo and behold, I found myself signing in alongside Guy Wolstenholme whom I had met, and played with, in the Boys' Championship at the Bruntsfield Golf Club on the west side of Edinburgh in 1946.

Together we would keep the Red Hordes at bay! He suggested a game, and had the boldness to telephone the Secretary, the formidable Guy Farrar.

We arrived. Mr Farrar couldn't have been more charming, and then we set off resplendent in Air Force attire. It was the beginning of July, the weather was hot, we rolled our sleeves up (which was our only concession to the 80-degree heat) and then, in smooth leather-soled boots, we began. I circumnavigated the course in 67 shots which, looking back, was probably the best round of golf I ever played in my life!

National Service completed, and a life in the ranks of professional golf came, and with it visits to Hoylake where the pros played the amateurs.

Oh, what fun those occasions were! The plan was to tune up the various teams, ie Ryder and Walker Cups. We played foursomes.

I remember on one occasion Bernard Hunt and I took on Joe Carr and fellow Irishman Sam McCready. That was ok, but we had to give them a four-up start. I think that was negotiated by our Captain so if we were heavily beaten we had a reasonable excuse! We were heavily beaten, so the excuse came in handy!

1967 saw me playing in The Open Championship, which was won by Roberto de Vicenzo. I pulled some back muscles trying to extricate myself from a grassy bank somewhere on the first nine, and that was that. I was carried back to the clubhouse, and another chance to win the Championship had gone, another memorable visit had passed, but it was made most attractive by the fact that my wife and I were offered accommodation by one of the members, a certain Gus, and Bettina, Lowe who, when sending me directions to their house, said, "You can't miss us, we have a lighthouse in the garden," and so they had!

There have been many changes at Royal Liverpool, or Hoylake as it's perhaps better known. The fabled Claret Jug has been away from Royal Liverpool for far too long. I can assure you, it will test the very finest of golfers.

Chapter Fourteen

14th hole

Hoylake: A View From America

by Jay Rains, United States Golf Association (USGA)

"There are places I remember all my life, though some have changed,
some forever not for better, some have gone and some remain.
All these places have their meaning, for lovers and friends I still can recall.
Some are dead and some are living, in my life I love them all."

I was born in 1956, nearly 10 years before John Lennon and Paul McCartney wrote the words to the song 'In My Life'. Eight years later I was captivated by four young men from Liverpool when the Beatles appeared on the Ed Sullivan Show. I became a Liverpudlian that night, but little was I to know that the place that I would remember and love most in my adopted second home would be Hoylake.

Both the history of golf in America and the United States Golf Association have tremendous roots at Hoylake. For well over a century our paths have crossed, often bearing witness to some of the game's greatest moments and personalities.

I was deeply honoured to be asked to reflect on the view of Hoylake from America and even more pleased to reflect on the Club's long and rich relationship with the USGA. What follows is certainly not meant to be exhaustive (to do so would require a book unto itself) but merely a taste of one of golf's enduring relationships: Hoylake and America.

In the late 19th century Liverpool was the second city of the realm. In America, we struggled to recover from the lingering effects of our Civil War, while the industrial foundations of the great Midwestern cities, such as Chicago, Detroit and Cleveland, began to take shape and the more adventuresome at heart pushed west toward what seemed a limitless sea of wild frontier and opportunity.

The early history of golf in America is firmly rooted in the class structure of the time. Golf was proposed as a leisure activity for the well-to-do and its popularity and the number of clubs grew quickly and in no time debate raged over the proper manner to organise and conduct an

American national championship. Given the lack of respect accorded professionals at that time, the focus was primarily on an amateur competition to be held among "proper gentlemen". The United States Open was an afterthought. The situation reached boiling point after a contentious 'national championship' was hosted by the St Andrews Golf Club of Yonkers, New York and won, by the way, by Laurence Stoddard, who had learned his golf on the links of Hoylake.

To resolve this issue, on 22 December 1894 representatives of five clubs, agreed to form an independent non-profit organisation, the United States Golf Association, charged with organising and overseeing our national championship. Ten months later, in October 1895, the inaugural championship, the United States Amateur, was won by America's 'Golf Evangelist', Charles Blair Macdonald, over the links at the Newport Golf Club. With little fanfare or attention the inaugural US Open was won the next day by Horace Rawlins over the same course.

Charles Blair Macdonald was born in America of Scottish origin, studied at St Andrews' university and while there became obsessed with the game that would dominate his life and make him famous as a player, golf club organiser and course architect. His book, *Scotland's Gift Golf* is one of the most important volumes in American golf literature. Macdonald was a driving force in the creation of the Chicago Golf Club and the founding of the USGA. His course designs endeavoured to recreate much of the inspiration he experienced at the Old Course, North Berwick, Prestwick and Hoylake. His signature creation, The National Golf Links of America, is living testimony to his passion to communicate golf in its purest form.

Between 1878 and 1883, Macdonald travelled extensively to Hoylake, becoming an overseas member of The Royal Liverpool Golf Club in 1879 and spending six weeks there the same year and again in 1883. Twenty-seven

Jay Rains, a club member who is also a member of the United States Golf Association

years after becoming a member, and 11 years following his victory in the inaugural US Amateur, Charles Blair Macdonald returned to Hoylake as a contestant in the 1906 Amateur Championship, losing in the second round to CC Lingen, the eventual runner-up. There is no doubt that the links at Hoylake and the Club atmosphere heavily influenced Macdonald's American course designs, his view of how a proper club should be organised and governed and how competitions should be conducted.

Eight months prior to the founding of the USGA the 1894 Amateur Championship was held at Hoylake and the winner was Hoylake's favourite son and, with the exception of Bobby Jones, arguably the greatest amateur golfer to ever live, Johnny Ball. Ball, along with John Graham (Jnr) and Harold Hilton, formed the great Hoylake Triumvirate. Three years later, in 1897, Hilton won The Open Championship at Hoylake, while in America, at the Chicago Golf Club, another Hoylake man, Joseph Lloyd, known as the 'General', was crowned The Open Champion of the United States.

So taken by Hoylake's golfing dominance of the time, HJ Tweedie extolled the virtues of Ball, Hilton, Horace Hutchinson and even Charles Blair Macdonald in *Golf* in January 1898, noting: "We all admit that we love to play at St Andrews just as good horsemen like to race at Newmarket; but we do wish that the golfing world would admit

The United States Amateur team, 1921. From left: WC Fownes, Bobby Jones, P Hunter, FS Wright, Francis Ouimet, J Wood-Platt, Jesse Guilford

that two of the present champions – one of the United States and the other of Great Britain – learned their golf on the keen putting greens of Hoylake."

In the early 20th century, America's new-found passion for golf was fanned by the barnstorming visits of many of the great British players. Of particular significance were the visits in 1900, 1913 and 1920 of the great Harry Vardon. While Ball and Graham did not compete in America, Hilton did, entering the 1911 United States Amateur at the age of 42. Hilton's presence in the event, at the Apawamis Club in Rye, NY, created great excitement in America as he already held the British Amateur title for 1911, a title he had also won in 1900 and 1901 to go with his victories in The Open Championship in 1892 and 1897.

Hilton did not disappoint. In the qualifying competition, he took the Gold Medal with a two-round score of 150, barely edging out the highly regarded young American, Charles 'Chick' Evans Jnr. A mild controversy swirled around the matchplay draw with some insisting that the USGA had favoured the British champion so as to ensure continued interest into the late rounds. If this was true, the USGA sacrificed one of their own in the process as Hilton demolished Robert C Watson, the Secretary of the USGA, 11 and 10, in the third round. In the semi-finals, Hilton faced one of America's best, Jerome Travers, the winner of the 1907 and 1908 US Amateurs. In a tough contest, Hilton held off Travers's

1921. Playing from the 'cross bunker' in front of the 6th green

surge in the afternoon round, securing a three and two victory. Travers would win the US Amateur in the next two years, as well as the US Open in 1915.

In the final, Hilton faced Fred Herreshoff of the Ekwanok Club in Vermont, who had bettered defending champion WC Fownes Jnr and Chick Evans on his way to the final. Despite an up-and-down performance, Hilton managed a 75 to Herreshoff's 81 for a three-up lead as the players retired for lunch. Hilton started strongly in the afternoon and after five holes was six up and cruising.

The Ekwanok man was a tough competitor, however, and Hilton's fortunes shifted rapidly as Herreshoff won five of the next seven holes to reduce Hilton's lead to one hole as the players went to the 13th. The next three holes were halved but when Hilton failed to save par from the bunker at the 16th, the match was all square. Hilton righted the ship to halve the 17th and 18th, barely avoiding defeat as Herreshoff's birdie putt grazed the edge of the hole. Still shaken from his apparent collapse, Hilton drove wildly at the 37th hole and his approach was badly sliced, heading into the trees and certain defeat when the ball struck a rock and, miraculously, caromed onto the green. Completely unnerved, Herreshoff topped his approach and failed to get up and down while Hilton two putted to win the match and the Championship.

In his account in *The American Golfer,* the editor, the great Walter Travis, winner of the 1900, 1901 and 1903 US Amateurs and the 1902 Amateur Championship, congratulated Hilton but fired the first shot in transatlantic golf competition. "Mr Hilton's win," noted Travis, "will so focus general attention on the game, arising from the fact our Amateur Championship is now held by a foreigner, that pressure, if any were needed, will be brought to bear from these outside influences on the vast body of golfers throughout the country to create an irresistible desire to 'get even' – to send a team of our representative players

Opposite: The 12th green looking west as dusk falls

abroad to try and capture the British Championship. All of which, quite irrespective of the issue, is bound to make for the good of the game generally."

Hilton returned to defend his title the next year at the Chicago Golf Club, with some uncertainty as to the reception he would receive due to some unflattering remarks he had made upon his return to England concerning the quality of the competition in the prior year's Championship. While a more positive re-appraisal of American golfing talent was requested in *The American Golfer* following Hilton's early exit from the 1912 US Amateur, won by Travers, it was nevertheless reported that the crowds were very supportive of him and the other competitors respectful, even if they secretly desired to thrash the great champion. Hilton suffered in the record-breaking Chicago heat and his inability to adapt to a new driver, and was beaten in the first round of matchplay two and one by CG Waldo and also lost a play-off for the medal prize by three shots to Chick Evans.

The visit of Hilton to compete in the 1911 and 1912 Amateurs, along with the visits of Vardon and Ted Ray, were important milestones in the development of a competitive championship identity among American golfers. The top Americans had seen the best and, while inspired and at times in awe, had determined that they could and would compete.

For many years, though, Americans had a distinct inferiority complex when it came to competing against the more seasoned British players. This, coupled with the cost and time of travel, acted as an impediment to the participation by all but a few Americans in the Amateur and Open Championships in the early 1900s. When The Open returned to Hoylake in 1913, the field contained a number of Americans, including the reigning US Open Champion, John McDermott and a Scottish immigrant, Stewart Maiden, the professional at East Lake in Atlanta, Georgia and the teacher of a young prodigy named Bobby Jones. Of the Americans entered only McDermott excelled, even though he finished with a disastrous 83 in driving rain and gales in the final round. McDermott finished fifth, nine shots behind the winner, JH Taylor, which was good enough to land him on the prize list (£7), the first American professional to achieve that.

The brash McDermott, a native of Philadelphia, won the United States Open in 1911 and 1912 but was one of the tragic figures of American golf. Suffering from mental illness, McDermott spent the last 65 years of his life in mental institutions, dying there in 1971. Nevertheless, in his prime McDermott and his attacking style of play were a sight to behold and his play in the 1913 Open paved the way for the many American professionals who would follow.

Three months after the 1913 Open Championship at Hoylake the psyche of American golf changed forever at the Country Club in Brookline, Massachusetts, outside

Boston, when a 20-year-old former caddy and amateur named Francis Ouimet defeated Harry Vardon and Ted Ray in a play-off to win the United States Open Championship. Ouimet remained an amateur throughout his life and is one of the most highly respected men in the history of American golf. The following year, a young Walter Hagen (who would win The Open at Hoylake in 1924) captured the US Open at Midlothian outside of Chicago and the inferiority complex of Americans was no more.

Hagen, followed by Bobby Jones, were to change the order at golf's high table after the end of World War I.

When I became a member of the Executive Committee of the United States Golf Association in 2003, I was told that I was the first member of Royal Liverpool to hold such a position. Given my love for Hoylake that made me very proud. Subsequently, I found out that I was not the first but the third to have such a dual honour. Assuming he retained his membership until 1894, the first was Charles Blair Macdonald, a member of the original Executive Committee of the USGA and the second was Bobby Jones, who was an honorary member from 1930 until his death in 1971 and was also a member of the Executive Committee of the USGA from 1928 to 1930. Any personal connection with Jones and the roads he travelled, no matter how small or trivial, makes me feel extremely honoured and humble.

1921 International Match, Great Britain & Ireland versus USA. The 9th green, which was further to the right in those days, making the approach a 'blind shot'

The 1953 Amateur Championship at Hoylake, won by JB Carr, sported a field containing two of the greatest American amateurs of all time, Harvie Ward (who lost in the final to Carr by two holes) and Bill Campbell. A member and captain of numerous Walker Cup sides, Campbell would go on to become President of the USGA and Captain of the Royal & Ancient Golf Club of St Andrews, the only person to hold both positions in their career in golf administration. Maybe of greater interest, however, was the presence in the 1953 matchplay draw of a passionate golfer and crooner of some renown, Bing Crosby. Crosby, whose son Nathaniel would follow his footsteps to Hoylake as a member of the 1983 Walker Cup team, won his first-round match before bowing out in the second round.

In the year of my birth, 1956, Peter Thomson won his third Open "on the trot" at Hoylake. Unfortunately, this was a period of time when many top Americans elected not to make the trip due to the cost of travel and small purse compared to what was available in the States. One American who made the trip, however, was the ageing but effervescent Gene Sarazen. Sarazen qualified for the Championship but withdrew to attend the funeral of a friend killed in a plane crash over the Grand Canyon. Before leaving, however, Sarazen conducted daily tutorials with the many young players in the field, particularly focusing on bunker play. In the front of the class each day was a 19-year-old South African, Gary Player, destined to become one of the greatest bunker players of all time, particularly in major championships. The top American finisher in the Championship, Mike Souchak, finished eight shots behind Thomson but praised our links, noting, "I rate Hoylake with Pebble Beach and Pinehurst No 2."

The last American individual to triumph at Hoylake in a major competition did so in the 1975 Amateur Championship. The Championship followed the

Opposite: Royal Liverpool member Nick Wainwright ponders a missed putt

Walker Cup, which had been held at St Andrews the preceding week and, as a result, contained one of the strongest fields since the days of Ouimet, Jones, Wethered and Tolley. The American contingent included future two-time US Open Champion Curtis Strange, US Amateur Champion and future Masters Champion Craig Stadler, US Amateur Champion and future US Open Champion Jerry Pate, not to mention Gary Koch and Jay Haas. The British competitors included future Masters and Open Champion Sandy Lyle, three-time Masters and Open Champion Nick Faldo, future undefeated Walker Cup Captain Peter McEvoy and future Ryder Cup Captain Mark James. Add to this field a young man from Rhodesia named Nick Price and the two great amateur warhorses, Bill Campbell and Michael Bonallack, and you had one of the strongest fields of all time.

But the man that stood tallest among this group was the 1972 US Amateur Champion, Marvin M Giles III, better known as Vinny. Thanks in part to a putting tip from his wife, Giles worked his way through the draw, finally dispatching the hayfever afflicted James, eight and seven, in the final. A star-studded and eventful Championship with the winner a great career amateur, Vinny Giles.

In 1921, recalling Walter Travis's call to arms of 10 years earlier, Francis Ouimet led a group of American amateurs into battle against a side of talented British amateurs in the first international team competition between America and Britain. Certainly, this informal competition was put into perspective by the Great War that had ended just a few short years before, where Americans and Britons had stood shoulder to shoulder in battle, not the last time they would do so. The American side fared much better than they would in the Amateur later in the week, taking the match 9-3. Americans, who struggle in modern-day Walker and Ryder Cups in foursomes, took to the format like fish to water, winning all four matches, including a five and three win by Evans and Jones in the opening match.

In 1983, 62 years after Evans and Jones strode from the first tee in the opening foursomes match, the Walker Cup came to Hoylake. Winning for the 26th time in 29 matches, the United States side broke an 8-8 deadlock by winning five of the final afternoon singles matches to secure a 13½-10½ victory.

Nine years later, the GB & I Ladies returned the favour by handing the Americans a 10-8 defeat in the 1992 Curtis Cup match at Hoylake. The weather on the first day proved formidable, driving rainstorms, gusts of 25 miles per hour, temperatures hovering just above freezing; in other words, an average summer day in Hoylake. "Their side is more used to these conditions," said former USGA President Judy Bell, herself a former Curtis Cup player and captain. "You win matches by inches, not by yards. They do all the little things right in the weather like that: hold the umbrella properly, keep as dry as possible, and stay warm. They add up over the course of a match." And add up it did, to an impressive 6-3 lead for the GB & I side at the end of the first day. As we all know, if you don't like the weather in Hoylake, just wait a couple of hours because it is likely to change, frequently in a dramatic fashion. On day two, blue skies and a mild breeze accompanied temperatures hovering in the mid-70s. The play of the American side warmed as well, but the GB & I team played strongly and the teams went to lunch with GB & I leading 7-5.

The most notable achievement of the morning foursomes was the victory of Carol Semple Thompson, the greatest woman amateur in American history, who set an all-time Curtis Cup record with her 12th victory in seven appearances. Carol added several more victories in Curtis Cup matches that followed the 1992 competition and her career record is unlikely to be broken.

The GB & I team stormed strongly from the gate in the afternoon singles winning the first two matches. The Americans refused to concede defeat, however, and after winning the next three matches, the fate of the Curtis Cup would be decided by the two youngest competitors, 18-year-old Caroline Hall for GB & I and 19-year-old Vicki Goetze of the United States. The match came to the final hole all square but Hall won her match, and the Curtis Cup, when her par bettered Goetze, who failed to get up and down from Hoylake's difficult greenside bunkers. The quality of the sportsmanship and competition was

1921. 9th green taken from what is now the forward 10th tee

Titleist

only matched by the polite and respectful enthusiasm of the crowds, a hallmark of all Walker and Curtis Cups.

The relationship between The Royal Liverpool, the USGA and American golf and golfers has always been and continues to be very special. "I was the de facto Manager for our Walker Cup team in 1983, my first visit to Hoylake," said David Fay, now the Executive Director of the USGA. "I remember the obvious strength of the links and, much like The Old Course, how the layout – its pacing and nuances – grows on you each time you walk the course. I remember the character of our hosts, very warm (translation: great party givers!) and full of humour. Americans have always felt at "home" when at Hoylake and our 1983 Walker Cup experience certainly reinforced that belief.

"When I returned in 2003 as Jay Rains' guest nothing had changed except the course, as subtle as ever but an even more stern test than before (although I'll admit I was a little saddened to see that the 7th hole is less devilish than in the past!). Without surprise, the hospitality shown to my wife Joan and me was outstanding, in every way, in the Hoylake tradition. Particular thanks to Doug Norval, Blyth Bell, the Secretary, Chris Moore, and the Captain, Sean Duncan, not to mention Jay for his guided tour of Beatles sites! I am delighted that the British Open will be returning to Hoylake and that the great links will be showcased for the world of golf."

The President of the USGA in 2004, Fred Ridley, was the 1976 US Amateur Champion, a member of the United States Walker Cup team in 1977 and the Captain of the American side in 1987 and 1989. When asked for his reflections on Hoylake, Mr Ridley noted that "along with the R & A and the Honourable Company of Edinburgh Golfers, American golf probably owes a greater sense of gratitude to Hoylake than any other place. The Club's obvious influence on Charles Blair Macdonald, the inspiration for the Walker Cup in 1921 and the stage for Bob Jones's Open victory in 1930 are all well-known. But more important than these famous moments are the everyday strolls around Hoylake's sacred links by visiting American golfers accompanied by gracious Royal Liverpool members.

"Every time an American shakes the hand of his Hoylake host at the 18th or raises a glass in the clubroom, we draw closer to our roots and the inalienable bond between the USGA and Royal Liverpool grows stronger."

Like I said before, I am a Liverpudlian. Whether it's walking down Mathew Street, strolling under "the clear suburban skies" on Penny Lane, singing at Anfield, closing The Ship (three hours late) or just enjoying the serenity and camaraderie I feel at Hoylake, I am a Liverpudlian. As they say, when you are in Liverpool, 'You'll Never Walk Alone', and I never have.

Overleaf: Waiting on the 7th, with players driving off from the 10th tee

Swedish Connection

In 1931 Djursholm Golf Club was established in a very attractive residential area by the Baltic Sea, only a few miles north of Stockholm. One of the first professionals at the Club was James H Dodd, commonly known as Jimmy. He had eloped with Joan, daughter of the President of Leek Golf Club in Staffordshire, whom he later married, and they ended up in Sweden. It goes without saying that Joan's father was against this relationship.

I grew up in Djursholm and was taught by Jimmy Dodd. During our long, cold winters we hit balls into a net in the men's locker room and, somehow, Jimmy slowly became adapted to life in Sweden. It did not come easily, though, and he spoke our language as if it were something not quite to be trusted.

Ted Roberts, professional at Stockholm Golf Club for 64 years. Son of a Hoylake solicitor

His eyes were blue and piercing and he was blessed with a simple and graceful swing that served him well. Competing against other senior professionals he won regularly, scoring lower than his age. He saw life the same way as he regarded the game, black and white, either/or, straight, a man with tremendous integrity.

Jimmy was born in Hoylake, the son of the stationmaster on the Liverpool-Hoylake line. He was an only child and at first contact fell in love with golf. Every free minute from his early school days was spent around Royal Liverpool Golf Club, where he swept the floor in the professionals' shop, changed spikes on shoes and grips on clubs and played whenever RLGC would let him.

He saw Arnaud Massy win The Open in 1907 but, more importantly, he caddied for Charles Hutchings, who at 53 became the oldest ever to win the Amateur in 1902. Hutchings was a member of RLGC and when he was carried into the bar to celebrate Jimmy was left on the final green with Hutchings' clubs, alone under the endless, darkening sky.

A few days later Hutchings turned up at the Club and pressed 10 gold coins into Jimmy's hand, a fortune, a year's salary at the time. Jimmy was 16 years old and he ran home to his mother, who replaced the coins with a sixpence.

When he told his story many years later he also spoke of the three Hs – Hutchings winning at Hoylake with the Haskell ball, the first time the Championship had been won with the rubber core ball. More than anything, he mentioned Hoylake with respect and gratitude, for here had he learnt everything about the game, and then some. He felt he owed Hoylake; at least that was the way he put it.

Why, then, did he choose Sweden, one of earth's most remote places? Surely, not for the weather.

In 1930 there were 10 golf clubs in Sweden, with a total of 1,300 members. Golf had been introduced informally at the tail end of the 19th century. The first official golf club was established in Gothenburg in 1902. One of the earliest professionals to work for Gothenburg Golf Club was George Roberts of Hoylake. There were three brothers – Charles, George and Edwin, or Ted as he was called, and they all became golf professionals. Their father worked in Liverpool, a solicitor. For sons of a solicitor to choose golf as a profession must have raised a few eyebrows at the turn of the last century.

I met Ted Roberts many times, but never asked him about how his parents had reacted. His father did not play, nor was he a member of any club. What did they talk about at dinner, for instance? Obviously, the three sons were engrossed in the game.

A hundred years ago a golf professional normally started his career caddying,

The Duke of Windsor playing with Ted Roberts in Stockholm

helping in the shop, sweeping the floor, doing the odd jobs, living hand-to-mouth and, more often than not, ending up where he had started, caddying.

For those who managed to find a position at a proper golf club it still meant very hard work for very little. It took a long time before anyone really understood what a professional did, or could do.

The most important source of income during the early years was, of course, club-making and repairing equipment. This is why Hoylake and Royal Liverpool provided such an ideal environment for anyone who wanted to learn the trade. It was a club where The Open Championship and other major events were played; there were visitors, there was knowledge, prestige, Harold Hilton and John Ball.

At Hoylake a young man could find his footing in the business. With luck.

Charles Roberts, the oldest brother, was the first to leave Hoylake. He found work at Woolton Golf Club in Liverpool and brought George along, as an assistant, but George found another opening. He travelled to Switzerland where, as luck would have it, he ran into Admiral Henry Lindberg, the then President of Stockholm Golf Club. The Admiral offered George the opportunity to teach in Stockholm for six weeks, a well paid, one-off deal, and George went. This was during the summer of 1910.

Going back to England meant travelling westwards across Sweden to Gothenburg, where George played an exhibition match for the members. He scored 85, a new course record, and was promptly offered the position as golf professional.

In 1911 George Roberts became the first full-time professional in Sweden and he remained until his untimely death in 1927. During the years in Gothenburg, though, he was the most sought-after club maker in Sweden; he won the first Scandinavian Professional Tournament in 1916 and was asked by many to be an advisor on subjects ranging from the use of water, general greenkeeping and how to keep bunker faces from collapsing.

He also persuaded his younger brother Ted to work as professional at Stockholm Golf Club in 1914. The club was to move to several places around Stockholm before it settled at Kevinge, north of Stockholm and very close to Djursholm.

The Kevinge course was laid out by John Morrison and the opening game was played by the Prince of Wales, Duke of York, Crown Prince Gustav Adolf of Sweden and Ted Roberts. The latter, a slightly built man with a beret placed dead centre on his head, outplayed his illustrious company and behaved as if this was just something you had for breakfast. He was as happy as always and very impressive.

Back to Jimmy Dodd. Having found his lovely Joan at Leeks Golf Club, and realising that this match never would be accepted in England, he called his long-time friend Ted Roberts and moved to Sweden. There was

work waiting, clubs to be made, shoes to be polished and swings to be taught. The couple moved into the Djursholm clubhouse, living in an area which today is the kitchen, and remained at the club for the duration of their lives. The Dodds became synonymous with the golf club.

My uncle Bruno was a member of Gothenburg Golf Club in 1911, when George Roberts became attached to the club, and a few years later my father became a member. He in turn moved to Stockholm to join Ted Roberts' club before ending up with Jimmy Dodd in Djursholm.

I had heard of the out-of-bounds behind the short 7th hole, of the snow-capped mountains in Wales in the early spring, of the Hilbre island bird sanctuary and the fact that John Ball actually played club competitions off a handicap of plus nine before I even knew what Hoylake was, or where. But it helped me to realise that we, who are involved in golf in Sweden, owe a debt to those who are today mostly forgotten, people who set standards for us, people who lived by these and never compromised.

The Roberts brothers – another Roberts, a nephew incidentally, worked at Upsala Golf Club before moving to Caldy Golf Club on the Wirral – and Jimmy Dodd have had a great impact on golf in Sweden, not only teaching the swing or making clubs but, more importantly, passing on the tradition in which they were fostered, in Hoylake.
Göran Zachrisson

Examples of the distinctive 'Ted Roberts' Swing'

Chapter Fifteen

15th hole

1968-1987: Relative Decline

by Bob Chadwick

After a lifetime at the top of the golfing tree, Hoylake slumped into decline. As golf became a major leisure industry boosted by television coverage, and by the charismatic characters at the top of the professional game – Palmer, Nicklaus, Player and Britain's own Tony Jacklin – so Hoylake seemed to stand still.

Attendance at The Open grew from 36,000 during the week in 1967 to virtually 30,000 per day by 1970. There was simply not the room on the course, nor the hotel and transport infrastructure around it, to accommodate the 'big one'. There was, though, a constant stream of top amateur events, and one European Tour event, in the next 20 years. But the absence – and, worse, the growing belief that it was a permanent absence – of the acclaim that only The Open can bring was hard to bear. There were those who tried to comfort their fellow members by saying that "we don't really want The Open any more", or "Hoylake is the home of amateur golf", but it was difficult to accept the loss of status.

It was also difficult not to feel affected in some way by the negative images that grew up around the Liverpool and Merseyside region. This beautiful city, that should have been nothing but a source of pride, became a pariah. The worldwide kudos of producing the Beatles and many other Merseybeat groups, followed by almost 20 years of dominance of English football by Liverpool FC and, briefly, Everton were incredibly strong positives. That the city's image deteriorated so badly in the face of these successes is even sadder.

The trouble with Liverpool's image did not, however, begin only in the 1960s. In retrospect and in the modern politically correct climate it should not be a source of pride that Liverpool's growth was founded on the 'triangle of trade' that took slaves from Africa to America in return for cotton to the mills of Lancashire.

Manchester's later overtaking of Liverpool in the second part of the 19th and first part of the 20th centuries was based on cotton and allied trades and the creation of the Manchester Ship Canal in 1894 was the start of Liverpool's relative decline.

Like many of the great seaports in the world, Liverpool grew by rapid immigration. But density of population meant poverty and disease and right from the start the city's image was not a pretty one. There were riots over food shortages in 1855. Many of the citizens had fled in the 1840s from the potato famine in Ireland and were damned if they were going to go short of food again.

So, even at its foundation, there might have been good reason for the good gentlemen members to refer to their club as 'Hoylake' rather than 'Liverpool', a brand dilemma which remains to this day.

If lack of space was the major cause of Hoylake's move into the shadows, the course remained highly regarded by all who played it. In 1971 Palmer and Jacklin were making a TV series called 'The greatest 18 holes of golf in Britain'. They spent the morning filming at Birkdale and were due at Hoylake for lunch and then to film two of Hoylake's holes – two out of the best 18 isn't bad! The chosen two were the 1st and the 7th, both renowned for their out-of-bounds.

A large crowd of members had gathered in the clubhouse to greet these two heroes. Palmer had been a significant force in turning golf into a worldwide industry. Although he had re-awakened the American interest in The Open from 1960 onwards, he had been

Liverpool's majestic waterfront

unable to play in 1967. This then was his one and only visit to Hoylake. Jacklin was the answer to Britain's sporting prayers and his wins at Lytham in 1969 and in the US Open at Haseltine in 1970 were hugely important in raising interest in the game in this country. He had played in the 1967 Open as a virtual unknown, but was already under Mark McCormack's management. He played his practice rounds in the company of Player and Nicklaus etc and then finished a superb fifth.

The two players arrived in a large limousine which pulled up right outside the front door. They stepped out, still wearing their golf spikes, and into the hallway, which was linoleum-covered in those days, to be greeted with the warmest applause by assembled members. They walked up the carpeted stairs and into the clubroom (still wearing their spikes) and were applauded every step of the way.

If ever there was a demonstration of how far and how fast the image of the golf professional had changed since the immediate post-war years then this was it. Just 20 years previously Henry Cotton had used his car as his changing room, as professionals were not allowed in the clubhouse. What a breakthrough! Spikes in the clubroom and applauded for it.

The two heroes entered the clubroom to be confronted by the best buffet you could wish to see. But – and here's the tribute to Hoylake – they walked around the buffet table to the picture window and Jacklin showed off his local knowledge to Palmer for at least 10 minutes by pointing out the various features of the 1st and other holes on view. Only then did they think of eating.

Liverpool's image had deteriorated yet further as a result of the National Dock Strike of 1966. Whilst other ports returned to work after days or weeks, Liverpool's dockers held out for a whole year. Liverpool's militant image was born. Strikes seemed to be a persistent feature of local life for the next two decades. 'Militant' became the name of a political movement embraced by large parts of the local Labour party. The media had opportunity after opportunity presented to them to show the city, and Merseyside as a whole, in a bad light.

Of course, on the international scene, our local difficulties would hardly have been noticed.

The mention of Liverpool abroad would continue to mean the Beatles and football. But even the latter cause for pride was turned against us with the terrible tragedies in the 80s at the Heysel and Hillsborough stadiums. Liverpool's fans were cruelly portrayed as outright hooligans in the first tragedy and a mindless mob in the second, when dozens of fans were killed by nothing more malicious than an overfilled stadium and inadequate supervision.

The Club had its own problems. There were two major crises. The first occurred in the inflation ravaged mid-1970s and was a product of poor management. The second was a failure by professional employees.

Inflation raged throughout the early 70s and there was reluctance at first to keep subscription levels fully in step. This may well have been born out of the fact that many members – either retired or "of independent means" – were in fact living on fixed incomes that were fast losing their purchasing power and there may have been reluctance to demand inflationary increases to subscriptions.

Whatever the cause costs in 1973, mainly wages, were running way ahead of income and the financial reserves were exhausted. It was also recognised that both the course and clubhouse had received far too little investment for many years.

Eventually the bullet was bitten. Inflation in 1973 was 24%, but subscriptions for full members were raised from £50 to £80 per annum, a 60% increase. There followed a record number of 13 resignations with effect from 1 January 1974.

The finances continued to cause problems and all sorts of ideas were considered. Some members suggested selling the clubhouse and erecting a new one overlooking the Dee estuary, accessed via Pinfold Lane. Another idea was to raise capital by selling Life

Centenary Dinner, 1969. Selwyn Lloyd congratulates Michael Bonallack, winner of the Amateur played at Hoylake that year. Also pictured, from left: Gerald Micklem, Joe Carr, Richard Jones, Dr Bill Tweddell, Alex Kyle

Memberships, but this was rejected after actuarial advice. In fact, Life Memberships had previously been used as a fund-raiser, back in 1910, to help with the purchase of the freehold from Lord Stanley.

However, one revenue-raising imperative was to increase the size of the Club's membership. By word of mouth this was 'advertised' amongst neighbouring clubs and a series of 'extraordinary' Council meetings were held in mid-1975 to elect large numbers of new members.

Ninety-eight members were elected over a seven-month period, nearly all of them in the Full Gentlemen category, which represented a 40% increase to that category. Such an influx was not, however, unprecedented: a recruitment campaign took place in the mid-1930s when failure of the world economy (not just Liverpool's) led to large numbers of resignations followed by a cohort of new members known as the 'hungry hundred' due to the enthusiasm and ambition for social status.

Around the mid-1970s it was also recognised that some of the management problems were caused by a lack of continuity in the leadership of the Council and the Club itself. Each year's Captain had about five months from November to April to "play themselves in" and then took over what was effectively the managing director's job for just 12 months.

Meanwhile, given our prominence in local golfing circles, the Captain had to attend countless dinners and give countless speeches as guest of honour. Although the important role of Honorary Treasurer provided some continuity, it was decided to create a new role of Chairman of Council who would take on the Club management role and leave the Captain to concentrate on his social responsibilities.

The Chairman/Captain shared leadership has been almost entirely positive ever since. The Chairman has generally served for a four-year term and usually been an ex-Captain, but these are guidelines, not rules.

By having a longer-serving Chairman the management of finances and development projects has been much more business-like. Also the supervision and, if necessary, replacement of the senior employees (Secretary, Greenkeeper, House Manager and Professional) has been much better handled.

It was good management, married to happy coincidence, that a series of changes of senior personnel took place from the mid-1980s onwards. John Heggarty took over as Professional from John Morgan in 1981; the House Manager's role, after a few incumbents who had strengths but also some weaknesses, was taken up by Janet McCartney who helped to raise the standard of catering and the image presented to our many guests. Probably most crucial of all, Derek Green became Greenkeeper in 1985 until his tragic death in 2005.

The state of the course had been a long-running problem in the late 1960s and 1970s and outside help was called for in the shape of agronomist Jim Arthur, whose services were paid for in part by the R & A. Although some improvements were made it became clear that the green staff were not being managed well enough to carry out the required work. Derek Green joined us from Woburn, an inland and fairly new course. His arrival led to immediate and visible improvement in the general tidiness of the course and, over the next 20 years, he oversaw the revitalisation of the course to the general delight of members and admiration of visitors. Derek Green became a nationally recognised leader in his field.

With the arrival of Group Captain Chris Moore in the early 1990s, the Club's team of senior employees had been completely replaced in a relatively short space of time. They (and worthy successors as House Managers) have become a major strength that has contributed enormously in lifting us from the relative doldrums of the 1970s and early 1980s.

However easy it was to become negative about Liverpool and its travails, the Club members had little time for pessimism as there was always a sense that things could be better. As much fun was being had on the golf course as ever before and more fun than ever was had in the clubhouse as regular discos, dinners and private parties became the norm compared with the rather stuffy post-war era. A bar downstairs, and the Mixed Lounge, had only been created in 1965. The bar facilities in particular were subject to a series of improvements about once every 10 years. The entrance hall was upgraded twice and the museum displays and honours boards added. The large inner hall had a dance floor under its carpet for some 20 years and this became the focal point of countless happy, indeed merry, evenings. In more innocent and less politically correct times, you might even have called it gay.

In 1969 the Club celebrated its centenary. Being one of the oldest clubs in the world, it was an almost unique event and deserved to be celebrated properly. The year began with a New Year's Eve dance attended by a large number of members. The novelty of such an event is difficult to appreciate now, but it is probably true to say this was the biggest mixed, or indeed unmixed, social event the Club had ever staged. New Year's Eve dances became an annual feature of the social programme. One unfortunate casualty of the big start to the centenary year was the reigning 1968 Captain, John Lawrie, who slipped on the ice in the car park on the way back to his car and broke his leg. John, who was a marvellous golfer and a long-serving R & A committeeman, had a terrible stutter and his telling of the story of how he saw in the centenary year was highly amusing though somewhat protracted.

Chosen to serve as Captain in 1969 was Selwyn Lloyd, the local MP and former Chancellor of the Exchequer, Foreign Secretary and Home Secretary. He subsequently

Overleaf: Secretary Chris Moore tees off from the 10th watched with great interest by fellow club member David Berstock and two Swedish guests

became Speaker of the House of Commons before becoming Lord Selwyn Lloyd of Wirral. He was not a golfer of note in his adult years but he had won the Boys' Medal and he presented a distinguished figurehead for the Club in this important year.

The R & A did us the honour of staging the Amateur here that year. A major celebration dinner was held to which many famous amateur golfers, past and present, were invited, as well as local club captains and other dignitaries.

The Amateur itself culminated in a final between two genuine lifelong amateurs, Michael Bonallack of Thorpe Hall, Essex, and already the winner three times, and Bill Hyndman of USA, aged 45, a competitor for almost 20 years and once a beaten finalist.

Hyndman reached the final by beating a young South African, Dale Hayes, in the semi. Hayes was a prodigiously long hitter and a great future was expected of him.

He did indeed play on the European and South African pro circuits for several years but never really made it to the highest levels, although he has stayed in the golfing limelight as a presenter on South African TV. In one of his earlier rounds, he was being caddied by another young South African. The match reached the 18th and went into extra holes. It was a very hot day and the caddie,

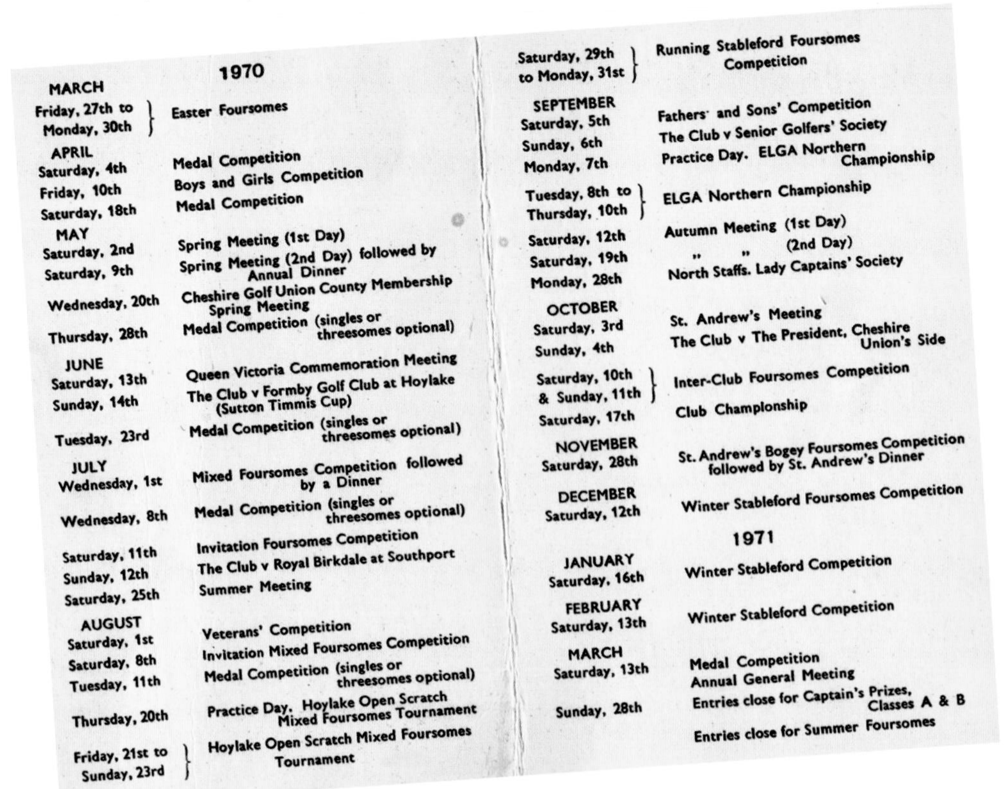

Date	1970
MARCH	
Friday, 27th to Monday, 30th	Easter Foursomes
APRIL	
Saturday, 4th	Medal Competition
Friday, 10th	Boys and Girls Competition
Saturday, 18th	Medal Competition
MAY	
Saturday, 2nd	Spring Meeting (1st Day)
Saturday, 9th	Spring Meeting (2nd Day) followed by Annual Dinner
Wednesday, 20th	Cheshire Golf Union County Membership Spring Meeting
Thursday, 28th	Medal Competition (singles or threesomes optional)
JUNE	
Saturday, 13th	Queen Victoria Commemoration Meeting
Sunday, 14th	The Club v Formby Golf Club at Hoylake (Sutton Timmis Cup)
Tuesday, 23rd	Medal Competition (singles or threesomes optional)
JULY	
Wednesday, 1st	Mixed Foursomes Competition followed by a Dinner
Wednesday, 8th	Medal Competition (singles or threesomes optional)
Saturday, 11th	Invitation Foursomes Competition
Sunday, 12th	The Club v Royal Birkdale at Southport
Saturday, 25th	Summer Meeting
AUGUST	
Saturday, 1st	Veterans' Competition
Saturday, 8th	Invitation Mixed Foursomes Competition
Tuesday, 11th	Medal Competition (singles or threesomes optional)
Thursday, 20th	Practice Day. Hoylake Open Scratch Mixed Foursomes Tournament
Friday, 21st to Sunday, 23rd	Hoylake Open Scratch Mixed Foursomes Tournament
Saturday, 29th to Monday, 31st	Running Stableford Foursomes Competition
SEPTEMBER	
Saturday, 5th	Fathers' and Sons' Competition
Sunday, 6th	The Club v Senior Golfers' Society
Monday, 7th	Practice Day. ELGA Northern Championship
Tuesday, 8th to Thursday, 10th	ELGA Northern Championship
Saturday, 12th	Autumn Meeting (1st Day)
Saturday, 19th	" " (2nd Day)
Monday, 28th	North Staffs. Lady Captains' Society
OCTOBER	
Saturday, 3rd	St. Andrew's Meeting
Sunday, 4th	The Club v The President, Cheshire Union's Side
Saturday, 10th & Sunday, 11th	Inter-Club Foursomes Competition
Saturday, 17th	Club Championship
NOVEMBER	
Saturday, 28th	St. Andrew's Bogey Foursomes Competition followed by St. Andrew's Dinner
DECEMBER	
Saturday, 12th	Winter Stableford Foursomes Competition
	1971
JANUARY	
Saturday, 16th	Winter Stableford Competition
FEBRUARY	
Saturday, 13th	Winter Stableford Competition
MARCH	
Saturday, 13th	Medal Competition Annual General Meeting Entries close for Captain's Prizes, Classes A & B
Sunday, 28th	Entries close for Summer Foursomes

The fixture card 1970-71. Rather less busy than today

although an accomplished golfer, was obviously not an experienced caddie. He needed a drink, or some other comfort, and marched off the 18th green to the clubhouse carrying the bag but leaving only the No 1 wood on the 19th tee. Hayes was compelled to use his driver. Unable to hit a four or five iron down the middle of the fairway, he took aim straight over the out-of-bounds and carried it to finish halfway up the second part of the dog-leg. This shot went down in the folklore of Hoylake and earned him his semi-final place. However, the veteran Hyndman saw him off three and two the next day.

In the 36-hole final Bonallack was always in control. Hyndman's age may have caught up on him and dulled his game slightly. Bonallack won three and two, to retain the title that he had won at Troon the previous year and he would win again in 1970 at Newcastle, Royal County Down, once more beating poor Hyndman in the final. This was the only occurrence of a repeat final in successive years although back in 1888 and 1890 our own John Ball twice beat Johnnie Laidlay. After a few more years at the top of the amateur game Bonallack retired from competitive golf and in 1984 moved on to become Secretary of the R & A for many years.

In 1975 the Amateur returned. This was a year when the Walker Cup was played in Great Britain and, by tradition, all the USA side were competing.

It had virtually become a tradition, too, that one of them won it: 1951 RD Chapman; 1955 JW Conrad; 1959 Dean Beman beat Bill Hyndman; 1963 was an exception when Britain's Michael Lunt beat John Blackwell. In 1967 Bob Dickson beat team mate Ron Cerrudo at Formby; and in 1971 Steve Melnyk beat team-mate Jim Simons, who had beaten one Tom Kite in the semi-final. The tradition would continue in 1979 when Jay Sigel beat Scott Hoch.

The 1975 USA team included three future major stars in Craig Stadler, Curtis Strange and Jay Haas as well as other lesser lights like Jerry Pate. Also in the team, 24 years after his first Cup appearance was 'Big' Bill Campbell who was to become one of the very few American Captains of the R & A.

None of these luminaries, however, reached the latter stages of the Amateur, but Stadler left behind a reputation on two fronts. Firstly, his prodigious hitting, which was reputed to include a drive at the 8th which carried the cross sand hills. Secondly, a less than sunny personality, which resulted in his caddie throwing down his bag and storming off the course with a string of expletives.

The final turned out to be a battle between the home and away Walker Cup teams. The GB & I representative, destined to go on to be the most famous member of the team by far, was Mark James. In the semi-final he beat Geoff Marks, twice before a Walker Cup player but not in 1975, by three and two. In the other semi, Marvin (Vinny) Giles III, who

Above top: 1986 John Behrend tees off as Captain of the R & A

Above: Awarding the caddy who claimed his drive, John Behrend claimed two firsts: he had a practice swing, and was the first Captain to 'drive in' without wearing a tie(!)

Opposite: All holes have names. The 16th is named after the Club's third Captain, John Dun

was making his fourth successive Cup appearance, beat team-mate Dick Siderowf who was to play in four Walker Cup matches.

The final was played on a lovely June day. Unfortunately for James the weather was also just right for creating a high pollen count and he suffered dreadfully all day with hay fever. He was famous for his hang-dog expression and matching gait and they were much in evidence, particularly in the afternoon.

After 18 holes Giles was two up: on the 19th James played much the better second shot to find the green whilst Giles was mid-fairway but about 10 yards short. Giles' running chip hit the flag and dropped in and he whooped and pirouetted with delight.

James was not able to hole his putt and what had looked like a possible one down had become three down. Thereafter the force was with Vinny Giles who pulled away to win eight and seven.

Our Captain who presented the Amateur trophy was Vernon Sangster. He had founded one of Liverpool's two hugely successful football pools companies, Vernons. He was our oldest Captain ever, and his best golfing days well gone, but he was a charming man who was very generous to the Club during some of its darkest financial hours.

1985 marked the centenary of the first Amateur, which had of course been at Hoylake in April 1885. Although we did not host the Amateur in 1985, it was decided to celebrate the centenary by inviting many distinguished golfers to play in our own Spring Meeting and attend the Spring Dinner on 27 April.

Among the guests were the Presidents of the Golf Unions of England, Wales, Ireland and South Africa, the Captains of 25 other clubs that had hosted the Amateur, the captains of many local clubs who would normally attend our Spring Dinner, and 10 former winners who had

ROYAL LIVERPOOL GOLF CLUB
FAR
SURE
AND
Dun
16
460
YARDS
LGU

won the title 17 times between them: Michael Bonallack (5), Joe Carr (3), Trevor Homer (2), plus Count de Bendern (known as John De Forrest when he won in 1932), Charlie Yates (USA), Doug Bachli (Australia), John Beharrell, Michael Lunt, Gordon Clark and Duncan Evans (all once each). There was also a suitably large representation from the R & A including several past captains of whom Gerald Micklem was the most famous, and their current Captain who was Hoylake's own John Behrend.

Behrend could claim to be our most distinguished member since Ball and Hilton. Although not quite getting a Blue, as a Dinner Match (first reserve) player he became a stalwart of the Oxford and Cambridge Golf Society and played with distinction in the President's Putter at Rye for many years. He won the Worplesdon Foursomes with Jessie Valentine three times in the early 60s, played for Cheshire for years, was President of Cheshire, Captain of RLGC in 1976, served on various R & A committees, wrote several golf books including the history of the R & A for its own 250th anniversary, and in 1984 became Hoylake's only modern-era Captain of the R & A.

At the R & A's customary ceremony, where the incoming Captain 'drives himself in' off the first tee and the local caddies have a competition to retrieve the ball and be rewarded with a medal for themselves, John managed to create a unique humorous moment. As the Captain's first shot is struck, a cannon is fired from some 20 yards away – in a safe direction. John, however, decided to take a practice swing that had not been rehearsed with the cannon-firer. Off went the cannon, there was a moment's stunned silence and then several minutes of laughter all round. He had to wait while the gun was reloaded before being able to truly drive in. Another, unique at the time, feature of this ceremony was that 'JB' was the first to drive in without wearing a tie.

Other leading amateur events during this period included the English Amateur Strokeplay Championship (the Brabazon Trophy) twice. In 1972 this was won by Peter Moody, a Cambridge Blue and England international, and in 1977 the winner was Sandy Lyle, then aged 20.

Three years earlier Lyle, from Hawkstone Park in Shropshire, had been favourite for the British Boys' Championship when it was held for the first time at Hoylake. He did reach the final but lost surprisingly to Toby Shannon. Of course it was Lyle who went on to great things whereas Shannon was not really heard of again.

Also paying his first visit to Hoylake in that event was Nick Faldo. He had only taken up the game four years earlier and his speedy rise to the top of the Boys' ranks was very much noticed by the R & A officials and English selectors, so he attracted much attention. He got through a few rounds of matchplay before being beaten by Lyle in the quarter-final.

The English Amateur of 1982 was only the third staging of that event at Hoylake since the first one was held there in 1925 (and won by T Froes Ellison of the home club). The winner this time was Andrew Oldcorn, who went on to play on the European Tour for a couple of decades with a fair amount of success. However, the event was more notorious because it was being played 12 months before the Walker Cup was due at Hoylake and the

Opposite top: Sandy Lyle, winner of the Brabazon Trophy, 1977

Opposite below: Sandy Lyle, runner-up in the 1974 Boys' Amateur Championship, being presented by John Turner. Nick Faldo pictured to the right

Left: Walker Cup 1983. The green's not in the greatest shape course was in a very poor state. In particular, a fungus had affected many of the greens, leaving large bare, brown, patches and the R & A were giving serious thought to moving the Walker Cup away. Fortunately we were reprieved by some fine spring weather. Within a few years the greenkeeper had been changed and the condition of the course improved and improved thereafter.

The 1983 Walker Cup was a delightful event to host. The players, officials and supporters from both sides mingled with each other and with Club members over the week that they were at Hoylake. The match was played in true old-fashioned spirit and the medium-sized crowds that came were, by definition, all golf enthusiasts who knew how to behave.

From the days up to the 60s when there were always several top amateurs on either side (Bonallack, Carr, Hyndman, Campbell etc in more recent years) we had reached the era when the sides were predominantly youngsters who hoped to progress to the professional ranks.

The USA side, to be fair, had four of their 10 players in their 30s with their Playing Captain (quite a rarity in these matches) Jay Sigel being the eldest at 39. Great Britain & Ireland had only two, George McGregor at 38 being six years older than the next most senior, Arthur Pierse of Ireland.

Of the USA side (apart from Sigel who actually turned professional for a short while to play on the US Seniors Tour) the most famous names were Nathaniel Crosby, youngest son of golf-mad Bing, who unfortunately died before being able to see his son represent his country, and Brad Faxon who became one of those best players never to have won a major. Of the GB & I side, there was Oldcorn, Philip Walton who went on to European Tour success and won a crucial singles in the European Ryder Cup win of 1995, and Philip Parkin who, though not quite living up to high expectations on the Tour, has become a respected commentator for Sky television.

The Cup was tighter throughout than the final score of 13½-10½ to the USA might suggest.

On the domestic front, the Club produced a regular stream of Cheshire players – and many other county level golfers joined RLGC as their second club. None of our men rose to international level, however in Audrey Briggs we had a Welsh champion and long-standing international.

Through Audrey's marketing efforts the Hoylake Open Scratch Mixed Foursomes in the early days attracted substantial numbers of lady internationals from all the home countries, and a few male internationals as well. The event remains one of the top mixed foursome events in the calendar.

Such was the enthusiasm for the mixed game – and the off-course social aspects – that the Squirrels (rhymes with Wirral) Golf Society was formed in 1972 to allow participants from the Hoylake Open Scratch Mixed Foursomes, and others of lesser golfing ability, to meet for mixed foursome golf at various venues around the country but at least annually at Hoylake.

The leading light of the Squirrels was Donald Turner, a single figure golfer of no mean ability in his prime, but definitely a scratch party animal. Donald was one of those people who enlivened every room he walked into and it was a sad loss for the Club that he had to resign in the early 1980s when his business affairs went wrong. His health declined and he became seriously ill. He was re-admitted as a member in 1990 but died the following year.

In 1975 there was an occurrence unique in the Club's history when Audrey Briggs and Robin Biggs won their respective Cheshire Championships.

Before the large increase in membership in 1975, on non-competition days at the weekends the number of golfers playing was very small. One could almost expect to turn up at the Club and walk onto the first tee on any Saturday or Sunday morning. There was no objection, therefore, and no difficulty in block-booking the starting times, when

Amateur Championship Centenary, May 1985. Standing, from left: Gordon Clark, Duncan Evans, Trevor Homer, Michael Lunt, John Beharrell. Seated: Joe Carr, John de Benders, Doug Bachli and Michael Bonallack

the Winter League was formed in 1967 to give the better players in the Club a regular weekly reason to play through the winter months. The Winter League was run for many years on an all-play-all basis. It is still going strong though the format has changed on a number of occasions.

For the first 20 years of its existence the League was organised and managed by John Howard. A Cheshire player, originally based at Wallasey, John was a true golf enthusiast, particularly with regard to technique and equipment. Any conversation with John would soon turn to his latest theory for taking two shots off his game, or adding 20 yards to his drives. He spent many long but happy hours on the practice ground and probably, over his lifetime, single-handedly removed its entire surface at least once.

Another advantage of the lightly-used course was that it was much easier to "cut across" and miss out parts of the course. The 8th and 9th were as much underused as the 17th and 18th during the winter; or a group could play the first four holes then "cut across" to the 12th.

This shortening of the course suited many of the older members, and it also meant that it was much easier to fit in an 'extra nine' in the afternoon after a morning round and a longish lunch. Another way to shorten the trip back to the clubhouse was to play a hole or two backwards. Thus, one might play the first 11 holes and then, subject to no traffic in the correct direction, play down the 3rd fairway aiming to hole out on the 14th green. From there the last hole of the day might be across the rough to the first fairway and holing out on the practice putting green to a nominated hole or any hole according to choice.

One of our elder members, Bill 'Basher' Hayes was reckoned to have played more holes backwards than forwards. He would often go out on a quiet Saturday or Sunday afternoon to play a few holes on his own; then he would find a two- or three-ball to attach himself to and would soon have them following his eccentric habits and inventing new cross-country holes!

A further entertainment on quiet days, or in the early evening when serious medal play was ended, was to play one-club golf for two very long holes: firstly from the 1st tee to the furthest extremity of the course to hole out on the 8th green – and then back to hole out on the practice putting green. This could be played as singles (with any number of players) or as a team game (again, with any number of participants) with each team member having to play in strict order, even if that meant trying to extricate from a bunker with a driver or putter!

Finally, in the fun golf category, mention should be made of Operation Speed. This was a competition played several times in the mid-70s to see how fast a single ball could be

Leisure Craft
Leisure Craft
Leisure Craft
Leisure Craft
Leisure Craft

CLASSIC
2004

propelled around the course, using a large team of golfers, some of whom had to be young enough to run! Having played the game amongst ourselves, just against the clock, there were then a series of challenges against local clubs Caldy and Heswall (home and away) and a telephone challenge against the Guinness Book of Records world record holders, Titirangi of New Zealand. The All Blacks won easily but Hoylakers like to think the New Zealanders played a much easier course.

Only one European Tour event was played during this era, the European Open of 1981. As its name implies it was, after its origin at Walton Heath in 1979, regarded as one of the highlights of the tour's year. In those days many more of their events were played on GB & I soil. Brian Waites, a late developer at the game, set a course record of 64 but the contest came down to a battle between Graham Marsh of Australia and Spain's Seve Ballesteros. Graham Marsh, younger brother of the Australian cricket wicket-keeper Rodney, played the last few holes a couple of shots better than Ballesteros and came from one behind to win by one.

In the locker room afterwards, no doubt thinking he was on his own, Seve was seen and heard by a passing member to be kicking the locker doors and using his most expressive Spanish to castigate himself and his brother Baldo who had just been caddying for him.

At the same time as the Club was enjoying its professional exposure, the 1970s and 80s saw Liverpool experience one of its darkest hours with the Toxteth riots.

The riots represented a clear low point. Margaret Thatcher appointed Michael Heseltine as Minister for Merseyside, but more significantly in the long run she also created the Merseyside Development Corporation (MDC) – a quango which enabled government money to be poured into the region without having to go through the hands of the demonised Liverpool City Council or

Opposite: Young members in preparation for the Easter Foursomes. From left: Kenham Cornwall-Legh, Kim Pinnington and Nicky Beazley in the clubhouse

Merseyside County Council. It was the MDC who compulsorily purchased the south docks area and started the regeneration process.

The Club continued its slow improvement.

One contributory factor, originally conceived as a fund-raiser but now seen as an essential piece of public relations each year, was the first annual brochure in 1986. Then, as now, advertisers were rewarded by bringing guests to a Company Day in September. The brochure has become a high-quality, colourful production, recording major events, as well as giving visitors a welcome, a guide to our facilities and a memento to take away.

Many members have demonstrated their literary talents in the brochure over the years, none more so than John Behrend and John Graham (Jnr) who were encouraged to write several books between them. The fact that the Year Book, as it has now become known, has always made a profit for the Club is an added bonus. The 19 editions up to the publication of this book have proved an indispensable mine of information.

An era had passed. Liverpool, and The Royal Liverpool Golf Club, knew that there were still many more steps on the road to restoring its image, but the future was certainly looking brighter for both of them.

Speed Golf 1971. The team pictured includes eight future Captains of The Royal Liverpool

Four Ball or Foursome?

It was the early tradition that golf was a two ball game and that was, and still is, the format at most of the other great clubs in the country. So why have we also played four ball games at Hoylake?

Michael Pearson informs me that four ball play has certainly, since World War II, been the favoured method of playing on a Saturday afternoon and Sunday morning. Now, there is little wrong with a four ball as long as the players understand what they are playing.

The reasons are quite simple. Most golfers felt that "as I am only playing once a week (certainly in the winter) I wish to play 'my own ball'". Also, a good competitive four ball match is the greatest of fun.

Many sympathise with the two ball game, but unless the whole field plays at that speed it will be chaos as four-ballers will naturally be slower. There is little reason for slow play when playing four balls if all golfers adhere to some simple but firm practice.

Four ball golf produces all sorts of characters. Though it will seem slightly self-indulgent to name too many who play on a Sunday morning, I should mention those who tee off in the winter dark, namely Peter Canevali, Brian Gourley, Gerry Maxwell, Carrick Peters and Keith Dodman, who have been joined by Peter Smith, Tony Aldwinckle and Mike Brabner, amongst others. They play their own form of golf and I am never too sure if they are enjoying the golf as much as they do tucking into the champagne as soon as they finish play.

The picnic lot follow, with Tom Ellison, Paul Griffies and Malcolm Clark, amongst others, never allowing their minimum of three stops to hamper their progress on the course.

The advent of the 8.36 am golfers was by chance. David Beazley and I were approached by Pat Healy when the starters came into operation in 1992. We used to tee off at the 8th hole and arrive at the 1st just before the frostbite started at 10.30 am. Pat would have none of this: "You will play at a proper time. Do you want to play before or after us?" Quick as a flash, Beazley elected before. So, from that moment onwards, we teed off in front of Pat and his men at 8.36 am. Michael Groves and Kieran O'Brien joined us, quickly followed by many others, an open band of members. Pat Healey's men follow, now marshalled by Tom Wynne.

Chapter Sixteen

16th hole

Roberto de Vicenzo: Essay to a Champion

The saddest thing of all is how the world at large will remember Roberto de Vicenzo.

At Hoylake, where he is loved, worshipped and admired in equal measure, he will always be the man who won the 1967 Open on The Royal Liverpool links. In his native Argentina de Vicenzo is feted alongside Maradona and Guillermo Vilas as the greatest sportsmen that proud nation has produced.

But to the rest of a cold-eyed world which feasts and dwells on the cruel and quirky, Roberto de Vicenzo will always be the man who lost the Masters in the most heartbreaking of circumstances. His playing partner Tommy Aaron mistakenly marked him down for a four instead of his birdie three at the penultimate hole, and when de Vicenzo signed his card without spotting the error he was penalised one shot. The Argentinian therefore missed out by just one stroke to Bob Goalby.

Everyone who loves golf will recall his famous remark: "What a stupid I am!" Only those who know the depth and excellence of this remarkable man will appreciate the context. What he said was this: "I am so unhappy to make five on the last hole, and Bob, he gave me so much pressure on the last hole that I lose my brain.

"I play golf all over the world for 30 years, and now all I can think of is what a stupid I am to be wrong in this wonderful tournament. Never have I ever done such a thing before. Maybe I am too old to win."

No pity, just humility, humour and a true understanding that the game is always bigger than the individual.

It is the man, not the golfer, that Hoylake loves most, and every member of a certain age will have a de Vicenzo tale to tell.

De Vicenzo first played The Open in 1948 and consistently performed well in the tournament. But as the years slipped by it seemed he was destined never to lift one of the game's greatest prizes. At Muirfield in '48, he finished third, while two years later he was runner-up to Bobby Locke at Troon. Thereafter there were numerous top six finishes.

Left: Roberto de Vicenzo back at Hoylake in 2000, while Philip Stern looks on in admiration

Then came Hoylake, and rounds of 70, 71, 67, 70 to beat off the challenge of the mighty Nicklaus by two strokes and give the man from Buenos Aires his first major title at the age of 44. In doing so he became the oldest winner of The Open Championship in modern times.

That day, behind the statistics, beat a heart like a lion in the body of a man who stood up and seized the day. He had watched Nicklaus birdie the 16th in the group ahead of him. He knew he needed a four, too. With the eyes of the world on him he hit a magnificently bold three wood second over Hoylake's graveyard of an out-of-bounds and onto the green. The birdie duly followed.

His playing partner was Gary Player. In a gesture of goodwill to a great champion we'll say he was trying to help when he said to de Vicenzo on the 17th tee: "Well, Roberto, The Open Championship's yours now."

"Oh, my God," was the best reply de Vicenzo could manage. With immortality beckoning he threw down his ball on the 17th tee. No tee peg. Nothing, he was to say later, would he allow to come between his club head and the ball at this seminal moment. He struck a true three wood up 17 and parred home. As he walked down 17 people were literally weeping with joy. He was that popular. That special. Nicklaus was awesome. Player

TORO

tenacious. Jacklin the golden boy. But the one the crowds loved was Roberto.

Victory was as self-effacing, as gentle, as the man himself. He'd stayed the week with a club member, Roy Smith, the pair having struck up a friendship through Smith's business interests in South America. As he left the Club as Open Champion, he flung an arm round Smith's shoulder and said: "Amigo, I only came here to see my friends and I've ended up winning the bloody Championship!"

The great man came back to Hoylake in 1981 for the European Open and was made an honorary member of the Club. He returned in 2000 when he played a memorable challenge match with Sam Snead, Jacklin and Sandy Lyle. What is not as well-documented is the practice round he played the day before the four ball: aged 77, de Vicenzo hit all four par-fives in two.

That day, he stood in the back of Hoylake pro John Heggarty's shop and talked golf with the other three great champions. Lyle and Jacklin began talking technique and Jacklin quizzed the Scot on the position of his hands at the top of his backswing. After 10 minutes, Roberto, one of the most natural golfers the world has seen, could stand it no longer. "You kids," he exploded, waving a finger at ex-Open Champions Jacklin (in his 50s) and Lyle (in his 40s), "you talk a lot of sh** about swing planes and hand positions and stuff. I tell you the only thing that matters – the six f***ing inches before you hit the ball and the six f***ing inches afterwards."

In Argentina, de Vicenzo remains a legend. In 2003, two Hoylake members were invited to his 80th birthday celebration in Buenos Aires. They arrived to find a guest list from the Who's Who of Argentinian sport, entertainment and politics. The former President, Carlos Menem, was there. So was World Cup winning footballer Ossie Ardiles, the tennis greats Vilas and Sabbatini. Each

1960

On occasion Fairbrother used the legendary caddy Campbell. Requiring a club, Campbell handed him a seven iron, all he managed was to scuff the ball left of the green. "Why did you give me a seven iron, I missed the green?"

"It wouldn't have made any difference if I'd given you an effing umbrella Mr Fairbrother."

In the early 60s, as the Wallasey club was distinctly unsure of its future as the lease with the local council was due to run out, over 80 members joined The Royal Liverpool Golf Club.

Wallasey's most famous son, Dr Frank Stableford, had been a member of Hoylake for years but amongst the new intake were Malcolm Fairbrother, who reserved his greatest laugh for his own jokes, and Woodley Benson, both great characters.

Malcolm, after a hole-in-one, went to professional John Heggarty for a lesson. Heggarty looked quizzically at him and remarked that he believed that he had just aced the 13th hole! "But" said Malcolm "it only just went in."

Opposite: Mowing the fairways. Golf course maintenance equipment is now of the highest standard, essential as over 40,000 rounds of golf are played annually on The Royal Liverpool course alone of them approached Roberto with awe, shook his huge hand and uttered the same word of greeting: "Maestro."

The "Maestro" it is estimated, won 230 tournaments worldwide in his career. As a striker of a ball he was unmatchable; his game only blighted by persistent problems with the yips when he had a putter in his hand.

Golf Digest described his swing as "drowsy and surprisingly powerful. A very solid ball striker who kept mechanical thoughts to a minimum." Lee Trevino was typically less po-faced. SuperMex said: "to me only three players have looked entirely natural swinging a golf club – Christy O'Connor, Roberto de Vicenzo and Neil Coles."

Always, always though, golfing genius second, nice guy first. He once won an American tournament, and after receiving the cheque and smiling for the cameras, he walked alone to his car and was approached by a young woman. She congratulated him on his victory and then told him that her child was seriously ill and near death.

De Vicenzo was touched by her story and took out a pen and signed his winner's cheque over to the woman. "Make some good days to the baby," he said in his characteristic broken English as he pressed the cheque into her hand.

The next week he was having lunch in a country club when a USPGA official came to his table. "Some of the guys in the parking lot last week told me you met a young woman there after you won the tournament." De Vicenzo nodded. "Well," said the official, "I have news for you. She's a phoney. She's not married. She has no sick baby. She fleeced you, my friend."

"You mean there is no baby who is dying?" said de Vicenzo. "That's right."

"That's the best news I heard all week," said de Vicenzo.

Hoylake. 15 July 1967. To everyone at Royal Liverpool it will always be the day the nice guy came first.

Chapter Seventeen

17th hole

The Return of The Open Championship

By 1987 there was a more positive mood to the Club. Economic recovery was evident and wealth was beginning to spread throughout the land. Reduced taxes at the higher level meant that there was more disposable income and one of the sports that benefited was golf, with extra revenue coming into clubs. Those intent on leisure found themselves, in many cases, with the money to indulge their hobbies. At the Club, a new generation was making itself known. It was a generation that had not known war, just a little austerity and rationing. In 1988, Nicko Williams, then in his late 40s, became Captain, followed the year after by Tim Marshall, son of Michael, so making three generations of the same family to captain Hoylake (his grandfather Roland was in office in 1935).

Nicko's enthusiasm was infectious. A new links manager, Derek Green, had been appointed a few years earlier and had transformed the course in a short time.

The company days followed and added to the efforts of members, who were working hard for the Club and income started to increase. But Hoylake was still not enjoying the revenue from overseas visitors in the same way as Birkdale and Lytham, who regularly hosted The Open Championship.

The new yearbook, however, was promoting the Club to a wider audience. Not only did it bring in much-needed revenue but it awoke literary skills in some of the members, none more so than John Graham (Jnr) and John Behrend. Behrend was already making a name for himself with some of his own specialist writings, including that marvellous book *John Ball of Hoylake* and, latterly, with *Challenges & Champions* (the history of the Royal & Ancient Golf Club from 1754 to 1883, written in conjunction with Peter Lewis).

John Graham (Jnr), with his deep knowledge of Hoylake made some telling contributions. I particularly like his first offering in the 1988 edition. Reminiscing on his first 60 years of golf at Hoylake he mentioned the equipment. Graham observed that since the inception of

iron-shafted clubs in the early 1930s little had changed! Little did he or we know what was about to happen to our golfing equipment.

Since his remarks every aspect of the game has changed. The ball now flies further, the woods, or should I say metals, have made the game so much easier for the average club golfer and have actually extended their playing lives. A poorly struck shot can have an acceptable conclusion. This is fine for the club golfer, but the top players are making many courses little more than a drive and a short iron to the green.

In the 1970s the position of Chairman was created. There were two reasons for this: the Captain in the Centenary year was the Rt Hon Selwyn Lloyd MP, an eminent politician who just could not make all the Council and other meetings that took place, let alone all the speeches that are required of an RLGC Captain. Further, it was decided that the proper way to run a club was not on a yearly basis with an annual change of the key decision-maker. The Chairman's role provided much-needed continuity and essential strategy. So, after lengthy discussion among senior members, the first Chairman of the Club took office in 1974 – a former Captain, Michael Marshall – a most consorpiant choice. I make no apologies for the use of 'consorpiant' – the eloquent Marshall never did. It means, in Marshallese, 'just perfect'; his legacy to the English language.

We have continued with the Chairman philosophy ever since and I believe it is the best way to secure the future of our Club. There must be continuity and the next generation must be allowed to take the reins.

With this new-found continuity, progress was being made, slowly for sure, but progress nonetheless. We still had financial problems but there was now a platform to progress. By 1989 there were rumblings within the Club that the Hoylake of old was awakening and mention was made, if only quietly, of The Open returning. Joe Maxwell, who was Chairman of the Club at the time, referred to this in the Club brochure of 1988. I say he mentioned The Open, but almost as an afterthought. It was still only a dream and was not spoken about with belief.

The good news was that after the British Ladies' Championship that year it was announced that the Curtis Cup would be played at Hoylake in 1992, and what an event that turned out to be! Played over two days, day one was awful – rain, thunder, the lot! On day two the skies cleared and what a wonderful contest unfurled. The outcome depended on the last putt on the last green and it secured victory for the Great Britain & Ireland team.

Both sides were delightful, true sportswomen, smartly dressed, and a pleasure to meet; no one more so than the American Captain, Judy Oliver. Elegance personified and dignified in defeat. I can see her now, as the winning putt was holed by the home team. She gracefully arose from her sitting position next to the green, took off her hat and warmly congratulated Liz Boatman the GB & I Team Captain and all the team members. Judy had style. And in Liz Boatman the GB & I team had a charming and skilful Captain. But graciousness in defeat is never easy and when Judy visited the Club some years later I mentioned this moment to her. She thanked me and expressed relief that her real feelings had been contained. I assured her that she appeared in total control. She smiled. It was with the greatest sadness that we learnt of her early death in 2002. She holds a special place in the hearts of many Hoylake members, a sheer delight. God takes His petals.

After a 20-year break the Amateur was played again in 1995 at Hoylake – the 100th playing of the event first played for on these links in 1885. The winner was Gordon Sherry, for whom great deeds were predicted. Unfortunately, not long after he suffered health problems and to date has not achieved the success his ability promised. It demonstrates the fine line between success and failure in the game of golf. In that Championship other notable players of the future included Ryder Cup men Padraig Harrington and David Howell, both completely outshone by Sherry.

There were many compliments about the course. A number of Americans who had not been fully aware of Hoylake were overwhelmed at the standard of the links. "Why don't they play more great events here?" "This is a sensational course," and other comments of

Preceding page: John Graham (Jnr) from a painting by Nancy Metcalfe. The Graham family have been part of the Hoylake golfing fraternity from the very early days

Left: The old 7th with the Cop (a local word for bank) stretching down the right side: anything over was out-of-bounds. This caused such controversy that a new approach was designed and out-of-bounds abolished in 1993 similar praise were common. These comments rather took the breath away, but certainly restored a little extra self-confidence. I remember that wonderful golf writer, the greatly missed Michael Williams, writing in the *Daily Telegraph* commented that: "Hoylake's fairways, greens and bunkers are in wonderful shape, the wind was brisk from the west and the waving rough menacing to anything other than a properly struck shot. What a day it would have been, if the clock could have been turned back, for The Open Championship." John Hopkins of *The Times* was equally complimentary. For Hopkins, the words of praise were the beginnings of wholehearted support that would lead to the announcement of The Open returning to Hoylake.

To celebrate the Centenary Amateur a dinner took place attended by our new Patron – His Royal Highness, The Duke of York. It was a splendid affair with speeches from former amateur winners, the great Joe Carr and Michael Bonallack, who were made honorary members on the night by the Captain, Nick Wainwright, who kept the evening going with his telling wit and legendary enthusiasm. There was little doubt as our guests headed for home that Hoylake had taken a small but significant stride forward for the first time in many years. There was once again positive reaction to the links of The Royal Liverpool Golf Club.

Right: The 1995 Amateur Dinner, the great and the good. From left: John Graham (Jnr), Michael Marshall, Gordon Jeffreys (Captain of the R & A) Alan Waterworth (Lord Lieutenant of Merseyside), Councillor Sidney Dunn, Mayor of Wirral, Nicholas Wainwright (Captain of RLGC), HRH The Duke of York, Joe Carr, Michael Bonallack, Anthony Shone

In 1996, Anthony Shone was appointed Chairman of the Championship Committee by the new Club Chairman, Tim White. Between them they had seen the ups and downs of Hoylake since the 1950s, so were well placed to gauge the situation. Tim White was Chairman of Council until he was succeeded by Gerry Maxwell, in March 1997, and then by Nicko Williams in March 2001. During their periods in office major events important to regaining The Open would be concluded.

For the Club to make an Open possible the major problems were finding sufficient space for the hospitality areas and a large enough practice range area. Finding that amount of space was not easy to resolve, but resolved it was, albeit slowly. In May 1995 the Club became aware that land alongside Meols Drive might become available. The Club's Championship Committee sought approval from Council to start the information gathering process to enable a bid to be made for The Open Championship.

In January 1996 we learnt that a company had been appointed by the receivers to dispose of the Leas School site and in March Council re-assessed the Club's position and sought and obtained a suitable loan facility from its bankers to support a possible purchase. The site was divided into an area for housing with the balance of 8.5 acres to be treated as green belt. In November a developer made an offer to acquire the development land subject to planning and RLGC was offered an option to acquire the green belt portion. Early in 1997 the Club made a verbal offer and in October that year contracts were exchanged, though there were numerous delays ahead of completion, particularly caused by a Public Inquiry, to be held in July 1998. Eventually, in December 1998, the Inspector's report was placed before the Secretary of State and in January 1999 the planning proposal was approved. The developer then required planning permission approval for their development but, finally, on 27 August 1999, the contract was completed and the Club became the owners of the Leas Green Belt site. It had taken four years for a possibility to become a reality.

While all this was going on, the opportunity arose for the Club to increase its space further. Hoylake Conservative Club was considering the sale of its bowling green and car park. Negotiations with them were concluded satisfactorily, with the help of the members, an external loan and the use of available Club resources. The Club could now extend its car park and possibly its putting green area, once again providing better facilities for a club with ambitions to host The Open.

These two acquisitions demonstrated to the R & A Championship Committee that we had solved one of the major problems of having the space to stage an Open and, by then, we had opened discussions with Wirral Borough Council for the provision of Open practice facilities on the nearby Hoylake municipal golf course.

Ahead of these developments, the increase in housing alongside the Meols Drive boundary with the links had created playing difficulties. In January 1995 some of the property owners alongside the 8th fairway had complained of golf balls landing in their grounds and a 30-ft fence was planned. The planning authorities rejected this and, in 1996, mounds were developed to direct the drive away from the boundary. It was substantially effective. The 7th hole was also reviewed and in the latter part of 1998 was redesigned.

Following the successful staging of the 100th Amateur in 1995, the Ladies' British Open Amateur in 1996 and the English Amateur in 1997, by April 1998 there was positive interest in Hoylake as an Open venue. In a letter to us the R & A highlighted a number of potential problems for the Club were we to hold The Open, but their interest was strong enough to make the Club look at every part of the links and the facilities needed. Following visits from the R & A early in 1999 a report was prepared on RLGC as an Open venue resulting in consultation over preliminary course changes.

Brian Gourley once again became Chairman of the Green Committee in 1999 and in June of that year his committee decided that a five-year plan should be obtained from two course architects with an Open in mind.

The plan submitted by Donald Steel was accepted, with the major changes being the re-siting of the 3rd and 17th greens. Our willingness to change the links was vital if we were to attract an Open. The changes in the links opened up space. They created more room for tented accommodation, spectator stands and sponsor facilities as well as allowing for easier movement of spectators around the course. So, when the R & A Championship Committee Chairman visited Hoylake in August 1999 he became much more interested in the idea of The Open's return to the links.

Above: Michael Bonallack in his prime. He won his third consecutive Amateur at Hoylake in our centenary year – 1969

Overleaf: The view out to the Irish Sea will have looked somewhat different for Michael Bonallack

In the latter part of 1999 a concerted effort was made to ensure interested parties were prepared to pledge support. In December we met the Wirral Borough Council and Merseyside Passenger Transport Authority, both of whom were key players. Their general and enthusiastic support was confirmed and, with Hoylake already named as the venue for the 2000 Amateur, a groundswell towards The Open's return was evident. In February and April of 2000 the R & A, RLGC and Wirral Borough Council met with the staging of The Open on the agenda. Confidence was strengthening and just after the April meeting the R & A Championship Committee walked the course to inspect the changes to be made to the links.

The Club then learnt that the Championship Committee of the R & A was at the final stage of considering Hoylake as an Open venue and Council at its monthly meeting was unanimous that the offer, if made, would be accepted.

In June, the R & A set down the conditions to be met. Principally these were that suitable practice facilities were provided at the municipal course, that adequate car parking was available within four miles of the course, that Wirral Borough Council would provide infrastructure assistance and, finally, that the Club implemented the changes to the links in accordance with the agreed plans.

Curtis Cup 1992. The flowers were placed in the urinals, 'due deference' being shown to the British ladies who were obliged to make use of the gentlemen's changing rooms

Practice facilities at the municipal course were vital as the Club's own facilities were insufficient. Using an area of the municipal course freed up our practice ground for public amenities and stands. This required significant changes to two holes on the municipal course, providing a teeing area of adequate height and size and a suitable chipping green, together with watering and drainage systems. The closure of the railway line between Hoylake and West Kirby had to be agreed with the Mersey Public Transport Authority so that players had constant access across the line to the practice ground. This would not be possible with trains every 15 minutes in both directions.

By the end of July 2000 Wirral Borough Council had confirmed their commitment, the availability of 18,000 car parking spaces, and the provision of suitable practice facilities at the municipal course.

In October 2000, Gerry Maxwell, the Chairman of Council, travelled to St Andrews to meet Peter Dawson, the Secretary of the R & A. At that meeting Peter Dawson advised that the R & A proposed to announce that RLGC was to be placed on the list of venues for The Open. They would not decide on a date yet. Funds to help with changes to the links were confirmed.

And now a further problem reared its head. The owner of the Leas site had retained a one-acre plot adjacent to the Greenkeeper's cottage and the Club's green belt land. If a house was built on the plot and the owner became hostile to the use of the land for a 'tented village', this might cause serious disruption and put Hoylake's Open ambitions at risk. The site owner was intent on marketing the plot with planning permission for a house and the 'Sale by Tender' process was to close on 15 December 2000. With little time to act and seeing how this could put our plans at risk, Gerry Maxwell telephoned Peter Dawson to discuss the situation and the importance of acquiring the land. Barry Owen of Mason Owen and a long-standing member of Hoylake was then asked to act for the Club and the R & A and to use his best endeavours to acquire the plot.

Happily, before Christmas, Barry Owen was able to tell us that he had successfully tendered on our behalf for the one-acre plot. Properly, the Chairman's letter to him was fulsome in its praise for his efforts and the achievement of a successful conclusion in somewhat unusual circumstances. "Not only did you help in the appreciation of the potential value of the site, but you were instrumental in persuading the Club and the R & A of the need for quick and decisive action. Both the Club and the R & A will benefit enormously from the acquisition. We are now set to stage The Open again at Hoylake, sooner rather than later."

After all the drama, the hard work, the determination and desire, the changes, the ups and downs, the highs and lows, on 25 January 2001 the formal Open Championship

Agreement was signed by the RLGC, R & A and Wirral Borough Council for a 25-year term. The R & A agreed to add RLGC to The Open venue list. The Passenger Transport Authority agreed the closure of the line between Hoylake and West Kirby for the Championship. As a result, in February 2001, the Captain, Kieran O'Brien, was able to write to the members confirming Hoylake was back as a venue for The Open. The following Monday a Press briefing took place at the Club to announce the return to the world at large.

The aim, to stage the greatest golfing championship, had been achieved. Credit is due to all those who served on Council and who, over many years, kept this aim in sight. Credit is due to Anthony Shone for his continuous efforts on the Club's Championship Committee, which resulted in Hoylake regularly staging Amateur Championships for both men and women. Credit is also due to Brian Gourley for his work as Chairman of Green, especially for his foresight in establishing a five-year plan which identified the links changes necessary for an Open. Finally, credit is due to Gerry Maxwell for preserving a frank, open and straightforward dialogue with the executive of the R & A on all matters for which their help and support was sought.

This approach was appreciated and contributed greatly to ensuring the successful return of The Open to Hoylake.

In 2001 Gerry Maxwell, having seen The Open become a reality for the Club, was succeeded as Chairman of Council by Nicko Williams. In December 2002 the date of July 2006 was confirmed for The Open's return. A small reception for an anticipated handful of journalists was arranged. Little did the Club expect the 150 members to arrive to mark the occasion. It was a fitting end to a long, difficult, but ultimately successful journey.

There was though a twist in the tail as the R & A ventured that the finishing hole should be the current 16th, a 520-yard brute fraught with risk and reward due to the ever-present threat of out-of-bounds. This would enable greater spectator stand seating to be provided and ease spectator flow around the finishing hole.

For over 100 years the basic outline of the course had remained the same. There was no statutory out-and-back pattern leading to the 9th and with the 18th finishing next to the clubhouse. This in itself offered scope for flexibility. The possibility of a player standing on what would become the 18th and needing an eagle to win The Open Championship became attractive.

For The Open at least, the decision was taken. Thus was created the 'Open Course 06'. This new sequence has merit but, for many, the old 1st, with its own out-of-bounds challenges, was one of the finest opening holes in British golf. When the dust has settled and the Champion Golfer for 2006 is announced, only then will the Club take time to reflect on the change of order and its long-term future.

"The Royal Liverpool is a club with a long and distinguished history and we are delighted that we are able to bring The Open back to this wonderful course"

Peter Dawson, Secretary of the Royal & Ancient Golf Club of St Andrews

Left: The St Andrews Dinner 2004. Pre-dinner drinks upstairs for the former Captains before descending the stairs to announce the new Captain

Above: Captain Graham Brown walking through the contenders, even though the Captain to be has accepted, one cannot hope feeling that some members think "it could just be me"

Overleaf top left: The contest over, Johnny Turner is taken upstairs to the greatest acclaim

Overleaf below left: Captain Brown enthusiastically performs the demise, the 'chieftain of the pudding race'

Overleaf right: Peter Bromilow, the Club's head chef, offers his finest haggis to the members

9

The Atlantic Trophy

On Tuesday, 28 September 2004 the first Atlantic Trophy match took place between a team from The Royal Liverpool Golf Club and the North American combined side, taken from 11 different clubs. The players representing those clubs were:

Essex County Club	Gerry Dockert	&	Craig H Deery
Fisher Island	Steve McPherson	&	Ged Parsons
Kittanset	Newcomb Cole III	&	Michael Kane
Myopia Hunt Club	Denny Ryus	&	Michael Valentine
Newport Country Club	Peter de Bar	&	Barclay Douglas
Peachtree	Sam Hatcher	&	John Duncombe
Pine Valley	Michael Brown	&	Michael Forgash
Royal Montreal	Tom Harrison	&	Rick Patee
Somerset Hills	Bob Callander	&	Richard M Boudria
Stanford Golf Club	Richard Harris	&	Tom Isaak
The Country Club	Pete Ingram	&	John D Rusher II

The morning matches were played in a four ball format, followed by foursomes after luncheon. In the evening a dinner was held for the competitors. The Hoylake Captain, Graham Brown, spoke with affection of the link between this part of the world and North America, sentiments that were universally appreciated. John D Rusher II of the Country Club spoke eloquently of golf in the UK.

The event was the inspiration of Nick Wainwright and Kieran O'Brien, who felt that, as we had so many friends in North America, it would be a splendid idea to spread the friendships throughout the Club. There is little doubt that many members of our Club will appreciate their initiative and those who travelled across the Atlantic to participate in the event enjoyed the Hoylake experience.

It is the intention to play for this trophy on a biennial basis, with the next event to take place at the end of September 2006.

Chapter Eighteen

18th hole

The Dinner Party

In 1899 on St Andrews Day, the Club gave a dinner in honour of Johnny Ball who was about to leave for the Boer War (where he served with heroism) after winning his fifth Amateur, a feat which caused the Club to name the clock tower after him.

I often look and marvel at the menu for that special evening, and we reproduce overleaf.

I think, too, how wonderful it would be to call upon the finest, the most significant golfers ever to have walked down a fairway and invite them to sit down with Johnny who would, reluctantly, host the evening.

The Club would, naturally, reproduce the menu of 1899 and somewhere in a quiet corner myself and a few selected members would sit and listen.

At the table would sit the following company:

The first great golfer was YOUNG TOM MORRIS, who won four Open Championships and also the Grand Challenge Event at Hoylake in 1872.

He would be joined by JOHNNY BALL, whose win in the 1890 Open was the first by an Englishman. This changed the balance of power, wresting it from the links of Scotland.

Sat there, too, would have to be the Great Triumvirate of HARRY VARDON, JH TAYLOR and JAMES BRAID, with 16 Open Championships between them in 20 years; need I say more?

After the Great War, the American professional began to dominate and joining us for dinner would be the charismatic WALTER HAGEN, along with his only competition for complete mastery, BOBBY JONES, legendary conqueror of the 'Impregnable Quadrilateral' in 1930.

There were many great golfers from both sides of the Atlantic both before and after World War II, but the next seminal figure must be BEN HOGAN, who popularised the game to a huge extent despite a near-fatal car crash, from which he emerged to win more major tournaments.

In the 1950s the first great Australian golfer, PETER THOMSON dominated The Open, winning his third successive title at Hoylake in

Royal Liverpool Golf Club
St. Andrews Day - 1899

Menu

Anchovies & Olives
Clear Turtle Scotch Broth
Soles a la Normandie
Fried Sparlings
Whitebait
Vol au Vent Quenelles Financiere
Pate in Aspic
Haggis
Saddle of Mutton
Boiled Turkey
Grouse
Ice Pudding
Cheese Souffle
Dessert

1956. There was criticism that there was not a great deal of competition from the Americans in this period, but he gave lie to the slur by winning twice again with the Americans present and vanquished.

At table, of course, are ARNOLD PALMER, GARY PLAYER and the Golden Bear, JACK NICKLAUS. Little needs writing as between them they glamourised the game for millions in the bold new television era.

Space, too, for TOM WATSON five-times Open Champion and the winner of four more majors to boot. What a shame he never had the opportunity to add Hoylake to his list.

By the 80s, invitations had been earned by NICK FALDO and SEVERIANO BALLESTEROS as the pendulum of power swung back towards Europe.

This was until the advent of one TIGER WOODS who bestrides the game like a colossus.

What of Old Tom Morris, you ask? Vijay, Ernie, Olazabal, Lyle? What of Greg Norman, or Trevino, Cotton, or Locke? Ouimet, Sarazen, the great Hilton, de Vicenzo? Sam Snead? Soup and sandwiches in the Spike Bar as our honoured friends?

No. Instead another bounteous banquet where the giants of the Pantheon invite their own special guests.

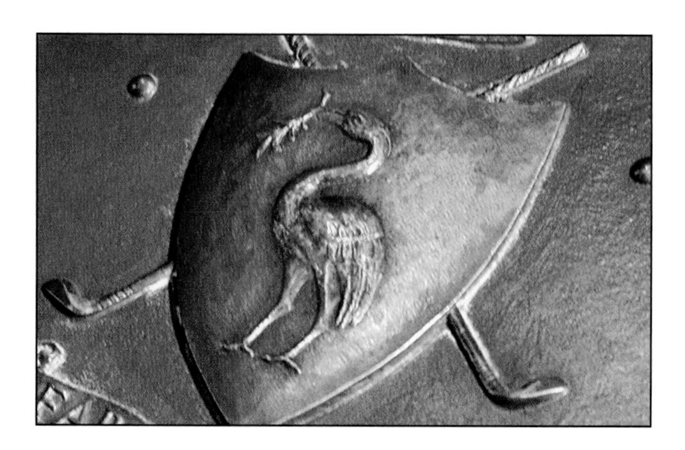

The Future ...

In 1933, Guy Farrar's history of The Royal Liverpool Golf Club ended with a question. "What," he asked, "will become of the Hoylake Club in the years ahead?" And 73 years later, I conclude by asking the same.

I draw a similar conclusion to Farrar.

The answer rests with the members. This is a members' club, one of the few remaining on The Open Championship rota. I hope upon hope it will always remain so. And as The Open returns we must ask whether, in the modern age, a great members' club can also be a great championship course. I have to believe it can. To do so it must constantly adapt and build upon its strengths. And to move this great Club forward, I humbly venture, requires consideration of six principles.

Firstly, we must never forget that Royal Liverpool belongs not just to the members but to the world of golf. It is part of the fabric, part of the story. To understand the significance and importance of that requires us as members to put aside the selfish thoughts that creep in from time to time.

Chris Moore, Secretary, explaining a 'missed putt', while Duncan Fraser appears convinced

The Royal Liverpool Golf Club Council 2006
Seated, from left: Chris Moore (Secretary), Johnny Turner (Captain), Mavis Barlow (Captain, The Royal Liverpool Ladies' Golf Club), Jill Oddie, Tim Marshall (Chairman), Maureen Richmond, Michael Barton, Peter Smith (Treasurer)
Standing: Rob McBurney, David Vaughan, Andrew Collinge, Doug Norval, Alistair Beggs, Nigel Lanceley, Nick Peel

1952-1953
1954
1958
1960
1963

Opposite: Chairman of the Championship Committee 2006, Doug Norval

Secondly, we must always believe, as Farrar was at pains to point out, that the golf is of paramount importance. We must look after the links and the way we play upon it. Hoylake is about golfers who care for their surroundings and care about how they play. That passion for place and for performance must be cherished and preserved.

Thirdly, for Hoylake to be great we need the city of Liverpool to be great too. This is a place that once stood proud as the second city of the Empire. Now, as I write, she makes plans to become the European Capital of Culture. Between times, there have been dark days and neglectful ones. The comparisons with Hoylake as The Open returns are stark, compelling, delightful and sometimes uncomfortable. Let Liverpool prosper.

And then there is the agenda for change. Compared with 1967, The Open of modern times is a huge and voracious beast. To accommodate it we have had to change both the stabling and the mindset. Make no mistake, from now on change will be with us always. We must not allow change to be hamstrung by tradition, but nor must we allow change to be dismissive of it. Tradition is at the very core of what marketers would call the "Hoylake brand". Every change we make must build on tradition and never once must a change be allowed to erode a precious heritage. It is a complex equation.

A fifth tenet for a proud future is a commitment to understatement. Hoylake is a special place because of it. There are no allocated parking places and Heaven forbid there ever will be. There are no "Captain's drive-ins", no "Captain's chair". There are no plaques on the course saying "Bobby Jones chipped in from here" or "Roberto de Vicenzo hit his three-wood clincher from here". At Hoylake things just happened. They just are. It is a traditional club but not a stuffy one. Of course, like other clubs, we have an honours board in the lobby and any member can have their name upon it – all they have to do is win The Open or the Amateur Championship.

A sixth and final principle requires Hoylake to again be a cradle for champions. A conveyor belt of world-class golfers. Once there was Ball and Hilton, playing in the same era, Hoylakers both, dominating world golf and living just a few yards apart. A phenomenon? Perhaps. But great champions are products of their surroundings as well as their genes and efforts. If we truly, rigorously and faithfully encourage junior golf, then Hoylake will again be the breeding place of giants.

So, 73 years on, when the next chroniclers of Royal Liverpool will ask themselves what legacy they have been left. I hope they look at this book, look across at the links and the golfers upon it and feel a decent job has been done. If so, I hope they say thank you – we understand the essence of Hoylake. We will build upon it, but we will never betray it.

Joe Pinnington, May 2006

Captains

1869-70	J Muir Dowie	1903	F Holroyd
1870-71	J Muir Dowie	1904	G Pilkington
1871-72	Lieut-Colonel EH Kennard	1905	HCR Sievwright
1872-73	Lieut-Colonel EH Kennard	1906	Peter Brown
1873-74	John Dun	1907	AM Paterson
1874-75	John Dun	1908	GE Godwin
1875-76	Wyndham CA Milligan	1909	AG Lyster
1876-77	Henry Houldsworth Grierson	1910	WB Stoddart
1877-78	George R Wilson	1911	E Ramsay Moodie
1878-79	Lieut-Colonel Briggs	1912	EA Beazley
1879-80	Charles Cook	1913	EV Crooks
1880-81	Alexander Brown	1914-19	JH Clayton
1881-82	Francis Muir	1920	CH McDiarmid
1882-83	James Mansfield	1921	Gershom Stewart, MP
1883-84	Charles D Brown	1922	Edward B Orme
1884-85	James Cullen	1923	JP Brocklebank
1885-86	B Hall Blyth	1924	AJ Graham
1886-87	John Graham	1925	WE Mounsey
1887-88	Alexander Sinclair	1926	James Baxter
1888-89	Alexander Stewart	1927	A Kentish Barnes
1889	James B Fortune	1928	Stuart Downs
1890	Charles Hutchings	1929	Kenneth Stoker
1891	HW Hind	1930	JGB Beazley
1892	SG Sinclair	1931	Frank Brocklehurst
1893	T Leslie Ferguson	1932	PW Leathart
1894	Horace G Hutchinson	1933	James Pegram
1895	Helenus R Robertson	1934	Roland Marshall
1896	GCH Dunlop	1935	FD Sharples
1897	TW Crowther	1936	Sir Percy E Bates, Bart, GBE
1898	Finlay Dun	1937	Vivian D Heyne
1899	WS Patterson	1938	WB Charles
1900	George R Cox, Jnr	1939-45	E Otho Glover
1901	E Evans, Jnr	1946	F Leslie Orme
1902	AG Rankine	1947	RJ Hodges

1948	David M Ritchie
1949	Thomas W Harley
1950	Dan Tobey
1951	AJ Kentish Barnes
1952-53	ER Orme
1954	Norman W Roberts
1955	JL Postlethwaite
1956	JA Graham (Jnr)
1957	G Gordon Beazley
1958	GF Williamson
1959	JDW Renison
1960	JM Marshall
1961	E Birchall
1962	ANL Warnock
1963	Roy H Smith
1964	WTG Gates
1965	AGL Lowe
1966	W Stanley Hulme
1967	MH Williams
1968	JC Lawrie
1969	Rt Hon Selwyn Lloyd MP
1970	DHL Shone
1971	AS Booth
1972	AHT Crosthwaite
1973	T Draper Williams
1974	JR Turner
1975	VE Sangster
1976	JE Behrend
1977	D Staveley Taylor
1978	TG Leighton
1979	L Briggs
1980	JA Brocklehurst
1981	AW Shone
1982	RT Robinson
1983	J Rees Roberts
1984	DHS Pain
1985	JH Spence
1986	KV Dodman
1987	JA Colvin
1988	NC Williams
1989	TJ Marshall
1990	LM White
1991	FDM Lowry
1992	GA Maxwell
1993	DG Beazley
1994	JDW Maxwell
1995	NA Wainwright
1996	PL Caneval
1997	AW Renison
1998	JN Kennefick
1999	PJM Stern
2000	KJA O'Brien
2001	DP Norval
2002	JCB Pinnington
2003	SB Duncan
2004	GH Brown
2005	JG Turner
2006	AJ Cross

Honorary Treasurers

1869-73	James Tweedie
1873-76	Charles D Brown
1876-79	A Sinclair
1879-81	J May Somerville
1881-82	James Cullen
1882-88	Charles D Brown
1888-90	JE Perrin
1891-93	HJ Simpson
1894	John Graham
1895-1900	Harold Janion
1901	GR Cox, Jnr
1901-19	GR Cox
1920-24	WE Mounsey
1925	GR Cox
1926-27	WE Mounsey
1928	LG Wall
1928-30	James Baxter
1931	GV Wall, Jnr
1931-35	GV Wall
1936-	AS Chambers
1946-49	Vivian D Heynes
1950-51	JL Harvey
1952-60	AJK Barnes
1961-63	WTG Gates
1964-65	JR Turner
1966-70	AHT Crosthwaite
1971-73	MH Williams
1974-77	Norman W Roberts
1978-79	JA Brocklehurst
1980-82	JH Spence
1983-84	JNL Packer
1985-88	FDM Lowry
1989-91	LB Goodwin
1992-96	MS Potts
1996-2000	JRJ Greenhalgh
2000-06	WP Smith
2006-	N Lanceley

Chairmen

1975-78	JM Marshall
1978-80	ANL Warnock
1981-83	JE Behrend
1983-86	AS Booth
1986-89	JDW Maxwell
1989-93	AW Shone
1993-97	LM White
1997-2001	GA Maxwell
2001-05	NC Williams
2005-	TJ Marshall

Honorary Secretaries

1869-72	George Leslie
1872-73	James Steven
1873-81	James Tweedie
1881-82	Jabez Gould
1882-94	Thomas Owen Potter
1922	WE Mounsey

Secretaries

1895-1900	W Ryder Richardson
1900-22	Harold Janion
1923	Major HC Forbes-Bell
1944-58	Guy B Farrar
1958-74	HG MacPherson
1974-90	J Davidson
1990-92	R White
1993-	Group Capt CT Moore CBE

Index

Q

R

S

Bibliography

Golf at Hoylake, John Behrend & John Graham

John Ball of Hoylake, John Behrend

Amateur 1894, Blyth T Bell & David I Hamilton

Yesterday's Wirral, Ian Boumphrey

History of Golf, Robert Browning

Tales from Links Cottage, John Graham

The Royal Liverpool Golf Club, Guy B Farrar

Harold Hilton, John LB Garcia

My Golfing Reminiscences, Harold Horsfall Hilton

Sixty Years of Golf, Robert Harris

Leas School Scrapbooks, CB Meyer

Royal Liverpool Yearbooks, 1986-2005

Technical note: The book refers to the holes before The Open 2006.

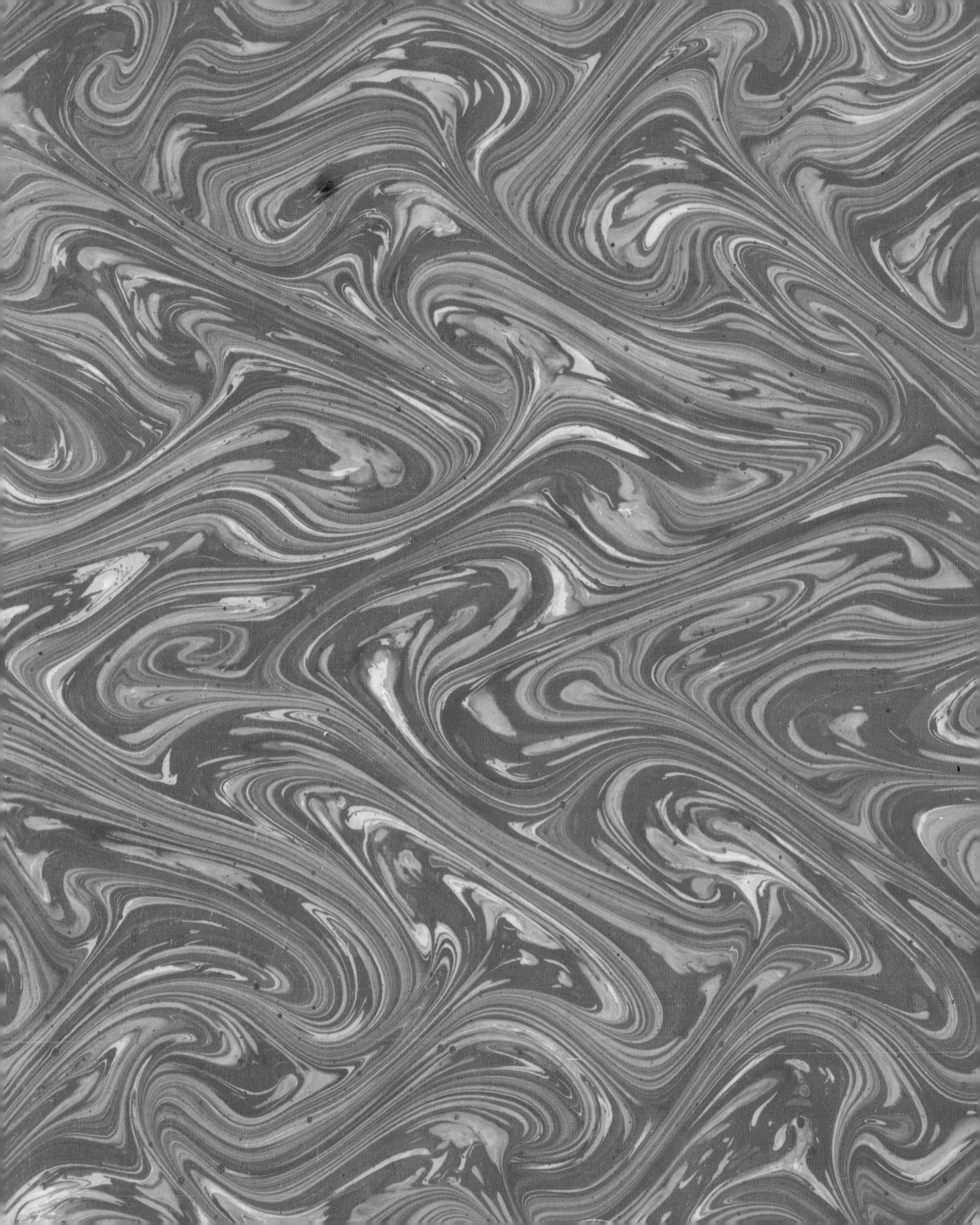